CAMBRIDGE TEXTS IN THE
HISTORY OF POLITICAL THOUGHT

MUSA SADR
Modernity, Shiʿism, and Islamic Humanism

Musa Sadr was a leading force in Lebanese politics from the early 1960s until his disappearance in Libya in 1978. Like now, this was a time of turmoil, violence and change in the Middle East. Sadr has been portrayed as primarily a charismatic man of action whose inspirational qualities led Lebanon's Shiʿi Muslims to the center of the political stage. This book also reflects his position as a thinker whose actions were firmly rooted in universal ethical and religious values, and for whom Islam was social philosophy as well as faith. With twelve texts taken from lectures or talks given by Sadr between 1966 and 1977, an introduction and a chronology of Sadr's life, the book situates Sadr within currents of humanist intellectual thought. Detailed contextualizing footnotes accompany the translations, highlighting the enduring relevance and topicality of Sadr's ideas.

Chibli Mallat is Presidential Professor of Law Emeritus at the University of Utah. His previous publications include *The Renewal of Islamic Law* (Cambridge, 1993), which won the Middle East Studies Association's Albert Hourani Award, *Philosophy of Nonviolence* (Oxford, 2015) and *Democracy Redefined* (Edinburgh, 2025). As the lawyer of the Sadr family, he established the responsibility of Muammar Qaddafi for the disappearance of Musa Sadr in Libya in 1978.

CAMBRIDGE TEXTS IN THE HISTORY OF POLITICAL THOUGHT

Cambridge Texts in the History of Political Thought is firmly established as the major student series of texts in political theory. It aims to make available all the most important texts in the history of political thought, from ancient Greece to the twentieth century, from throughout the world and from every political tradition. All the familiar classic texts are included, but the series seeks at the same time to enlarge the conventional canon through a global scope and by incorporating an extensive range of less well-known works and previously marginalised voices, many of them never before available in a modern English edition. Where possible, the texts are published in complete and unabridged form, and translations are specially commissioned for the series. However, where appropriate, abridged or tightly focused and thematic collections are offered instead. Each volume contains a critical introduction together with chronologies, biographical sketches, a guide to further reading and any necessary glossaries and textual apparatus. Overall, the series aims to provide the reader with an outline of the entire evolution of political thinking on a global scale.

For a list of titles published in the series, please see end of book

MUSA SADR

Modernity, Shiʿism, and Islamic Humanism

EDITED BY
CHIBLI MALLAT
University of Utah

CAMBRIDGE
UNIVERSITY PRESS

CAMBRIDGE
UNIVERSITY PRESS

Shaftesbury Road, Cambridge CB2 8EA, United Kingdom

One Liberty Plaza, 20th Floor, New York, NY 10006, USA

477 Williamstown Road, Port Melbourne, VIC 3207, Australia

314–321, 3rd Floor, Plot 3, Splendor Forum, Jasola District Centre,
New Delhi – 110025, India

Cambridge University Press is part of Cambridge University Press & Assessment,
a department of the University of Cambridge.

We share the University's mission to contribute to society through the pursuit of
education, learning and research at the highest international levels of excellence.

www.cambridge.org
Information on this title: www.cambridge.org/9781009736930

DOI: 10.1017/9781009736947

When citing this work, please include a reference to the DOI 10.1017/9781009736947

First published 2026

Front cover illustration: Digital Vision Vectors/Getty Images

A catalogue record for this publication is available from the British Library

A Cataloging-in-Publication data record for this book is available from the Library of Congress.

ISBN 978-1-009-73693-0 Hardback
ISBN 978-1-009-73692-3 Paperback

I dedicate this book to Gareth Smyth, who spent years working on it. His essential contribution and coauthorship are acknowledged in the Introduction.

He died suddenly on January 15, 2023, a few months before the manuscript was completed.[1] *From the start of the project in 2018, he insisted on explanations with a copious set of footnotes that would help the educated reader who is not necessarily conversant with Middle Eastern arcana. He also left his mark on this improved and expanded version of the work when four chapters were added to the original collection, by enriching it with a precise set of comments and references. The notes in Chapter 1 show his mastery of the literature.*

As correspondent of the Financial Times *in Iran for several years, Gareth's subtle understanding of contemporary Iran, Iraq and Lebanon was unmatched. He never tired of consulting colleagues and experts to find the most adequate wording in the book. He was a taskmaster of details in his intensive work with the two other central contributors to this book, Hawra al-Sadr, the Imam's daughter in Tehran, and Zeinab Charafeddine, his*

[1] See obituaries by Michael Karam, "From the Levant to the Holy Mountain," *Diwan* (Carnegie), February 21, 2023; Khaled Yacoub Oweis, "British-Irish Journalist Gareth Smyth: A Middle East Specialist for Whom Subtlety Was Key," *National*, January 30, 2023; David Donaldson, "Gareth Smyth – Obituary," *Guardian*, April 21, 2023; Chibli Mallat, "Gareth Smyth, grand journaliste de l'Orient," *Ici Beyrouth*, February 2, 2023.

lifelong partner in Beirut. They always responded diligently to nuances in Arabic and Persian drawn from the rich, dual cultural rootedness of the Imam.

In the margin of the Word documents, I would find many queries to clarify or discuss. We spent hours on Skype discussing equivalents to legal and esoteric words in English. He was often far ahead of the academic experts. For instance, in the first chapter of Sadr's autobiography, he wrote in the margin:

> This is Ijtihad, rendered as "jurisprudence" – Chibli, this is an issue. I think we need for sure to use ijtihad (Arabic) at first mention in the book, and I'd prefer to use it throughout rather than render as "jurisprudence," which to me means something more like philosophy or theory of law. If it's rendered as jurisprudence I think that will create loads of problems given the way Sadr uses the term in some chapters.
>
> *Ijtihad* is very important to Sadr, and maybe one could argue that common law, ie judges – including Saudi judges – making decisions is a form of *ijtihad*?

Having researched, discussed, written about and taught ijtihad *as a central legal concept in the Islamic legal tradition, when all has been said, the most powerful insight for the Western reader is Gareth's last sentence. One not only "could" but should "argue that common law, ie judges – including Saudi judges – making decisions is a form of* ijtihad.*" Gareth's definition of the word is the best. In the present use of the term, this is what judges do, when they render a decision. Any modern court report is simply an "ijtihad."*

Now that Gareth is no more, these comments in the form of personal addresses are particularly moving. There would have been no book without him, and the book would have been a far better one had he seen it to publication.

Contents

Acknowledgments

This book was several years in the making. Michael Scott provided the initial translation of the first eight chapters. Chadia Nohra and the Language Platform company translated four chapters added to the original submission following outside reviewers' comments. They are warmly acknowledged. The book benefited also from the continued support of Muhammad Reza Kalantari.

The research greatly benefited from qualitative contributions by Zeinab Charafeddine, and from the active engagement of Hawraʾ al-Sadr, the daughter of Imam Sadr, who initiated the project and stood at each and every turn behind the painstaking collective endeavor resulting in the book. Julie Flint helped revise several chapters with substantive and stylistic comments.

I am extremely grateful to Michael Cook for his early support for this project, to the anonymous reviewers at Cambridge University Press for their enriching comments, to Liz Friend-Smith for her professional follow-up, to Muhammad Ridwaan for copyediting the manuscript and to the in-house editors of the series for their help in seeing this book to publication.

Introduction

CHIBLI MALLAT AND GARETH SMYTH

I.1 Musa al-Sadr's Islamic Humanism

This book introduces Musa Sadr less as a leading political figure in modern Lebanese and Middle Eastern history than as a thinker whose actions were firmly rooted in ethical and religious values. For him, Islam was social philosophy as well as faith.

The book consists of twelve addresses, lectures and interviews given by Sadr since his social and economic concerns in Tehran in the late 1950s through his meteoric rise and leadership in Lebanon, which was cut short by his invitation and kidnapping by the Libyan ruler on August 31, 1978. This is the first such collection in English by Imam Musa, as he is widely referred to in the region. Several collections of articles, speeches and interviews were collected in a series of books published by the Imam Sadr Center for Research and Studies in both English and Persian (and some in other languages).[1] The present book focuses on his intellectual contributions.

The collection confirms Sadr's intellectual preeminence in a wider world perspective by setting forth a living vision of a thoughtful political and civil society leader. In sharp contrast to both "religious" and "secular" regimes that have brought disaster upon disaster on the Middle East, it offers a vision of a man immersed in a complex and troubled

[1] For a sample, s.v. "Ṣadr, Mūsā," Bibliography.

region, in his own words, at key moments of a remarkable career. The reader will be struck by the relevance and topicality of his ideas.

The occasions gathered present Sadr's ideas on the centrality of justice and free will in Islam, his views on press freedom, individual and social responsibility, "Islamic economics," humanism and civil society, sect and sectarianism in Lebanon and the tumultuous history of the Middle East. They express Sadr's

> desire and feeling of wanting to give and to receive, the desire to fulfill obligations and duties toward others, and the enjoyment at having rights and obligations fulfilled by others; this is what we call "civic feeling." It is innate, inherent and natural in human beings. When Islam comes to this feeling it tries to make it more profound by approaching it philosophically.[2]

The texts vary in their formality and cover a wide spectrum, which ranges from a short philosophical treatise in Sadr's critical preface to the *History of Philosophy* by famed French scholar on classical Shiʿism Henry Corbin, to particular challenges and dangers of the hour – which Sadr consistently communicates in an accessible, engaging and sometimes ironic way.

The book also includes a chronology of Sadr's life and a recently discovered autobiographical text (see Chapter 1), which we chose to footnote heavily to explain the context of Sadr's actions and words for the larger, non-Middle Eastern readership.

These essays carry Musa al-Sadr's voice as it was most closely shared by his audience. Behind the apparent improvisation, for he worked sometimes from written notes, sometimes without any, the texts show his intellectual reach with, in addition to the autobiographical Chapter 1, a focus on recurring themes in three main parts: (i) Islamic thought on human values; (ii) social and economic considerations; and (iii) his approach to, and involvement in, the Lebanese crisis until his disappearance in 1978. The texts are divided across three main parts, organized thematically rather than chronologically.

A picture emerges of a political leader shaping, and reacting to, fast-moving events from a clear set of general principles, at the center of which stands the individual, together with her social responsibility, a spiritual connection with the divine, Sadr's attachment to the Shiʿi

[2] From Chapter 6, address in Senegal, 1967.

religious tradition, as well as a sustained criticism of the way politics operate in Lebanon. The reader will draw his own conclusions on the adequacy of these principles in the turbulent region in which Sadr worked, and on the larger humanistic appeal that underlines his action.

The remainder of this introduction examines various issues and themes intimately linked to Sadr the activist and thinker.

I.2 Context: "The Shiʿi International"

By any standard, Musa al-Sadr is a larger-than-life Lebanese leader.[3] Nearly five decades after his abduction in Libya, his image towers over an assertive Shiʿi community in Lebanon.[4] Sadr brought it out from a marginal status reinforced by a sectarian political system, and he did so without allowing it to appear as a threat to the other communities. In Lebanon, Sadr is adulated by the vast majority of Shiʿis and commands respect across the other religious groups. His place in the collective memory stems partly from a charisma compelled by his tall stature and elegant gait, his gentle personality, beauty in the face with luminous eyes, his willingness to listen and a special command of Arabic with a slight Persian accent. The continuous attachment to him comes mostly from a successful projection of his Shiʿi pride and convictions onto a more universal religious and human scene of which he sought to be part between 1957, when he was just short of thirty years of age, and his abduction in 1978. All Lebanese realize how irreplaceable Sadr remains to a fragile society lacking moderation, wisdom and equanimity, and his cross-confessional appeal is associated with sundry anecdotes. A famous one is Sayyed Musa, as he is also called less formally, taking people after prayer to buy ice cream from a Christian merchant in Tyre, a gesture

[3] See the Bibliography for extensive coverage of his life and works. Two good introductions are Fouad Ajami, *The Vanished Imam: Musa al Sadr and the Shia of Lebanon* (Ithaca, NY: Cornell University Press, 1986); and Rabāb al-Ṣadr, *al-Falsafa al-iṣlāḥiyya fī ruʾyat al-Imām Mūsā al-Ṣadr wa-aʿmālihi* [The reformist philosophy in the vision of Imam Musa al-Sadr and in his writings] (Beirut: Markaz al-Imām Mūsā al-Ṣadr li-l-Abḥāth wa-l-Dirāsāt, 2022).

[4] In the absence of evidence provided by the Libyan government to the contrary, the family considers the Imam to be still alive. We respect this strongly held conviction and use the present tense accordingly.

portrayed as a large embrace of all without heed to their religious community.[5]

There is, however, a much larger circle than Lebanon in the context of Sadr's life and works, and it does not carry the same universal reverence. Musa al-Sadr stands firmly at the center of "the Shiʿi International," described elsewhere as a network constituted by the historical convergence between traditional Shiʿi law and modern constitutionalism.[6] This transnational network came to dominate Middle Eastern politics, and the larger international scene, upon the access of religious leaders to power in Iran in 1979 in the wake of the Islamic Revolution. By doing so, it created a significant resentment in various parts of the Arab and Muslim world, including in Lebanon.

Yet Sadr's prominence antedates the revolution in Iran. He is the scion of a celebrated family of religious leaders across the Middle East, where both men and women have succeeded in shaping their proximate and less proximate environment with the values they believe in.[7] Visiting Iraq for the first time after the removal of Baʿthist rule, one of us (Mallat) was struck by the immediate embrace of several people of his Lebanese leadership and the inevitable mention in the same breath of their sadness and anger at his disappearance. In Baghdad, "Sadr City" covers almost half of the large metropolis and was renamed, in the wake of the fall of the Baʿth Party, after Muhammad Baqer al-Sadr, the Imam's younger cousin, and Sadeq al-Sadr, his cousin on his mother's side.[8]

In Iran, Muhammad Khatami, who was elected president twice with large majorities and established a period of moderation and growth between 1997 and 2005, is married to Sadr's niece, Zohreh. In Lebanon, Sadr's close kin is wedded into other prominent Shiʿi

[5] For this cross-religion appeal, see his church address at Lent 1975 in Chapter 10. Sayyed is a formal title for Shiʿis who descend from the Prophet Muhammad through his daughter Fatima, the wife of the first Imam in the Shiʿi tradition, Ali b. Abi Talib, also the cousin of the Prophet.

[6] See, generally, Chibli Mallat, *The Renewal of Islamic Law: Muhammad Baqer as-Sadr, Najaf and the Shiʿi International* (Cambridge: Cambridge University Press, 1993).

[7] For the family tree, see H. E. Chehabi and Majid Tafreshi, "Musa al-Sadr and Iran," in *Distant Relations: Iran and Lebanon in the Last 500 Years*, ed. H. E. Chehabi (Oxford: Centre for Lebanese Studies, 2006), 140; Sabrina Mervin, *Un réformisme Chiite: Ulémas et lettrés du Jabal ʿÂmil (actuel Liban-Sud) de la fin de l'Empire ottoman à l'indépendance du Liban* (Paris: Karthala, 2000), 437.

[8] Muhammad Baqer al-Sadr was executed by the Iraqi regime of Saddam Hussein on April 8, 1980. His cousin Muhammad Sadeq al-Sadr was assassinated with his two sons in Baghdad on February 19, 1999.

families, including the Sharafeddins in particular. In the late 1950s, Abdul Hussein Sharafeddin, respected religious leader of the Shiʿis of Jabal Amil, in south Lebanon, introduced the young Iranian religious scholar Sadr to the country and pushed him into prominence.[9] Sadr visited Lebanon for the first time in 1955 and made the decision to stay in the country after 1959. Lebanon has since been the terrain where he was most active.[10] His sister Rabab married a notable from Tyre, Hussein Sharafeddin, and has taken over the large social institutions that she founded with her brother in the 1960s.[11]

I.3 Nonviolence for Lebanon

In the light of the Imam's status nationally and regionally, his abduction during his visit to Libya in 1978 marks a turning point in Lebanese and regional politics. The sudden, unexpected disappearance from the public scene was, to borrow the words of a famous editorial by the French daily *Le Monde* a year earlier, an "insult to the future."[12] The editorial had been penned in reaction to the assassination in March 1977 of Kamal Jumblat. Within less than two years, Lebanon lost its two most compelling figures to crimes committed by regional strongmen in a double insult to the country's future. The pattern of assassinations has never stopped since.

Reference to Jumblat as another major figure of modern Lebanese history is purposeful, and one should mention in this context of Lebanese towering figures in the twentieth century a third exceptional leader, Raymond Eddé. From the very first day of Lebanon's descent into chaos in April 1975, Eddé, a traditional Maronite Christian notable, a prominent parliamentary deputy and minister and a lawyer by profession, remained committed to nonviolence. He also refused systematically to make the slightest compromise in his rejection of force and in his

[9] Abdul Hussein Sharafeddin is the author of *al-Murājaʿāt* (Sour: al-ʿIrfān, 1936), one of the most important books in the 1930s advocating a rapprochement between Sunnis and Shiʿis. He died in 1957.

[10] For details, see his autobiography, Chapter 1.

[11] On Hussein Sharafeddin, the grandson of Abdul Hussein and the author of a modern history of Tyre/Sour, see the obituary by Chibli Mallat, "Ghiyāb al-adīb Ḥusayn Sharaf al-Dīn muʾarrikh madīnat Ṣūr" [Passing of man of letters Hussein Sharafeddin, historian of Tyre], *al-Nahār* (Beirut), March 17, 2022. Sitt (respectful title akin to "Lady") Rabab published her informed doctoral thesis on Sadr as al-Ṣadr, *al-Falsafa al-iṣlāḥiyya*.

[12] Editorial, "L'Avenir insulté," *Le Monde*, March 18, 1977.

steadfast opposition to foreign governments meddling in Lebanese affairs. Together with Eddé and Jumblat, Sadr constitutes the third shining figure in a narrow pantheon of Lebanese leaders.[13] Eddé was forced to leave Lebanon after several attempts on his life in 1976 and died in French exile in 2000. Jumblat was assassinated in 1977 in Lebanon. Sadr was "disappeared" in 1978 in Libya. History was unkind to Lebanon and to the world by depriving the country of its most alluring leaders. With their absence, the crisis in which the country has been mired continues several domestic and regional wars later, with no end in sight after fifty years.

Lebanon first descended into violence in 1975, when Lebanese and Palestinians in Lebanon fought Lebanese factions, mostly Christian, over different views of the country and its role in the region. Jumblat was the leader of a Lebanese–Palestinian front responding to Christian militia exactions and ethnic cleansing. As the head of the Lebanese National Movement (LNM), Jumblat led a large armed opposition to the Christian militias and the then president of the country with a view to remove him from power and establish a reformist, left-of-center non-sectarian government.[14]

[13] On Kamal Jumblat, a good biography is Igor Timoviev, *Kamāl Junblāṭ: al-Rajul wa-l-usṭūra* [Kamal Jumblat: The man and the legend] (Beirut: Dār al-Nahār li-l-Nashr, 2000). See also on his thought and relevance, Chibli Mallat, *ʿAn Kamāl Junblāṭ wa-min waḥyihi* [On Kamal Jumblat and his inspiration] (Beirut: Badāʾiʿ, 2018). On Eddé, see Nicolas Nassif, *Raymond Eddé: Jumhūriyyat al-ḍamīr* [Raymond Eddé: The moral republic] (Beirut: Dār al-Nahār li-l-Nashr, 2002).

[14] The National Movement (al-Haraka al-Wataniyya) was a coalition of motley groups generally on the left and of secular persuasion that supported the Palestinian cause. It came to prominence after securing several military victories in late 1975 and early 1976 against the right-wing Christian militias that were opposed to armed Palestinian presence in Lebanon and fought them in the country. While the LNM included originally Sadr and his supporters, Sadr and Jumblat (with the PLO leadership) parted ways a few months into 1976 over Syria's increasing intervention in matters Lebanese under the rule of Hafez al-Assad. On the fraught relations between Sadr and the Palestinians at this crucial period, see Tristan Hillion-Launey, "Musa al-Sadr, les chiites libanais et les Palestiniens du Liban (4). Rivalités, divergences et affrontements," *Cahiers de l'IFPO*, March 29, 2021, https://ifpo.hypotheses.org/11058. Syria's military intervention in the summer of 1976 rolled the LNM back and forced a ceasefire that consecrated Syrian military presence in the country and the domination of Damascus over the Lebanese political scene for three decades. For an overview of the so-called two years' war (1975–76), see René Chamussy, *Chronique d'une guerre: Liban 1975–1977* (Paris: Desclée 1978); Samir Kassir, *La Guerre du Liban: De la dissension nationale au conflit régional* (Paris: Karthala 1994) (new ed. L'Orient des Livres/Sindbad/Actes-Sud, 2018).

Sadr took a diametrically opposed stance to the one chosen by Jumblat. Jumblat wanted to reform Lebanon in secular terms, while Sadr never jettisoned the religious component as central to change. As importantly, they differed in the means chosen. While Sadr's legacy is associated with a famous Arabic aphorism, "*al-silah zinat al-rijal*" (weapons are men's adornment), he rapidly took a reserved position toward the use of force inside the country:[15]

> Before I translate the needs of the deprived into this political, social, economic change that we demand, it is imperative to add the central foundation for this change: this foundation is our refusal to change by force, not only because it is a pity for this small nation to be subjected to violence and because the Lebanese structure is complicated, but also because it is prohibited to handle fire with one's bare fingers, so long as there are democratic means available in principle and their use possible and expected.[16]

This is a remarkable paradox in the position of Lebanon's two national figures at the outset of the Lebanese wars. Jumblat had embraced, for years, the nonviolent path pioneered by Gandhi. Sadr had not, and his writings and political philosophy support armed resistance. The paradox lay at the heart of the tragic beginnings of the long Lebanese history of unrest, with Jumblat taking up arms against the Ancien Régime despite his express advocacy of nonviolence, and Sadr's refusal to use force to remove the established order despite the association of his large following, prima facie, with armed resistance. It pits philosophically nonviolent Jumblat embracing violence for the sake of the oppressed

[15] On the expression *al-silah zinat al-rijal*, which is a statement widely ascribed to Sadr and associated with his political activities, he responded to criticism in an interview carried out a few months into the civil war: "In Lebanon, I believe that the complex local conditions and the looming dangers to the country and to the [Palestinian] resistance prevent the possibility of using violence for the sake of change, especially since change has become a wide national demand. There needs to be change in the means of change, i.e., in the electoral law so that change can happen." Interview for *Majallat al-Usbu' al-'Arabi* (weekly Arabic-language magazine in Paris) by Samir Shahin and Fatima Sarduk, "al-Thawra wasila la ghaya" [The revolution is a means, not an end], September 20, 1975, www.imamsadr.net/News/news.php?NewsID=6158.

[16] Mūsā Ṣadr, *Risāla ilā al-maḥrūmīn* [Message to the deprived] (Beirut: Markaz al-Imām Ṣadr li-l-Abḥāth wa-l-Dirāsāt, 2000), 11. This is the text of a long statement read at the press conference of Sadr on September 11, 1975, also entitled "*ibtihal al-watan*" (the supplications of the nation). On *mahrumin*, see n. 22 and accompanying text; on the historical context, see Rula Jurdi Abisaab, "Sayyid Musa al-Sadr, the Lebanese State, and the Left," *Journal of Shi'a Islamic Studies* 8, no. 2 (2015): 131–57.

despite a long-standing belief in nonviolence as political philosophy of change, versus Sadr, the founder of a revolutionary movement with an early military calling, shunning violence on the Lebanese political scene and adamantly refusing to involve his followers in the violent revolution/civil war engulfing the country.

This does not exclude Sadr's own contradictions. In addition to a long-standing closeness to the Syrian ruler Hafez al-Assad, whose military involvement in Lebanon he supported, the political party founded by Sadr was named Amal, the Arab acronym of which (*a-m-l*) means hope, yet represents the militia dimension associated with its birth as Afwaj al-Muqawama al-Lubnaniyya (Units [or Regiments] of the Lebanese Resistance).[17] This resistance included a military dimension, which came to the fore brutally after Sadr's disappearance in 1978. But Sadr was ambivalent when creating the movement, and his interviews in 1975 and 1976 show his deep unease with any armed group operating outside the Lebanese state's monopoly of violence.

When Jumblat was assassinated in March 1977, likely under the orders of Syrian president and ally of Sadr, al-Assad, whom Jumblat had just accused of turning Syria into "a large prison," Sadr's initially muted reaction gave way, two weeks after the assassination, to a dark premonition that he expressed in an interview condemning the murder:[18] "There is no doubt that political assassinations, especially in the present circumstances, must be considered a setback to peace."[19]

This is consistent with a track record that goes as far back as 1966, when Sadr reacted to the assassination of Kamel Mroue, a leading journalist who established two daily newspapers in Lebanon, *al-Hayat* and *The Daily Star*. Mroue was gunned down in Beirut on May 16, 1966, by assassins close to then Egyptian president Gamal Abdel Nasser. Sadr denounced the assassination in one of the most expressive statements of his legacy: "Assassination is one of the worst, most futile and cowardly ways to reach any goal, no matter what the goal may be. It is

[17] Hafez al-Assad emerged from the 1963 and 1966 coups in Syria to become president from 1971 until his death in 2000, when he was quickly succeeded by his son. A good biography is Patrick Seale, *Asad of Syria: The Struggle for the Middle East* (London: I.B. Tauris, 1988); on the closeness of Sadr and Assad, see 173, 352, 357.

[18] Ajami, *The Vanished Imam*, 176.

[19] "*La shakk anna al-ightiyal al-siyasi, wa-khassatan fi al-zuruf al-haliyya, yu'tabar intikasa fi masirat al-salam*"; interview with 'Isam Kheireddin, *al-Muḥarrar*, April 3, 1977, www.imamsadr.net/News/print.php?NewsID=6192.

also a dangerous social phenomenon, since trial, judgment and execution are undertaken by one single person."[20]

In the early months of Lebanon's violent trials and tribulations, as violence engulfed the country further every day, Sadr started a hunger strike in the ʿAmiliyya mosque in south Beirut in a Gandhi-like gesture:

> Violence had defiled the country; I have come to the house of God, and my sustenance is the book of God [the Qur'an] and a few drops of water. I will stay here until death, or until the country is saved. I have bid farewell to my family, to my wife and children, and have come here to ask God to save this country.[21]

Sadr did not waver from this position: two months later, in his *Letter to the Deprived*, he made clear that "just as we do not accept violence as a means of change, we do not accept violence to prevent it; otherwise, we would fall into a dictatorship. Better have a revolution."[22] There is no attested violence under his command between his hunger strike and his disappearance three years later. This does not mean that he is not perceived as having taken side with Syria's rulers, themselves part of "the Shiʿi International" as Alawis, a minor Shiʿi community in terms of numbers, but a politically dominant group in Syria from the 1970s to their violent removal from power at the end of 2024.[23]

I.4 Violence in a Regional Context

Because of Israel, Musa al-Sadr's attitude was different on nonviolence in a regional context. In addition to a long-standing enmity since the

[20] The speech at the commemoration of Mroue two weeks after his assassination includes several of the humanist traits one finds in Sadr's writings, "*La siyana li-l-hurriyya illa bi-l-hurriyya*" [No preservation of freedom except with freedom], May 31, 1966, translated here in Chapter 9.

[21] Cited by Ajami, *The Vanished Imam*, 165 (mentioning late June 1975).

[22] Ṣadr, *Risāla ilā al-maḥrūmīn*, 11. The last clause, "better have a revolution" (*khayrun minha thawra*), is intriguing and appears to contradict Sadr's appeal to nonviolence, but it must be seen in the context associated with revolutions, perceived then as naturally violent. On this association, which includes Hannah Arendt in a late text from 1969, see Chibli Mallat, *Philosophy of Nonviolence* (New York: Oxford University Press, 2015), 6n8.

[23] On the development of closer ties between Syrian Alawis and Twelver Shiʿis in the rest of the Middle East, including the Lebanese Shiʿis, see Chibli Mallat, *Aspects of Shiʿi Thought from the South of Lebanon* (Oxford: Oxford Centre for Lebanese Studies, 1988), n7, and accompanying text. The return of Syria to Sunni rulers in December 2024 marks a watershed in the region.

establishment of Israel over Palestine and the massive influx of Palestinians seeking refuge in Lebanon, on-and-off low-scale hostilities had persisted since Palestinians took up arms in the south of Lebanon in guerrilla warfare after the 1967 war.

The situation developed in a complex pattern, with the Palestinians as the main armed group established in the south. As trouble spread in Lebanon in 1975 and Syria invaded the country in October 1976, Israel established a small perimeter inside the country, dubbed "the good fence," with villagers within that zone isolated from the rest of the country and allowed to work in Israel. Considering the precedent of the West Bank, Sadr and most Lebanese were alarmed at the transformation of south Lebanon into a potential "North Bank," with land-grabbing settlements a tangible fear, compounded by the full military onslaught conducted in April 1978 and the occupation of about a fifth of Lebanese territory. Sadr supported armed resistance to Israel while denouncing Palestinians taking up arms within Lebanon.

Whether regarding Israel and other countries, Sadr's vision was never limited to Lebanon, on account of the "the Shiʿi International" and its regional network, which he personally embodied more than any other Lebanese leader in modern history. In his life, Sadr had three major moments, Iranian, Iraqi and Lebanese. Having studied in Iran at the traditional seminary curriculum at Qom as well as in the modern law school in Tehran, then in Iraq for a brief two-year period of "graduate studies" at Najaf in 1955–57 meant for apprentice scholars in the traditional fashion, Sadr honed his family and religious network in a way few other political figures in the Middle East succeeded in achieving. While the Lebanese moment was the latest and the most intense, it was never exclusive of the other two.

Various accounts are replete with recollections of major Iranian and Iraqi figures about the activities of Sadr in an intimate and intricate community of leaders in the making across the three countries.[24] In 1977–78, the star of Ruhollah Khumaini rose considerably in the popular revolt he led against a powerful US-backed shah, but the

[24] In addition to the works mentioned in n. 11, see Hussein Sharafeddin, *al-Imām al-Sayyed, Maḥaṭṭāt tārīkhiyya, Īrān – al-Najaf – Lubnān* (Imam Sayyed, historical moments, Iran – Najaf – Lebanon] (Beirut: Dār al-Arqam, 1996). We do not have clear testimonies on the relationship between Sadr and Khumaini. For a complex set of local and regional entanglements, s.v. "Khomeini" in Chehabi, *Distant Relations*, various chapters.

revolution did not succeed until early 1979, after Sadr's fateful visit to Libya. Like many people within and outside the Middle East, he was supportive of an extraordinary insurrection against the entrenched dictatorship in Tehran. From philosopher Michel Foucault to local Arab and Iranian folk, people across the globe were sympathetic to the rising rebellious tide against one of the most entrenched dictatorships on the planet. Disillusion came later.

Two days before Sadr arrived in Libya, he articulated his support for Khumaini and the rising revolutionary tide in an op-ed in *Le Monde*. Signing it as "President of the Supreme Shi'i Council of Lebanon," he noted that the popular mobilization unfolding in Iran was distant from right and left alike, and he underlined its "open humanism and revolutionary ethics."[25] His enthusiasm for the Iran revolution and its clerical leadership is evident.[26] This last published article before his disappearance shows his admiration for the Iranian Revolution about to sweep the Middle East. It is remarkable, reading it half a century later, how much Sadr is attentive to nonviolence. Sadr mentions twice in the brief op-ed his respect for the "unarmed people" (*peuple désarmé*) standing against the "Shah's regime ... which disposes at the moment the greatest stockpile of weapons in the Third World."[27]

This theme of "unarmed people" rising against dictatorship is of importance in the subsequent course of history and the many nonviolent revolutions, also known as "color revolutions," that have marked the world since the collapse of the Soviet bloc. In this book, the reader will find insights into the philosophy of Sadr mostly on the side of nonviolence as principle. While the subsequent history of Iran is disappointing for its rampant authoritarianism, the humanism that surfaces in

[25] Imam Moussa el-Sadr, "L'appel des prophètes," *Le Monde*, August 23, 1978.

[26] A book published in Iran shows the reverence of various first-rate Iranian personalities; see Mahdī Farrokhiān, ed., *Andīshe-ye rabudeh shodeh* [The thought that was stolen (with the disappearance of the Imam)] (Tehran: Imam Moussa Sadr Cultural Research Institute, 2006). See also Ḥabībe Jafariān, *Sayyed Mūsā Ṣadr: Haft revāyat khuṣūṣī* [Sayyed Musa Sadr: seven personal narratives] (Mashhad: Sepīdeh Bavārān; Tehran: Markaz-e Imām Mūsā Ṣadr, 2015).

[27] Sadr, "L'appel des prophètes." In Mallat, *Philosophy of Nonviolence*, 53–54, the question of nonviolence in the Iranian Revolution of 1978–79 is discussed at some length. The verdict is that, absent its conscious and deliberate commitment to nonviolence, it does not rise to being qualified as a nonviolent revolution. Sadr's emphasis on the "unarmed people" rising against the shah in the article published in *Le Monde* does not mean that Sadr was opposed, Gandhi-like, to all violence used in deposing the shah, but this was never tested.

Sadr's various lectures and writings comes down strongly on the side of human rights as his dominant philosophical outlook and in his rejection of violence as a political tool. But in his larger view of the region, his fascination with the budding unarmed revolution of Iran would probably not trump his support for armed resistance to Israel. This also explains his wide respect in Lebanon across the Shiʿi political/religious spectrum, including Amal and Hizbullah, the latter being founded in the wake of the wider occupation of south Lebanon by Israel in 1982.

I.5 Musa al-Sadr's Humanism

If one were to reduce Musa al-Sadr's legacy to a single idea, this monad would be humanism.

At the center of his writings rests the human being, *al-insan*, meaning both the individual per se and the individual within the larger collectivity. So recurrent is the reference to the word *insan* in the texts chosen that its translation falls short of projecting the intensity of references to all that is human in Sadr's view. In part, the word in Arabic corresponding to man/human has special connotations in its multiple uses. In English, "man" appears traditionally both in opposition to "woman" and as a synonym of human, as in man/humankind. In Arabic, *insan* is genderless, for the feminine *insana* is rarely if at all used in classical or modern texts. In addition, the concept of insan carries an abstract nuance one can render in English as humankind.[28]

Evidence of this nuance can be found in the Qur'anic verse joining the word *insan* with an adjective in the feminine gender, *basira*: "*bali-l-insanu ʿala nafsihi basiratun*" (a human [being] is responsible for her soul).[29]

[28] In this book, in line with Musa Sadr's known views on gender, we have generally used "humankind" and the pronoun "she" as well as "he."

[29] Qur'an 75:14. This is our translation, which emphasizes the feminine ending of *basiratun*. It does not appear in traditional English translations; e.g., see https://corpus.quran.com under 75:14:

> Sahih International: Rather, man, against himself, will be a witness.
> Pickthall: Oh, but man is a telling witness against himself.
> Yusuf Ali: Nay, man will be evidence against himself.
> Shakir: Nay! man is evidence against himself.
> Muhammad Sarwar: In fact, people are well-aware of their own soul.
> Mohsin Khan: Nay! Man will be a witness against himself.
> Arberry: Nay, man shall be a clear proof against himself.

The verse appears in one major Arab jurisdiction as the basis chosen by courts to root the individual's responsibility in the Qur'an.[30] In this literal reading of the verse, the courts derive legal consequences in terms of compensation for damages inflicted or the crime committed by the person who betrays this testimony/evidence/responsibility. It establishes for the jurist the individual's responsibility for her acts.

The consequence is to neutralize gender with a view to marking a preference in the translation by using alternatively man and woman for *insan*, save when the male/female difference is emphasized by Sadr, usually to show his deference to women in reading the tradition. As his nephew Sadeq Tabataba'i reports, "I recall, since childhood, that [Sadr] paid special attention to the kids in the family, both male and female without discrimination, and to be more precise, paid special attention to the girls."[31] This conforms with another, eminently practical report, arising from the Imam's social work. In Lebanon, "he established 'the home for girls' (*bayt al-fatat*) to elevate the social level of women, including a school to erase illiteracy, a school for manual work and for sewing and a technical high school for nursing."[32] While the alternative translation would have appeared slightly contrived a few years ago, there is little doubt that the "feminine condition" (Simone de Beauvoir) figures highly in the Imam's set of priorities. Sadr's genderless use of the word *insan* provides an objective platform for a gender-parity interpretation of the world.

This is also true for the humanist label more generally. The life and works of Sadr hold him as figure of choice for the "humanist" tradition. In Western modern history, the period generally associated with the beginning of humanism is the Renaissance, with Erasmus of Rotterdam as its archetype. In the deep history of the Middle East, there are several contenders to the humanist pantheon, as varied as Jewish philosopher and jurist Moses Maimonides (d. 1204), Syrian poet-philosopher Abu al-ʿAlaʾ al-Maʿarri (d. 1057) or Iranian philosopher Mulla Sadra al-Shirazi (d. 1640); let alone, lest we unduly forget him, a Middle Eastern person of choice, Jesus of Nazareth. Adding Sadr to that long list is easily defendable.[33]

30 See Chibli Mallat, *The Normalization of Saudi Law* (New York: Oxford University Press, 2022); for the use of the verse in Saudi courts, see 60, 83.

31 Sharafeddin, *al-Imām al-Sayyed*, 42.

32 Ibid., 129.

33 For more on this humanist roster of Middle Eastern figures, see Mallat, *Philosophy of Nonviolence*, 82–83nn38–39.

Sadr's humanism is Islamic.[34] This is inevitable for a man of religion as a profession and dedication. It is the more noteworthy since the Western tradition of humanism is historically linked to the detachment from religion as its dominant component. European humanism – read Western/world humanism – emerged in significant part as a secular movement against the power of the Church. Humanism rose in Europe against established churches, Roman Catholicism in particular. It sailed through the wars of religion that tore Europe for the better part of the sixteenth and seventeenth centuries as the philosophical harbinger of the separation between religion and state. In the West, secularism and humanism are cognates, even if humanism is also espoused in modern Christian philosophy. This is not the tradition of the East, not a Near or Middle Eastern tradition at least, where the relationship between religion, society and state remains deeply intertwined. In the Arab and Muslim Orient, or in the Middle East generally, the humanism of Sadr never turns its back to religion.

From a narrow Western perspective, that might disqualify Sadr from being a humanist. The way humanist religious leaders generally overcome the secular pull is to turn ecumenical. Sadr is always celebrated for his ecumenism. In different moments of his life, including his participation in the coronation of Pope Paul VI in the Vatican in 1963, interfaith dialogue on a world scale is central to his activity. A Christian reader will find herself at ease with most ideas and theological underpinnings in the present book. This is a mantra that was reinforced in Pope John Paul II's celebrated "Lebanon as message" joining East and West in 1989. It appears strongly in Sadr's belief in Lebanon as the model example of ecumenical humanism:

> Lebanon, at this particular stage in history, represents an essential model for the world. Firstly, because of the expansion of transport and communication, we feel that the entire world in the late twentieth century and at the beginning of the twenty-first century lives effectively like a single country. The distance between one country and another, in terms of physical travel time, seems no more than the distance between Beirut and Tripoli. In such an interconnected

[34] Our preference for "Islamic humanism" over "Muslim humanism" comes from the relatively more dynamic connotation of the word "Islamic." "Muslim" evokes state of fact. "Islamic" appears as a determined, dynamic choice. In contrast, there is no such nuance for the word "Christian" in English. One can only say "Christian humanism."

> world as ours, which includes different religions and coexistence among the peoples of the world, any efforts to create a universal state should link closely with and be greatly affected by the success of Lebanon's example . . .
>
> If the experience of Lebanon should falter or fail, this would harm and undermine the whole of human civilization for the next fifty years, at the very least. Therefore, we say that Lebanon is a civilizational necessity, now more than ever.[35]

In addition to the premonitory quality of this comment, Sadr's Islamic humanism is informed by several other traits also feeding into his philosophy.

One is egalitarian, with an insistence on the charitable dimension of Islam and the need to go beyond to the structural problems of inequality. In a full book on economic principles in Islam, one can see the convergence of his approach and worldview with the elaborate examination of his cousin Muhammad Baqer al-Sadr in *Iqtisaduna* (Our economic system) or the Persian oppositional cleric Mahmud Taliqani's *Islam and Ownership*.[36] In Lebanon, Sadr's name is associated with the struggle of the "*mahrumin*," those who have been "deprived" (also translated as "disinherited" or "dispossessed"). Both Sadrs' views are strongly anchored in a socially aware message to be achieved by the state for the poorer, exploited and deprived sectors of society.[37]

35 From Chapter 12.

36 Muhammad Baqer al-Sadr was executed by the Iraqi regime in April 1980. His main contribution is *Iqtisaduna* (Our economic system), published originally in two volumes in Najaf in 1961. Musa al-Sadr authored, just before the publication of this major book, a series of seven articles in Persian that appeared in the first year of the journal *Maktab-e Islam*, published in Qom ca. 1959. Many concepts and explanations are shared, and no doubt the two Sadrs must have exchanged conclusions of their research into the economic doctrine in Islam at the time. Musa Sadr's articles were collected in *Iqtiṣād dar maktab-e Islām* [Economics in the Islamic school] (Tehran: Mashʿal Dāneshjū, 1989), and translated into Arabic as *al-Madhhab al-iqtiṣādī fī al-Islām* [The economic school in Islam] (Beirut: Markaz al-Imām Ṣadr li-l-Abḥāth wa-l-Dirāsāt, 1998). See also Chapters 6–8. In Iran, Iraq and Lebanon, this egalitarian spirit was shared, until the Iranian Revolution, by prominent clerical figures, including foremost in Iran Mahmud Taliqani (d. 1979), author of *Islām va Malekiyyat* [Islam and ownership] (Tehran: Enteshār, 1965 [1961]). The position of Musa Sadr on property is more guarded and less redistributionist economically than his contemporaries, including Muhammad Baqer. He was closer to Khumaini in that respect.

37 Ṣadr, *Risāla ilā al-maḥrūmīn*. For more on his socioeconomic views, see the thorough contribution of Tristan Hillion-Launey, "The Islamic Economy according to Musa al-Ṣadr: The Avant-gardist Thoughts of an Original Shiʿi Reformist Cleric," in

Another anchor is spiritual, with Sadr's attraction to what he calls "a [special] type of Sufism":

> This type of Sufism differs from the more well-known ascetic type of Sufism, which is based upon ignoring desires deliberately in a quest for purity and perfection of the soul. Rather, desire is a transcendental need for man. What he can impose on himself by fulfilling his desires keeps him from a total dependency on his surroundings.[38]

A third overarching trait is legal. It is present in Sadr's works as both theory and practice. As theory,

> the separation between the principles of economic and social justice and those that obtain from Islamic beliefs is part and parcel of the tragedy in dissociating doctrine from the law. This separation, and the passivity of Muslims, has resulted in a loss of depth and strategy in the foundations of justice, so much so that economic, social and other applications of justice have become simply a social and political demand shorn [from the law].[39]

As practice, Sadr entrusts the responsibility to the religious law scholars, the *fuqaha'*:

> The responsibility of religious scholars in this field is great, highly delicate and urgent, as they are the trustees serving the community and its people, especially those deprived among them – these scholars alone can give a true picture of the struggle of the disadvantaged and the oppressed within societies and stand in the way of appeals to extremism and atheism. Religious scholars are especially capable of preventing the distortion and deflection of efforts to restore rights to people deprived of them. The oppressors and usurpers of justice and rights typically accuse movements that are struggling for justice of atheism or sectarianism. The best remedy in such cases is for religious scholars to stand with the deprived and oppressed and adopt their cause.[40]

The responsibility of scholars in the city is obvious for Sadr. Other than this passing reference, however, one does not find in Sadr's written legacy a more specific official role for religious clerics, in particular his

Proceedings of the Sixth Annual Conference on Shi'i Studies (London: Islamic College, 2021), 33–74.

[38] From Section 2.8. [39] From Section 8.1. [40] Ibid.

fellow scholars of traditional law. This is because in the period when Sadr was active, from the late 1950s through the mid-1970s, he was defending the social role of religious scholars and encouraging them to participate actively in social and political life, rather than assigning them governmental positions in the state. As the Islamic Revolution in Iran succeeded and endured, the concept known as "the rule of the jurist" (Arabic *wilayat al-faqih*, Persian *velayat-e faqih*) consecrated the role of "leader" to a top member in the Shiʿi religious leadership, both in constitutional text and practice, leading to a large controversy that persists to date.[41] This was not the case in the period during which Sadr was active in Lebanon, when his access to an official governmental seat was hard to conceive. Paradoxically, the sectarian constitutional system of the country does not encourage the religious leaders of the various communities to be in government.

Except for the passage above, the subject of religious leadership does not appear prominently in Sadr's written texts. His emphasis is more in the equivalent of Vatican II, perhaps even "the liberation theology" one finds in Latin America, with an advocacy for men of religion to be involved on the side of the poor and the deprived, not to lead the country as government officials. This is another important area where Sadr's views would have been of importance in the development of modern constitutionalism had Muammar Qaddafi not abducted him in 1978.

I.6 Musa al-Sadr's Trials

In 1996, Muhammad Khatami was emerging with a promise for stability and moderation in a revolution that had endured a long war with Iraq, during which it considerably hardened domestically.[42] As a self-styled reformist, the new Iranian president steered the country onto a moderate course. A close relative of Musa Sadr, Khatami had authored two books that provide the best entry point to understanding his general religious

[41] There is a large body of literature on *wilayat al-faqih* (rule of the jurist) as the central tenet of the Iranian constitution in Art.5 and Arts.107ff. A rich introduction on political philosophy in the contemporary Iranian debate can be found in Constance Arminjon Hachem, *Chiisme et État: Les clercs à l'épreuve de la modernité* (Paris: CNRS, 2013).

[42] This and the next section were primarily written by Mallat, to whom the personal references apply.

and political philosophy.[43] After the long interaction with Sadr's Iraqi cousin Muhammad Baqer, another intellectual expression of "the Shiʿi International" comes by way of Khatami.

Together with my interest in Muhammad Baqer and Khatami, in addition to the many remarkable people encountered in "the Shiʿi International," I developed with the Sadr family a lifetime journey of friendship and trust, of which the present book is one result. There were several others. The most meaningful career-wise was when the family of the Imam entrusted my law office in 2000 with bringing a legal case about his abduction in Libya two decades earlier. Together with two close companions on the trip, cleric Muhammad Yaʿqub and journalist Abbas Badreddin, news of his whereabouts abruptly stopped on August 31, 1978.

With the legal fight came unique challenges and some difficult moments. Central to the judicial effort was the Imam's son, Sadri, who bears his father's physical traits and endearing charisma, with whom a strenuous legal effort was carried out over five continents, including Australia,[44] to force out the responsibility of Muammar Qaddafi for the abduction of the Imam and his two colleagues.

The lawsuit on behalf of the Sadr, Badreddin and Yaʿqub families was brought in Lebanon on May 22, 2001, by their immediate relatives as *parties civiles*. For a lawyer entrusted with such momentous responsibility, the first question is to determine the central conceptual approach to secure progress, both procedurally and substantively. While moved by the same universal values of justice, the legal rationale for the case operated against a very different background to other international law instances that had developed the field of international criminal law beyond its traditional narrow boundaries.

Before the 1990s, only the pursuit of Nazi war criminals had yielded serious judicial results on the international scene. In the world at large, developments in international criminal law had been effectively halted since Nuremberg. They were revived with the demise of the Soviet Union in two main theaters: Iraq with the invasion of Kuwait by Saddam Hussein in August 1990, and Yugoslavia after its 1992 collapse

[43] On Khatami's worldview, see Chibli Mallat, "Khatami – A Man amidst the Waves," *Daily Star*, June 23–28, 1997 (in six parts). The two books by Khatami are *Az Doniā-ye Shahr tā Shahr-e Doniā* [From the world of the city-state to the city of the world] (Tehran: Nashr-e Nāy, 1994); and *Bīm-e Mawj* [In the middle of the waves] (Tehran: Sīmā-ye Javān, 1994).

[44] Natalie O'Brien, "Cracks in Case of Missing Imam," *Australian*, September 4–5, 2004.

into various smaller states and immense violence within them and on the newly established borders.

The first tangible result was the International Criminal Tribunal for the former Yugoslavia, which was established by United Nations Security Council Resolution 827 (1993). Several other international courts have since been established by the Security Council, including the 2007 Special Tribunal of Lebanon for the assassination of Lebanese former prime minister Rafiq Hariri in February 2005. The search for justice for grave violations of basic human rights culminated in the establishment of the International Criminal Court (ICC) at the Rome conference in 1998, with the ICC starting officially its work in 2002.

All these cases, as well as the trial for the downing of an airliner over the Scottish town of Lockerbie in 1988, are part of a heavy state-directed machinery and the United Nations. In the case of Lockerbie, the US and British governments actively supported the families of the victims by flexing their significant power in the Security Council to produce the special tribunal that sat in Scotland.

For several reasons, it was impossible in 2001 to imagine a special court getting established by the Security Council for the disappearance of Imam Musa al-Sadr, despite the generally unfailing national support in Lebanon. The country was beset with a weak government and an unending succession of civil and regional wars. The disappearance of the Imam had taken place in 1978, over two decades earlier, denting its legal appeal. Unlike Lockerbie, where 270 people were killed, the crime was "kidnapping," and only three Lebanese citizens had disappeared. It was not possible to argue that a crime against humanity had been committed, which generally requires a far larger number of victims. Even if the statute of limitations and the projection backward of the jurisdiction of the ICC had been possible, the competence of the ICC in such matters was hard to envisage.

This left open the national jurisdictions' route only. The most important precedent was formed by the Pinochet case in England. The case was brought by the Chilean dictator's victims before the London High Court. At the same time, other jurisdictions were solicited by relatives of victims, Belgium in particular, where new legislation allowed the successful prosecution of the so-called Butare four, including two nuns who had participated in the Rwanda massacres of 1994. By 2000, preparations for the trial for Sadr started, with his family's trust resulting from some success in rallying the fissiparous Iraqi opposition around a demand for an international trial of Hussein; and, more significantly, in the case of the victims of Ariel Sharon in the Palestinian camps of Sabra and Shatila, which I had brought in Brussels before the Belgian ordinary criminal courts in June 2000 on behalf of the victims' families.[45]

The hard facts in the case of the disappearance of Sadr and his two companions on August 31, 1978, are scant. Qaddafi invited Sadr around the time of the annual celebrations of the military coup that brought him to power nine years earlier, on September 1, 1969. The visit of his three official guests took place in the last days of August against a tense background in Lebanon and the region. In Lebanon, Qaddafi had mediated unsuccessfully among the various warring parties in 1976 (which did not include Sadr's Amal movement) as part of his then messianic belief of taking on the leadership of the Arab world after the death of Egyptian leader Gamal Abdel Nasser. Qaddafi was close to the leftist Palestinian coalition at the time, despite some privileged ties to the Assad family in Syria, whose rule lasted through the Libyan leader's demise in October 2011.

Alliances and disagreements are notoriously murky in the Middle East. Although Qaddafi negatively perceived the Imam siding with Syria against the Palestinians allied with the Lebanese left whom he supported, this was a while before he invited him, and the privileged relationship of Qaddafi with the Assad regime lasted until his demise in October 2011. When the Imam visited Libya on Qaddafi's invitation in late August 1978, the revolution in Iran was on the rise, with tension across the Middle East exacerbated by a coup in Afghanistan and a profound split in the Arab world, with Egypt going it alone for a peace treaty with Israel when the successor of Nasser, Anwar al-Sadat, visited Jerusalem in November 1977. Amid all this turbulence, various theories emerged on the reason why Qaddafi abducted his guest the following year. They all remain pure speculation.

The main legal episodes of the trial are discussed elsewhere.[46] To summarize procedurally complicated developments straddling

[45] For all these cases, see Mallat, *Philosophy of Nonviolence*, 263–68, including a bibliography.

[46] Ibid., 271–76. I conducted the trial on behalf of the families with my colleague at the law school, Dean Fayez Hage-Chahine. The threat materialized in a fax sent by Qaddafi's office to mine in August 2002. The bribes suggested were conveyed through various indirect "intermediaries," in the spirit of the large settlement that Qaddafi paid to the families of Lockerbie's victims. For text of the fax, see ibid., 275n95.

Libya, Lebanon and Italy, the criminal complaint of the families forced Qaddafi into publicly disavowing the fabricated story that prevailed over fifteen years, namely, that he had nothing to do with the three men's disappearance, and that the Imam and his two companions left Libya on an Alitalia flight to Rome on the evening of August 31, 1978. By forcing the collapse of the narrative, leading Qaddafi to publicly declare that the Imam had disappeared in Libya, the judicial fight in Lebanon drew the support of worldwide human rights organizations, especially Amnesty International. The case then saw Qaddafi indicted by the Lebanese prosecutor general and the investigative judge in charge concurring.

Qaddafi threatened the lawyers and sought to bribe the Sadr family. All threats and enticements were ignored, and the family's moral standing stood in sharp contrast to the acceptance of blood money for Lockerbie in the West. The case also defeated efforts to whitewash Qaddafi's name by way of the Italian judiciary. It created the only public opposition to him in the streets of New York as the United Nations opened its largest forum to him shortly before the revolution that swept him away in 2011. In short, the indictment scared Qaddafi, his family and his associates far more than any action taken previously to make him accountable, including repeated solicitations by Arab leaders for Qaddafi to come clean on Sadr's disappearance.

The efforts before the highest court (*al-majlis al-ʿadli*) in Lebanon reached their pinnacle in the summer of 2011, when the families put their arguments to the court as the massive popular revolt against Qaddafi was under way. Before judgment was rendered, Qaddafi died next to the sewers where he was hiding to escape the ire of his victims' anger, which had been pent up over four decades of continued tyranny in the country.

Ever since watching the poor-quality video of Qaddafi begging for mercy at the hands of the vengeful mob that killed him on October 20, 2011, I have in my mind a story that takes us back over 2,000 years in history. This was the rout of "Matho (or Mathos) the Libyan" and his execution by a mob in 238 BC, in a precedent that was immortalized in *Salammbô*, the magnificent novel of Gustave Flaubert published in 1862.

Matho was a soldier and mercenary who rose to power during Carthage's heyday in the third century BC. In the *Histories* of Polybius (d. 118 BC), Mathos rallied other Libyan mercenaries shortly after the end of the First Punic War in 241 BC to march on Carthage. "This was the origin and beginning of the mercenary, or, as it is also called, the

Libyan war."[47] After three long years of internal strife, Matho was defeated by Hamilcar Barcas, Hannibal's father, and brought down by a popular revolt in 238 BC. He died in horrendous conditions. "For the last act in the drama was performed by the young men conducting a triumphal procession through the town, and finally inflicting every kind of torture upon Mathōs."[48]

Polybius does not give any further details, but in his inimitable style, Flaubert built on the account the fictional story of Matho's lover Salammbô. The passages fictionalizing that obscure episode of Libyan history deserve to be quoted, for the parallels with the end of Qaddafi are just stunning. The description of Matho's execution by the mob comes from the fifteenth and last chapter of *Salammbô*, ending with the wide sense of relief among his victims:

> The sun sank behind the waves; his rays fell like long arrows upon the red heart. As the beatings diminished the planet sank into the sea; and at the last palpitation it disappeared.
>
> Then from the gulf to the lagoon, and from the isthmus to the pharos, in all the streets, on all the houses, and on all the temples, there was a single shout; sometimes it paused, to be again renewed; the buildings shook with it; Carthage was convulsed, as it were, in the spasm of Titanic joy and boundless hope.[49]

In Qaddafi's gory death fiction uncannily matched reality. For the Sadr, Yaʿqub and Badreddin families, the relief in seeing his comeuppance was marred by the faintness of the hope that the men, one of them, or two, or all three, might suddenly emerge from the dictator's underground jails. In October 2011, when Qaddafi's regime fell, Sadr would have been eighty-three years old, Yaʿqub sixty-three, Badreddin seventy-three. There was one case in Libya in which a political prisoner who had disappeared eight years before them had been suddenly released.[50]

47 Polybius, *The Histories of Polybius*, trans. Evelyn Shirley (London: Macmillan, 1889; Project Gutenberg), 1, §70, www.gutenberg.org/files/44125/44125-h/44125-h.htm.

48 Ibid., 1, §88.

49 Gustave Flaubert, *Salammbô*, trans. J. S. Chartres (Paris: Michel Lévy Frères, 1862; Project Gutenberg, 2006), chap. xv, www.gutenberg.org/ebooks/1290.

50 "In 2001 nearly 300 prisoners, among them political prisoners, were released. They included Libya's longest-serving political prisoner, Ahmad Zubayr Ahmad al-Sanussi, accused of involvement in an attempted coup in 1970." "Factbox: Qaddafi Rule Marked by Abuses, Rights Groups Say," *Reuters*, February 22, 2011.

It was not to be: 2011 was a special moment in history for Middle Eastern hope, but the counter-revolution prevailed there and elsewhere. Since then, the efforts to find the truth of what happened to the Imam and his companions have been frustrated. The fate of Sadr and his companions in Libya is as obscure in 2026 as the day they disappeared. We still do not know their exact whereabouts or fate. Every day is added torture for their families. The judicial indictment of Qaddafi and his Matho-like demise are no substitute for justice and truth. This is no less true for Lebanon and the Middle East, where thousands of victims have yet to see even a modicum of justice, in a world mired by the violence of dictatorships and massive inequality.

In Lebanon, the void occasioned by Sadr's disappearance is yet to be filled. This book is one opportunity to keep him and his message alive. Sadr's humanism is needed more than ever.

I.7 Conclusion: A Household Name

In Lebanon and in the Middle East, Musa al-Sadr is a household name. He was for me (Mallat) also, in a more personal sense. I retain a faint memory from when I was perhaps ten years old. It is a strong image of a tall man appearing with my parents in the early 1970s in the bedroom that I shared with my sister in our Beirut home to wish us sweet dreams. Clearly, a distinguished guest was visiting for dinner, but I was not sufficiently aware of Lebanese politics other than to recognize a famous name. I have other memories from my youth of the Imam, but I never saw him in person again. A picture dating from around 1973 or 1974 shows him with my father, probably at a meeting my father had with Sadr while presiding over the Beirut bar, or perhaps to celebrate the historical arrangement reached in a legal dispute known in the country as the *Rumul* case. The story of this case is worth recounting.

Rumul is "sands" in Arabic, and a long-standing legal dispute over large plots of sandy land in the southern suburb of Beirut involved powerful parties: the Maronite bishopric of Beirut, which had a century-old beneficial interest in *waqf* (trust) over the land, against the municipalities of Shiyyah (Chiah), Ghobeiry and Haret Hreik, owners of the land as commons. The dispute included, adventitiously, the people who had come to live on large parts of the land, namely, Shiʿi citizens from the south who had migrated to the Beirut suburbs in search of work and better living conditions.

This in Lebanon is a historical case by any measure, including the extraordinary rehabilitation of an obscure clause that my father, as the lawyer for the Maronite Church, had found in the nineteenth-century register of revenues received by the Maronite bishopric of Beirut. The old register, which served as evidence of an effective and continued interest in perpetuity for its Maronite beneficiaries, survived to provide the strongest argument for the fiduciary interest of the Church. The case proceeded slowly, over a period of thirty years, with a dual argument that the Lebanese civil courts accepted, all the way to the court of cassation and the administrative expropriation committees.[51] The first prong of the argument was the right to inscribe the Beirut Maronite bishopric as beneficiary of the trust in the land register; the second prong of the legal argument was administrative, namely, that perpetual beneficial interests in a religious waqf were at least tantamount to half the value of the property over which the waqf had been established.

The case was eventually decided by the Lebanese courts in favor of the bishopric against the claim of the ownership of the commons by the municipalities, but it had also long been the basis of a compromise that my father agreed upon with the Imam for a new ownership status for the land that benefited its residents. As the de jure leader of the Lebanese Shiʿi community since Sadr established the Supreme Shiʿi Council in 1969 and directed it until his disappearance in 1978, the Imam was naturally concerned about the well-being of hundreds of thousands of Shiʿi citizens who had been displaced from the south by poor economic conditions and by Israeli violence, and relocated to the southern suburb where the sandy land stood.[52] The al-Zahra hospital, still there today, was built on one of these plots.

In a symbol of Lebanese continuity, the Imam Sadr Foundation in the southern suburb of Beirut may well have been first built on part of the

[51] Case initiated before the Lebanese civil courts, decision of first instance court of Mount Lebanon December 30, 1958, confirmed on appeal on May 31, 1965, and in cassation on June 11, 1971. Decision of the expropriation first instance committee of Mount Lebanon dated March 30, 1996, affirmed by the expropriation appeal committee. (All files with author.)

[52] Because there had been state expropriation on top of the land dispute, the case continued with some momentous consequences: the Maronite bishopric benefited from a large financial compensation for its beneficial interests as recognized by the court and the committees, for much of the land had meanwhile been expropriated. It used the money in part to build the large Hikma/La Sagesse university building on the outskirts of Beirut.

land freed by the *Rumul* compromise.[53] Upon every visit to the foundation was some Schadenfreude bringing back that early memory of the Imam leaning in the doorway of our bedroom to wish us well, my sister and me, and the strong friendship and the purposeful professional interaction across the generations.

Since then, another Lebanon altogether has emerged since after half a century of violence, a far less compromising one. One does not know what the continued leadership of Musa al-Sadr would have meant for the country. The fate of Lebanon would have been far more humane, no doubt.

[53] This is not certain and requires some archival work. There is no doubt, however, that the present al-Zahra hospital is built on the *Rumul* land.

Note on the Text

Since this book is meant for a general scholarly audience, the transliteration does not include diacritics, except in the Bibliography (and related bibliographic notes). The reader of Arabic and Persian is unlikely to be confused.

The transliteration generally follows the system adopted by the *International Journal of Middle East Studies*. There is no capitalization in Arabic or Persian, so the rendering in English is serendipitous and follows context; for instance, "Allah" or "Musa" are capitalized, respectively. The Imam of the Shiʿi tradition is written with a capital I, as opposed to the imam who leads the prayer. I have generally preferred the use of "God" to "Allah" and removed traditional qualifications such as "Holy" in "Holy Qur'an" or the *basmala* formula ("In the name of God") often found at the beginning of a chapter. Again, this is to make the text easier for the general reader.

Common nouns like *sharīʿa*, *shaykh*, *jihād* and *ḥadīth* are used in their modern form now integrated in English dictionaries, so sharia, sheikh, jihad and hadith. I have sometimes left *umma* in Arabic and sometimes translated it as "Islamic nation," although "community" clarifies that it predates any modern notion of "nation-state" or nationalism.

Proper nouns such as Husain, Sharafeddin and Musa may be rendered, respectively, as Hussein, Hussain or Husayn; Charafeddine, Charafeddin or Sharaf al-Din; and Moussa or Mousa. Musa is the Moses of the monotheist tradition in the Qur'an and remains "Moses" in the text when cited in the Qur'an. An effort was made to standardize names, but I did not force a particular transliteration when several are used. For instance, both Musa Sadr and Musa al-Sadr appear in the text.

Mūsā al-Ṣadr (in proper transliteration) often appears in the literature and in newspapers as Moussa Sadr, in the French rendering common to several names in Lebanon, or Musa Sadr, also without the definite article "al-." Musa Sadr is the preferred spelling by the family, and I use it for the title of the book.

Depending on the use by Sadr of Qur'anic verses, the reference appears within the text of the chapter or in a footnote usually added by the editor. Most of the texts were recorded as spoken addresses, and there are a few notes that Sadr had written himself (these rare annotations are indicated where relevant).

Dates are all from the common era (CE), unless otherwise indicated. Square brackets ([ ]) are the editor's interpolations.

The book is footnoted to explain nuances in the Arabic, to give political/historic context in some passages or to provide full references for Qur'anic verses or hadiths – the sayings of Prophet Muhammad and of the Twelve Imams who form part of the canon in mainstream Shiʿism (which includes the vast majority of Shiʿis in the world, and to which Sadr belongs), as opposed to Sunnis, for whom hadiths are those related only to the Prophet. Notes also explain, where needed, terms drawn from Islamic law. Arabic and Persian titles of books and articles are translated, except for classical books on law and hadith that adopt metaphorical or rhyming titles.

The choice and content of notes reflect the intent to appeal to both specialists and general readers interested in the Middle East and include academic as well as more general books. Since the chapters stand separately, some notes are repeated for the reader not to have to constantly leaf through. The search facility commonly available in digital books helps considerably, but a traditional index is also included.

The translation of the Qur'an is adjusted depending on context to make it more accessible to the audience. N. J. Dawood's English translation of the Qur'an is generally adopted, with various editions (e.g. New York: Viking, 1978). For brevity, such citations are given, for example, in the form "Qur'an 2:130" (i.e., sura 2, verse 130).

The order of the chapters is not chronological, but thematic. More technical chapters on theology and philosophy are included in the end of Part I and carry a more elaborate set of notes. The reader can generally read a chapter irrespective of its order in the book.

Chronology

Musa Sadr's Interrupted Journey

Born in Qom, June 4, 1928. Abducted in Tripoli, Libya, August 31, 1978.

1928 Birth of Musa al-Sadr (Moussa Sadr) on June 4 in the city of Qom, Iran, to a family of scholars originating from Jabal Amil (south Lebanon). His great-great-grandfather, Sayyed Salih, was born in Shhur, a village in southern Lebanon, and Sadr's genealogy can be traced to the seventh Imam of the Shiʿi tradition, Musa b. Jaʿfar (d. 799).

1934 Enrols in Qom elementary school, finishing his secondary school studies in 1947.

1941 Begins his religious studies in the Qom Seminary (*hawza*), continuing his scholarly education to reach the rank of *mujtahid* (scholar authorized to issue rulings independently) at an unusually young age.

1950 Enrols in the Faculty of Law, Department of Economics, University of Tehran. Graduates in 1953. Sadr becomes the first Shiʿi religious scholar to receive a modern law degree while also continuing his studies and teaching in the hawza.

1954 Travels to the holy city of Najaf, Iraq, to pursue higher religious studies. Participates in the Muntada al-Nashr group in Najaf and joins its administrative committee. The Muntada organizes cultural forums with the leading intellectual figures of the city.

1955, 1957 Brief visits to Lebanon.

1958 Returns to the hawza in Qom, where he participates in establishing *Maktab-e Islam* magazine and soon becomes editor in chief. *Maktab-e Islam* is the first Islamic cultural magazine published in Qom and plays a leading part in Iran's intellectual renaissance.

1959 Participates with other leaders (including Ayatollahs Beheshti, Azari Qomi and Makarem Shirazi) in drafting reforms to the academic curriculum in the hawza.

At the end of the year, Sadr arrives in the city of Tyre (Sour) in Lebanon (after the two previous visits in 1955 and 1957), where he begins work as a cleric (imam), succeeding Abdul Hussein Sharafeddin, the country's leading Shiʿi scholar, with the encouragement of Grand Ayatollah Hossein Borujerdi, the leading Shiʿi *marjaʿ* (reference) of the time.

1961 Sadr launches his social and institutional work reorganizing al-Birr wa-l-Ihsan Association, a local charity that he overhauls and enlarges. Sadr establishes educational, vocational training, healthcare, social and religious institutions, seeking in particular to empower women. He runs literacy courses, succeeds in abolishing begging in Tyre and its environs, and establishes a charitable fund for a vocational school in Jabal Amil.

1963 After a two-month visit to Europe, Sadr announces that the tour's objective has been to improve his knowledge of other cultures and reach a better understanding of their progress. He expresses hope this will improve work methodologies in charity, social and religious institutions at home.

June 30 Sadr participates in the coronation of Pope Paul VI as the only Muslim cleric invited to the ceremony. In meetings in the Vatican, Sadr highlights the suffering of the Iranian people and religious scholars under the rule of the shah.

1964 Begins cooperation with members of al-Nadwa al-Lubnaniyya (the Lebanese Cénacle), which hosts him several times to give lectures on Lebanon. The forum, founded and directed by Michel Asmar (d. 1984), serves as an important venue for intellectuals and scholars, drawing participants from all Lebanese communities.

1966 (August) Holds a press conference at the Press Syndicate putting forward ideas for a better organization of Lebanese Shiʿis. Based on wide-ranging studies and consultations, Sadr's efforts lead to the Lebanese parliament approving a law in 1967 establishing the Supreme Islamic Shiʿi Council.

1967 Travels to West Africa for discussions with leading members of the Lebanese community to connect them more intensively with the homeland. Meets the presidents of Côte d'Ivoire and Senegal. Léopold Sédar Senghor, president of Senegal and man of letters, praises the Imam's efforts to spread kindness and nonviolence.

1969 (May 23) Sadr voted head of the Supreme Islamic Shiʿi Council. Calls for the unification of religious rituals among all Muslim sects. Warns against rising Israeli threats, emphasizing his support for Palestinian resistance.

June In a speech on June 2, states that the many sects of Lebanon are windows of culture to the entire world.

1970 Launches media campaign to defend south Lebanon against Israeli violations. Calls on people to stand their ground in their villages and not emigrate. Asks the government to arm citizens and train them for defense, to activate conscription laws and to implement development projects in the south.

May Forms the Commission for Assisting the South with the participation of the heads of the Lebanese sects. Calls for peaceful national strikes. On May 26, some 50,000 people gather near the Supreme Islamic Shiʿi Council in Hazmiyya, Beirut. In response, the Lebanese government forms the Council of the South, with a commitment to develop the region and alleviate its poverty.

August Tours several European countries in support of the Palestinians. Holds a press conference in Bonn to condemn the Judaization of the city of Jerusalem to the detriment of the other two world religions.

Speech at a press meeting in France: "The catastrophe of Palestine is a black smear on the world's conscience. The struggle of the Palestinian people is in defense of all religions and the sanctity of Jerusalem. Israel is a racist and expansionist state, and Lebanon's coexistence of religions is a religious and cultural need for the world."

March — In Cairo, stresses the coexistence of sects in Lebanon as a unique cultural experience in the world.

1971 — Sadr, now widely referred to as Imam, leaves Lebanon on a tour including to Morocco, where, upon the invitation of King Hassan II, he lectures at the University of al-Qarawiyyin in Fez. Visits Mauritania, Nigeria and Egypt. In Cairo, Sadr participates in the sixth conference of the Islamic Research Academy at al-Azhar, a leading center of Islamic thought since the tenth century CE. An active member of the academy since 1968, Imam Sadr presents the Azhar public suggestions on national and Islamic issues.

In Egypt, Sadr visits the front at Suez, where troops have been stationed facing Israeli forces since the 1967 war. Sadr spends several weeks meeting the military staff, acting as imam for prayers.

Calls for upholding religion and for jihad to free Palestine. Suggests a project of jihad bonds to activate grassroots participation in any war against Israel.

After reading in Lebanese newspapers of British vicar Herbert Adams highlighting developments in the Middle East, Sadr writes to Adams that "all of us, Muslims and Christians, felt and heard the voice of Jesus Christ ... becoming louder to awaken the conscience of the Christians in the West ... against Zionism, which has turned the city of worship [Jerusalem] into a den of thieves."

While emphasizing the positive role of sects in Lebanon, Sadr denounces the country's sectarian regime as evil covering up "political feudalism."

1972 — Issues a call from Jwaya, south Lebanon, about the dangers of Israeli violations. To bolster the resilience of the people in the region, Sadr intensifies his activities, with statements to the national and international media, lectures and sermons in mosques, churches and universities, warning of the dangers of the government neglecting its responsibilities both in defending the south and in developing Lebanon's deprived regions. Calls for a regime based on shared religious values rather than secular or sectarian structures.

1973 Sadr announces in successive Friday prayers that efforts to seek freedom in Palestine should aim also to free Islamic and Christian holy sites and be rooted in a universal approach to the freedom of all humankind. With the outbreak of the October/Ramadan War between Israel and the Arab countries, Sadr calls for jihad and leads a campaign to collect donations for the families of fighters.

1974 Convenes in March a rally in Baalbek, attended by 100,000 people, and another in Tyre in May, attended by 150,000. Participants take an oath to stay mobilized until no deprived person or area remains in Lebanon. The rallies lead to the creation of the Movement of the Deprived (Harakat al-Mahrumin), and the issuing of the "intellectuals' manifesto" in support of the movement. This is signed by over 190 leading public figures, representing all sects and segments of society.

1975 With the outbreak of civil war, Sadr pleads with all parties to end the violence and restore peace in Lebanon. Urges the Lebanese to respect their homeland, and Palestinians to preserve their cause at the heart of Lebanon. On his instigation, the Committee for National Peace is formed. He draws up guidelines for the committee that emphasize preserving coexistence and using dialogue and democratic means to achieve reform.

June 27 In protest against the continuing civil war, Imam Sadr begins a hunger strike in the ʿAmiliyya mosque in Beirut, spending his time in prayer and fasting. Sitting in a corner of the mosque he dictates a message: "Violence has defiled the country; I have come to the house of God, and my sustenance is the book of God and a few drops of water."

Imam Sadr ends the strike five days later as a national reconciliation government is formed and adopts his demands. Visits Qaʿ and Deir al-Ahmar, Christian villages in the Beqaa region, to lift a siege and end the local sectarian conflict.

Announces the birth of the Lebanese Resistance Units (or Regiments, Afwaj al-Muqawama al-Lubnaniyya), or "Amal" in the Arab acronym.

At his request, a spiritual summit for all the heads of the Lebanese religious communities is held. At the summit, Sadr warns of three dangers: the division of Lebanon, leading to conflict inside the homeland sparked regionally by the creation of Israel; continuing Israeli violations, which should be resisted on the basis of values and rights rooted in religion, history and nation; and the end of Palestinian armed action inside Lebanon. He describes Israel as a threat to Arabs, to Muslims, to Christians and to liberty and dignity.

1976 (May)	Participates in the Lebanese Islamic Summit, held in the town of ʿAramun, which adopts a constitutional document that he considers a prelude to peace and national harmony. Works to defuse tensions between the Syrian and Palestinian leaderships. States that cooperation is the only way forward, and that a clash between them will cause Lebanon to fall and resistance to end, harming Syria and the Arab cause to the sole benefit of Israel. Conducts intensive efforts with Arab leaders to halt the civil war, resulting in the Riyadh conference on October 16 and the Cairo summit on October 25, and leading to a ceasefire in Lebanon with the deployment of the Arab Deterrence Force.
1977 (January)	Emphasizes that Lebanon is a cultural need for the world, and that Lebanese coexistence is essential for the future of Islam and Christianity.
May	At a meeting of the Supreme Islamic Shiʿi Council, Sadr presents a working paper with suggestions for political and social reforms, and calls for the reconstruction of Lebanon along the lines of coexistence and resistance to Zionism: "Lebanon is a final homeland for all its sons and daughters." Expresses his support for the growing Islamic movement in Iran at a rally to mark the passage of forty days after the death of Ali Shariati, one of Iran's most prominent Islamic thinkers.

1978 (Summer) Imam Sadr starts an Arab world tour to meet several leaders after the Israeli invasion of south Lebanon. On August 25, Sadr and two companions, Sheikh Muhammad Ya'qub and journalist Abbas Badreddine, depart for Libya to meet government officials at the invitation of Muammar Qaddafi. The three men are last seen on August 31 leaving their hotel for a meeting with Qaddafi, and are never heard from again. The Libyan authorities say their guests have left Libya for Italy. Both Italian and Lebanese judiciaries reject their claims in the wake of extensive investigations. Arab and international pressure on Qaddafi meets denial and stonewalling.

2000 Start of judicial action in Lebanon in the name of the three families.

Twelve Texts on Humanism

1

By Way of an Autobiography

1.1 Beginnings

My father was a renowned religious scholar[1] and became a *marja'*.[2] He led the Grand Seminary in Qom, Iran.[3] My eldest brother[4] was also a religious scholar, and so was my paternal grandfather, Sayyed Isma'il al-Sadr,[5] a major religious figure who nearly became the recognized leader of the Islamic Shi'i community around the world. My maternal

[1] This chapter first appeared in 2022 in Arabic as a booklet, *Kalima huwa qā'iluhā* [Words he spoke] (Beirut: Markaz al-Imām Mūsā al-Ṣadr li-l-Abḥāth wa-l-Dirāsāt, 2022), including several photos. The Arabic text was discovered in 2019 and is based on taped interviews by Sadr carried out in a doctoral study on him in France that seems to have remained unfinished. The editors were unable to connect with the interviewer, Mona Makki, thanks to whom this remarkable text has survived. The exact date of the interview is unknown, but the various references (see nn. 113, 124) in the text suggest that it was carried out in 1977, after the lull that followed the "two-year" civil war in Lebanon in October 1976 and before the development of the popular revolt in Iran, which Sadr does not mention here, and which started shortly after the death of Ruhullah al-Khumaini's son Mustafa in Najaf on October 23, 1977. The subtitles adopted by the Sadr Research Center are for the convenience of the reader and stand in lieu of the questions put to Sadr.

[2] Sadreddine al-Sadr (1882–1953). See Muḥammad Muḥsin Āghābozorg Tehrānī, *Ṭabaqāt a'lām al-Shī'a* [Biographies of famous Shi'is] (Beirut: Dār Iḥyā' al-Turāth al-'Arabī, 1982 [1962]), 51:943–49. A *marja'* is a source of guidance for Shi'i believers. For details on how a Shi'i religious leader becomes a marja', and what the *marja'iyya* as an institution has meant since the eighteenth century, see Mallat, *Renewal*, 38–58, 61–89, respectively.

[3] The Qom Seminary (*hawza*), established in 1922 by Grand Ayatollah Abdul-Karim Haeri Yazdi (1859–1937), was the largest Islamic seminary in Iran. See Hamid Algar, "Ḥā'eri, 'Abd-al-Karim Yazdi," in *Encyclopædia Iranica*, www.iranicaonline.org/articles/haeri/?highlight=Haeri%20Yazdi.

[4] Reza Sadreddine al-Sadr (1921–94). Tehrānī, *A'lām*, 943–49.

[5] Isma'il al-Sadr (1842–1920). Born in Isfahan, he is the first scholar to be known by the last name of al-Sadr. Ibid., 159–60.

grandfather, Sayyed Hussein al-Qummi, was also a prominent religious scholar and an internationally recognized jurist.[6]

All of my ancestors were significant religious scholars in their day. The father of Sayyed Isma'il al-Sadr, Sayyed Sadreddine,[7] emigrated from Lebanon to Iraq as a child and later settled in Isfahan, where he became a well-known religious scholar. His father, Sayyed Salih,[8] had also emigrated during the Ottoman era under the rule of Ahmad Pasha al-Jazzar,[9] after Shi'i religious scholars were persecuted in Jabal Amil and two of his children killed. In emigrating to Iraq as a religious scholar, Sayyed Salih followed in the footsteps of several of our forefathers, including Sayyed Ibrahim Sharafeddin, Sayyed Ali Noureddine, Sayyed Noureddine Ali,[10] and others.

Our lineage can be traced back to Imam Musa b. Ja'far,[11] one of the twelve Shi'i Imams. All our forefathers were either religious scholars or pious believers. This has made us first and foremost a religious family, even though some members have been prominent politicians, such as Mohammad al-Sadr,[12] who became prime minister of Iraq and was a key figure in Iraq's independence, as well as my uncle Sayyed Mohammad

[6] Ayatollah Sayyed Hussein Tabataba'i al-Qommi (1912–2007) was born in Najaf, Iraq, before moving to Iran. Ibid., 653–55.

[7] Sadreddine al-Sadr (1779–1847), Musa Sadr's paternal great-grandfather. Ibid., 668–70.

[8] Salih Sharafeddin (1710–1802). Ibid., 661–62.

[9] A Bosnian who converted to Islam, Ahmad Pasha al-Jazzar (1722–1804) was the Ottoman governor of Sidon and Damascus who maneuvered between various communities and rival leaders, largely with the aim of collecting taxes for Istanbul in order to remain in power as the Ottomans' local representative. The nickname *jazzar*, butcher, refers to his uniquely brutal rule. In South Lebanon, he defeated the 1781 revolt of Nasif al-Naser, a Shi'i leader of Jabal Amil, prompting many Shi'i sheikhs to move to the Beqaa region or further afield. Jabal Amil is a hilly area in southern Lebanon and one of the oldest strongholds for the Shi'i community. The region's name is said to derive from Banu 'Amila, a Yemeni Christian tribe that migrated from southern Arabia and settled in the area, which generally corresponds to the Upper Galilee. See, generally, Mallat, *Aspects*, 1–3.

[10] The three forebears, all from the early lineage of the Sharafeddin family, are mentioned in 'Abd al-Hussein Sharafeddin, *Bughyat al-rāghibīn fī silsilat Āl Sharaf al-Dīn* [The object of desire in the lineage of the Sharafeddin family], ed. 'Abdallah Sharafeddin (Tyre: Markaz al-Imām Sharaf al-Dīn, 1991), 1:12–13, with further references to earlier sources. We are grateful to Raed Charafeddin for this information.

[11] Imam Musa b. Ja'far al-Kazem (745–99) was the seventh Imam in Twelver Shi'i Islam. He was called "al-Kazem" (in Arabic, the one who does not allow his anger to show) for his kindness and generosity toward his people. He was a prominent scholar of the Ja'fari school of law (*madhhab*), in modern times considered the "fifth" school of law in Islam, along the four other established Sunni schools; see nn. 26, 28 and accompanying text.

[12] Mohammad al-Sadr (1882–1956) was president of the Iraqi senate several times between 1929 and 1943, and briefly prime minister in 1948.

Mahdi,[13] who was also a religious scholar and played a major role in Iraq's independence. Many members of our family became politicians and experts in Iraq, Iran and Lebanon, but the overarching character of our family remains religious.[14]

1.2 Between Religious Duty and Academic Learning

I did not become a religious scholar just because I came from a religious family. It was rather a kind of a sacrifice I made for my father. We used to live in Iran, and the previous king, Reza Shah,[15] issued a series of laws, some of which regulated the work of religious scholars, imposed restrictions on them and conscripted their young men into the army.[16] Enormous pressures were exerted on the religious establishment during

13 On Mohammad Mahdi al-Sadr (1879–1939), who lived mostly in Iraq, see ʿAbd al-Karīm al-Dabbāgh, *al-Sayyed Muḥammad Mahdī al-Ṣadr* (Qom: Rāfed, 2017).

14 The term "Shiʿi International" (Mallat, *Renewal*) reflects the simple reality that Shiʿism was not dependent on the national state nor constrained intellectually or politically by state boundaries. "It is doubtful whether Sayyed Sadr al Din al Sadr, Sayyed Musa's father, thought of his move from Iraq to Iran in the 1920s as the crossing of an international frontier . . . Ties of faith, commerce, and family bound Najaf and Kerbala to the Persian religious centers across the borders." Ajami, *The Vanished Imam*, 35. Shiʿi religious leaders had to negotiate and manage relations with state authorities and were always vulnerable to charges of being "loyal" to a "foreign" power.

15 Reza Shah Pahlavi (1878–1944), known as Reza Shah, became emperor-king (shah) in 1925 after a coup d'état brought him to power in Tehran in 1921. He was the founder of the Pahlavi dynasty, which was overthrown by the Iranian Revolution in 1979.

16 *Khidmat al-ʿalam*, literally "flag service," refers to draft conscription. For a discussion of the army under the Pahlavi shahs, see Stephanie Cronin, *Armies and State-Building in the Middle East* (London: I.B. Tauris, 2014), chap. 4. Cronin explains that both Reza Shah and his successor, Mohammad Reza Shah, saw a large, conscripted army as part of "modernisation" developing a popular sense of nationalism based on loyalty to the monarchy. This, Musa Sadr suggests here, undermined the clerics' autonomy. "Conscription . . . [introduced in the 1920s] had encouraged an embryonic process of national integration and it certainly produced an impressively large army, but the resulting force continued to possess serious military and operational inadequacies. Furthermore, the vast amounts of money spent acquiring the most up-to-date weaponry from abroad resulted in the distortion of military priorities and led to unrealistic and complacent assessments of the army's strength . . . the conscript army of the 1930s was a parade-ground army, largely untried in battle" (ibid., 139). The Iranian army's disintegration in the face of Soviet and British intervention in 1941 was far from the end of the story, writes Cronin: "It was the Shah's [Mohammad Reza's] insistence on a particular model of military development, the building of a large army based on conscription, which proved to be his downfall [in the 1979 revolution], as a small, volunteer professional army would surely have proved to be much less vulnerable to external social and political pressures, more loyal to its creator and more effective in purely military terms" (ibid., 135).

his rule, which reduced the number of students at the seminary to under 300. Before and after these restrictions, seminary students were in the thousands.

During that time, people generally turned away from religious learning and from the clergy. Hardly anyone stayed close to religion – some of those who did came from various backgrounds while others were the sons of religious scholars.

Back then, my father believed that the calling[17] of religious scholars in Iran was under threat, and he urged me to follow the clerical path. I had just graduated from middle school[18] and received my national diploma (*brevet*). He told me that I had a religious duty to become a member of the clergy. I was disappointed to abandon my modern academic studies,[19] but I heeded my father's guidance and began religious training. A few years later, my father instructed me to pursue my modern studies in parallel with my religious learning. I applied to the first and second baccalaureate examinations and was admitted to the Faculty of Law.[20] I graduated from the Tehran Faculty of Law while pursuing my religious learning.[21]

The reason why I first began my religious studies was my father's instructions and my belief in his guidance. When political pressure began to rise, and after graduating from the Faculty of Law and reaching a fairly advanced level of religious learning, I had to make a choice. I was offered a high-ranking position in the judiciary, but I decided to stay on the path of religious studies because I felt that Shiʿi scholars were better positioned to assume a leading role in serving their community. I decided therefore not to abandon my religious studies, and, upon graduating, I moved to Lebanon to undertake the mission that I am here to accomplish.

1.3 Role Model

While the Islamic environment in which I grew up was pious, it was also open-minded. Our family was religiously observant, and I remember

[17] *Risala* (Persian *resalat*) often means "letter" or "treatise," but is translated better here as "mission" or "calling." A risala (more accurately *risala ʿamaliyya*, practical treatise) was also the crowning compendium and the most advanced contribution of a scholar who has reached the advanced stage that makes him a marjaʿ. See Mallat, *Renewal*, 13, 47–48.

[18] This was in 1947.

[19] Sadr uses an Arabized version of the English "academic."

[20] Sadr also studied economics, which was then taught within the law faculty.

[21] In 1953.

seeing my father praying very often, night and day. He was conservative and frugal; for example, we never had Persian carpets in our home. Our life was austere. My father was a man of literature, a historian and a poet – and he was immersed in modern culture. During his youth, he founded modern schools in Iraq and wrote a series of history textbooks. He wrote for some of the most prominent Arab magazines, such as *al-Manar*, *al-Huda* and the Egyptian and Iraqi issues of *al-Risala* – and for this he was criticized by conservative scholars during his youth.[22]

The environment in which I grew up was Islamic and observant in our style of life, but open-minded in terms of thinking and action. I remember that my father made several proposals to restructure and modernize the Qom Seminary, and to redesign its examinations. While some of his proposals were carried through, he was not able to achieve all that he had hoped for, because of the opposition by conservative members. He had progressive views on religious organization and Islamic affairs. He expressed modern opinions in his fatwas and in writings on Islamic law,[23] which show how open-minded and progressive his thinking was. He not only wrote about Islamic law and rules but also authored history books and an encyclopedic collection of the sayings of *ahl al-bayt* (the household of the Prophet)[24] in which he laid out in an organized manner speeches and stories attributed to them. He was deeply interested in Islamic unity, and he joined those who sought to bring Sunnis and Shiʿis together by writing a book entitled *Liwaʾ al-hamd fi-ma rawahu al-fariqan*.[25] "Let us transform," he used to say, "the Qur'an and what Muslims have attributed to the Prophet into axioms and agree on [as many] issues [as possible], and reduce the severity of the disagreements between Muslims." It is for these reasons that I regard my

[22] All three magazines were published in Egypt at the turn of or in the early twentieth century and were founded and/or edited by Sunni scholars.

[23] *Fiqh*, the technical aspect of Islamic law, designating the classical corpus.

[24] Literally, "People of the House," *ahl al-bayt* refers to the family of the Prophet Muhammad, including first and foremost his daughter Fatima and son-in-law Ali.

[25] *Liwaʾ al-hamd fi-ma rawahu al-fariqan* (literally, *The Fanion of Thanks in the Sayings Attributed to the Two Leaders [the Prophet and Ali]*) remains unpublished. In a speech given on January 10, 1969, Sadr mentioned the book as "an attempt to compile what Muslims narrated from various sects in all fields of belief and law, to serve as a common reference for all in accordance with the Qur'an. More precisely, it sought to unify the Prophetic Sunna [the hadiths, which are different for Sunnis and Shiʿis]." Speech available on www.imamsadr.net.

father as a role model in my life, and why I have such a great deal of respect and appreciation for him.

1.4 What It Means to Be a Shiʿi

This is a delicate issue. Shiʿis are regarded in our everyday life as a community that differs from other Islamic communities. Muslims themselves have contributed to this belief, as have scholars of various backgrounds. As far as I know, Shiʿism is not a separate Islamic community producing *fiqh* scholarship opposed to the other fiqh schools – the Hanafis,[26] Shafiʿis, Malikis, Hanbalis or even the Zahiris,[27] Ibadis[28] and other legal schools. Nor is it a separate school of *kalam*[29] that stands out from the Muʿtazila[30] or the Ashʿari[31] schools. Shiʿism, as described in its earliest references, is the ideology of the activist class, the vanguard, or what we now call "cadres."[32] *Ijtihad* (the creative interpretation of law) plays a major role in Shiʿism. Simply put, ijtihad is an advanced understanding of reality and of religion; it is an innovating vision. The Imams of the Prophet's House assumed this role, and they taught their companions, who are among the founding figures of Shiʿism, to do the same.

[26] The Hanafi school is one of four Sunni schools (madhhab, pl. *madhahib*) of religious law, following the teachings of the Imam Abu Hanifa (d. 767). The Shafiʿi school derives from the teachings of Muhammad b. Idris al-Shafiʿi (767–820); the Maliki school from the teachings of Malik b. Anas (711–95); and the Hanbali school from the teachings of Ahmad b. Hanbal (780–855). On the four schools, and what is known and not known sufficiently in histories of Islamic law, of their consolidation, and the role (or not) of ijtihad, see Chibli Mallat, *Introduction to Middle Eastern Law* (Oxford: Oxford University Press, 2007), 110–122; George Makdisi, *The Rise of Colleges: Institutions of Learning in Islam and the West* (Edinburgh: Edinburgh University Press, 1981).

[27] The Zahiri school, following Dawud al-Zahiri (815–33), believes in the strict adherence to the literal provisions of the Qur'an and Sunna, rather than resorting to more freely interpreting the text.

[28] The Ibadi school, founded by Abdullah b. Ibadh al-Tamimi (d. 708), originated in the Khawarij "secessionist" movement, which established itself as a "community" after 657. It is the dominant school of law in Oman.

[29] *Kalam*, literally "speech," is close to the Graeco-Roman "rhetoric."

[30] The Muʿtazila ("those who stand apart") appeared as a theological school/tradition in early Islam, emphasizing human free will and the createdness of the Qur'an.

[31] The Ashʿari school was a theological tradition stemming from Abu al-Hasan al-Ashʿari (d. 935), who believed in the use of reason to defend Islam and the divine nature of the Qur'an.

[32] *Taliʿa*, vanguard, a concept common in communist circles, and adopted in militant Shiʿi movements. Sadr also uses an Arabized rendition of the Franco-English "cadres."

As we all know, almost all of the Imams were martyred. In a well-known hadith, "We are all either killed or poisoned." The Imams always offered advice on how to improve governance, and they had followers. Rulers and caliphs were upset, and so the Imams often faced displacement and torture, sometimes martyrdom by assassination or poisoning.

When we examine the sayings of these Imams, we do not feel that they favor one school of thought over another. They call upon people to embrace Islam as a whole instead. The term "Shiʿism" was first used by the Prophet, as is mentioned in several commentaries, such as *al-Durr al-manthur* by al-Suyuti,[33] who says that the Prophet was once sitting when Ali came to him.[34] The Prophet welcomed Ali and said: "O Ali, you and your followers (*shiʿa*) will enter God's heaven satisfied and blessed."

Even in the days of the Prophet, the presence of followers of Ali (*shiʿat ʿAli*) was attested. By *shiʿa* are meant his followers, the companions that used to meet Imam Ali, to seek his assistance, and who regarded him as the perfect incarnation of a true Muslim and a perfect example of Muhammad's teachings, of Islamic teachings and of how we should bring up Islamic individuals. At the time, there was no purpose in establishing any "school of thought." The Prophet was still present. I prefer to think of Shiʿism as an "ideology"[35] – the ideology of the Muslim vanguard – rather than a separate school of thought.

At a practical level, Shiʿism is based on the religious principles of Oneness, prophecy and Judgment Day, which all Muslims adhere to. Justice – that is, divine justice – is considered one of its fundamental doctrinal beliefs.

Some Islamic schools of thought believed that there was no point in describing God as "just," because what is "just" is determined by what God does. Shiʿis, on the other hand, believe that God only does what is [already/independently] just. Others, including the Muʿtazila, agreed

[33] Jamal al-Din al-Suyuti (1145–1505) is the author of a famous Sunni *tafsir*, *al-Durr al-manthur fi al-tafsir bi-l-maʾthur*, available on www.wikisource.com.

[34] Ali b. Abi Talib (d. 661), the cousin, son-in-law and companion of the Prophet Muhammad, ruled as the fourth caliph from 656 until he was assassinated in 661 by a member of the Khawarij faction. He is the eponymic figure in Shiʿi Islam and the first Imam.

[35] Musa Sadr here uses an Arabized version of the English and French word.

with the Shiʿis.[36] This characterized Shiʿism at a certain point, even if few Muslims share this understanding of justice nowadays.

And then the Imamate. The Imamate is a pillar[37] of Shiʿism. The Imamate, or *wilaya*,[38] comes from the fact that the Prophet had two roles, which we can also refer to as two missions or responsibilities.

The first responsibility is that of prophecy,[39] delivering law and religion from God to the people. And the Prophet delivered the divine message of Islam trustfully.

The second role is that of wilaya, the task of implementing the rules of religion. In Medina, the Prophet was not only a messenger but also a leader who tried to build an Islamic society of good Muslim citizens:[40] "The Prophet has a greater claim on the faithful than they do themselves."[41] The Prophet was given the authority to rule, and Muslims were required to obey the Prophet, whose sayings, opinions, thoughts and choices had to be respected. Muslims could not favor their own beliefs over those of the Prophet; they had a duty of obeyance to enable him to build the Islamic society, which he did. Building this new society no doubt required time. Even the nine or ten years after *hijra*[42] were not sufficient for the Prophet to build the new society for which he had laid

[36] The Muʿtazila (see n. 30) went against doctrines based on an understanding of God as "all-knowing," holding the Qur'an to be uncreated and eternally existing and human actions predestined. Similar debates have taken place within other religions, including Christianity, and indeed within "nonreligious" philosophy (Ludwig Wittgenstein highlighted the differences between "predicting" that someone will follow an order, and gives the example of a gymnast listening to an instructor, and someone observing the regular reactions of different metals to acids: *Philosophical Investigations*, trans. G. E. M. Anscombe, P. M. S. Hacker and Joachim Schulte [Oxford: Wiley-Blackwell, 2009], 630). Ethical judgments are applied to actions, not events, to motives, not to scientific laws. Sadr consistently argued that human beings had free will and a choice as to whether to act justly or not.

[37] Sadr uses the word *rukn*, also applied to the "five pillars" of Islam: *shahada* (profession of faith), *salat* (prayer), zakat (alms), *sawm* (fasting) and hajj (pilgrimage). This is naturally a major difference from the Sunnis, for whom there is no particular theological recognition of any of the Twelve Imams.

[38] *Wilaya* (rule, governorate, guardianship) refers here to authority or "guardianship" exclusive to the Prophet and the Imams.

[39] This is "prophecy" in the original English sense, from the Greek root meaning to "speak on behalf of" another (a deity), rather than the later sense of foretelling the future.

[40] Muhammad moved to Medina (known then as Yathrib) from 622 following his "flight" (hijra) from Mecca. He returned in 629 as the new leader in the city. In Medina, the Prophet acted as arbiter in disputes, developing in effect a system of law. See, e.g., Martin Lings, *Muhammad: His Life Based on the Earliest Sources* (Rochester, VT: Inner Traditions, 1983), chaps. 33–39.

[41] Qur'an 33:70–71. [42] See n. 40.

the foundations. On the Day of Ghadir (*yawm al-ghadir*), the hadith tells us, when the Prophet was returning from his "farewell pilgrimage,"[43] he reached al-Juhfa, where a pond (*ghadir*)[44] lay by a crossroads. Pilgrims returning home to Syria, Iraq, the Hijaz or Yemen would part ways there.[45] The Prophet gathered them and declared that his time was near, that God had told him that he would die soon and said: "Do I not have a stronger affinity to you than you do yourselves?" to which they replied, "Yes." The Prophet then said: "He who has me as his master has Ali as his master."[46] We believe that the Prophet chose Ali at God's command, as the text indicates to us that God entrusted Ali to become a leader and an Imam to take forward the building of an Islamic society.

1.5 Shi'ism as Perspective

Shi'ism is an Islamic vision as doctrine. As far as fiqh or the sources of sharia are concerned (questions such as: What is fiqh? What are the rules of the sharia? What is halal and what is haram? What is right and what is wrong?), all Muslims agree that such matters should be decided on the basis of the Qur'an and the Sunna – that is, the Prophet's biography, sayings and deeds – as well as on *ijma'*[47] (the consensus of the Muslim community),[48] and on human reason.[49] There is no dispute between Muslims with regard to these four sources.

However, Shi'is add to these four sources the sayings of the Imams of the Prophet's House – namely, Ali, al-Hassan, al-Hussein, Zayn al-Abidin, al-Baqer, al-Sadeq, al-Kazem, al-Rida, al-Taqi, al-Hadi,

43 *Hujjat al-wida'* ("the farewell pilgrimage"). Shortly before the end of his life, Muhammad went to Mecca, from Medina, for a pilgrimage that established many of the rituals performed on hajj ever since.

44 *Ghadir* means stream or spring, but is understood in this context as a pool or pond. The stream was located in a valley close to Medina and known as Ghadir Khumm.

45 Bilad al-Sham corresponds to Greater Syria, comprising today's Syria as well as Lebanon and Palestine.

46 This is a saying celebrated by the Shi'is, in which the Prophet confers the mantle of his leadership to Ali. It is known as *hadith al-ghadir* (see n. 44). The Sunnis acknowledge the hadith but dispute the Shi'i interpretation of Ali as the designated political successor (*khalifa*) of the Prophet.

47 *Ijma'* refers to the consensus of Islamic scholars (or of the Muslim community) on a point of law.

48 *Umma*, nation, community of Muslims at large.

49 *'Aql*, reason. Sunni legal scholars do not usually include 'aql as a formal source, to avoid a freer interpretation of the Qur'an and Sunna.

al-Askari and the twelfth Imam. Shiʿis strictly abide by the sayings, deeds and choices of these Twelve Imams, just as they abide by those of the Prophet. Other Muslims do not agree with this view; they rely instead on the sayings of the companions of the Prophet[50] as the direct tradents of the [divine] revelation. By contrast, Shiʿis do not rely on all of the Prophet's companions, but only on a limited group of them whose sayings are documented in a verified text. This is the difference between Shiʿis and other Islamic schools of thought in terms of sources. That is why some ideas are different, but I must emphasize that this difference is not significant. Some Imams, such as Ali, al-Hassan and al-Hussein, were also companions of the Prophet, and their sayings are used by non-Shiʿi Muslims. Al-Baqer and al-Sadeq are also considered "successors," and the sayings of successors are valued. Shiʿis also adopt the sayings of some of the Prophet's companions. While this difference in the reliance on sources is real, it is not significant when compared to the main teachings of Islam, and it gets narrower by the day.

I would like to point out that over twelve generations the Imams observed the world develop and evolve. During that time,[51] Islamic society grew and came into contact with the global community, with global civilizations, such as the ancient Egyptian civilization, the Pharaonic civilization in Alexandria, the Greek civilization with its broad philosophical, scientific and artistic heritage, the civilizations of the Chaldeans, Assyrians and Ur, Hammurabi's legal thought,[52] Persian-Iranian civilization and Indian civilization. Toward the end of the first century, Islamic society began to expand and to interact with these civilizations, and it was exposed to new challenges in governance and administration, an immense territory and a large variety of ways of interacting and lifestyles.[53]

[50] *Sahaba* ("companions") is often taken to mean disciples and followers of the Prophet Muhammad who accompanied him throughout his lifetime.

[51] That is, between the death of the Prophet in 632 and the occultation of the twelfth Imam in 874.

[52] Hammurabi, a Babylonian king (r. 1792–50 BCE), established a legal code that influenced subsequent Middle Eastern law, including the law of Moses as rendered in the Torah. The code laid down specific penalties, including physical punishments. "In the 282 paragraphs of the Code of Hammurabi … 21 are devoted to criminal dispositions. The 'tooth for a tooth' concept of the Qur'an and the Bible are rendered verbatim in the Code." Mallat, *Introduction to Middle Eastern Law*, 17.

[53] By 660, expanding Arab rule, inspired by Islam, took in today's Iran, following the overthrow of the Sasanian Empire, and much of Egypt. By 750, the reach included Bukhara and land as far east as the Indus River. The notion that Arabia was then exposed to wider influences is summarized in Fred Donner, "Muhammad and the Caliphate," in

In its early days, Islamic society was faced with thousands upon thousands of new questions and issues. The Qur'an had been revealed in the days of the Prophet, and, of course, there was no new revelation after that. All the Prophet's companions had also passed away, as they all belonged to the same generation. That is why Shiʿi Muslims relied on the sayings of the Imams – in particular al-Baqer and al-Sadeq – who lived later. The Imams shaped Islam's position on various issues of life, guided Muslims and answered their questions. Shiʿi thought remained unified and cohesive, and the Shiʿis did not ban innovative interpretation (ijtihad), since they had established a robust framework that guarded against deviation from core principles. By contrast, other Muslim communities resorted to other [more reserved] methods of interpretation, in the form of preference (*istihsan*)[54] based on public interest (*maslaha*),[55] after precedent (*qiyas*)[56] failed to serve as a basis for governance. They found themselves issuing rules that resembled legislation more than mere religious opinion. This resulted in disunity and the threat of a deep schism between Muslims in departing from Islamic belief. In response to that threat, Sunni schools of law decided in the mid-eighteenth century to ban innovative interpretation.[57] That is why Shiʿi

The Oxford History of Islam, ed. John Esposito (Oxford: Oxford University Press, 1999), 1–61. Musa Sadr is making the point that a largely nomadic Arab society faced governance challenges in dealing with different societies: for example, the settled communities that had been under Sasanian rule in present-day Iraq and Iran. Albert Hourani, *A History of the Arab Peoples* (Cambridge, MA: Harvard University Press, 1991), chaps. 2–4, offers a graceful exposition of how this evolved in terms of economy, politics, language, culture and religion. See also Jonathan Berkey, *The Formation of Islam: Religion and Society in the Near East 600–1800* (Cambridge: Cambridge University Press, 2003). The sheer size of the Islamic world includes this wider influence that plays out, according to Musa Sadr, in different ways and different areas.

54 *Istihsan* literally means "to consider something good" and denotes the preference of the legal scholar for a particular legal interpretation among various ones.

55 *Maslaha* (benefit, interest), more technically *al-masalih al-mursala* (absolute, i.e., overarching, interests), is a legal concept. It denotes a juristic methodology by which certain things are allowed or prohibited based on whether they serve the public interest.

56 *Qiyas*, analogy, is the process by which the teachings of hadith are compared to those of the Qur'an in order to apply them to new circumstances. It corresponds to the doctrine of precedent in the common law.

57 Sadr refers here to a century-long controversy on tradition and innovation in law. For Shiʿis, innovation (ijtihad) is a central obligation that the legal scholar, the *mujtahid*, must practice to address controversies that arise in his age. For Sunnis, it was traditional to describe ijtihad as having been barred sometime in the classical age. Sadr refers to this "closure" as a mid-eighteenth-century occurrence. It is more probable that the reference is to the moment when a similar controversy between the Akhbari and the Usuli schools

jurisprudence with regard to religious judgments, Shiʿi thought with regard to doctrine and Shiʿi interpretations of the Qur'an enrich the human soul. This is perhaps one of the key differentiating features of Shiʿism.

Consequently, we do not consider Shiʿism to be a separate sect but rather an Islamic vision adopted by Imams from among the People of the House. True, there remain to date differences and variances between Shiʿi jurisprudence and thought and other Islamic schools of thought. We are working tirelessly to bridge the gap among Islamic schools of thought, both in terms of jurisprudence and other facets of Islam.

1.6 Beginnings in Tyre (Sour)

I came to Lebanon toward the end of 1959. I believe it was in November. Before I graduated, and following my father's death, I had moved to Najaf.[58] Prior to that, in 1956, while in Iraq, I received an invitation to visit Lebanon from Imam Abdul Hussein Sharafeddin,[59] who was a renowned religious figure and the most prominent Shiʿi scholar in the country. We are relatives, as he was my father's cousin, and our family was originally part of the Sharafeddin family. This first visit of mine lasted around a week. We discussed several different matters, and he treated me like a son.

After I returned to Iran and Iraq to finish my studies, Sayyed Abdul Hussein Sharafeddin fell ill, and he told some of his aides that it would be a good thing if Musa Sadr were brought to Lebanon after his death: he called this "an opportunity," which reflected his conviction and his well-known kindness.

He might even have believed that it would be a welcome opportunity for the people of Tyre to request my presence. I was less than thirty years old at the time. When he passed away, his remains were carried to Iraq.[60] I was among those who officiated at the funeral procession, and I met some of his friends and family members to offer condolences.

of legal interpretation led in the mid-eighteenth century to the dominance of the latter, innovative school since. See Mallat, *Renewal*, chap. 1. The controversy of the "closure of ijtihad" is complex and has not been fully elucidated. For a new reading of the controversy within the Sunni schools, see Mallat, *Introduction to Middle Eastern Law*, 110–22.

[58] In 1954. [59] See Introduction, n. 9.

[60] Sharafeddin died on December 10, 1957, and was buried in Najaf.

In 1958, I received a letter from people in Tyre asking me to come to their city and succeed Sayyed Abdul Hussein Sharafeddin.

It turned out that after Sayyed Sharafeddin's death, several people in Tyre attempted to invite various scholars to succeed him. They either were unable to come or there was no consensus as to who should take Sayyed Sharafeddin's place. The position remained vacant for nearly two years. It was then that they wrote to ask me to come.[61] I was a student at the religious seminary in Qom at the time, and I was the editor-in-chief of the journal *Maktab-e Islam*, which was the most prominent Islamic periodical in Persian up until it was banned by the Iranian government.[62] I received the invitation toward the end of summer, and I decided to give it a chance. I came to Lebanon and stayed in Tyre for nearly one month. I found that there was acceptance, consensus and love for me among the people and that it was a suitable place for work. I made the decision to move to Tyre and make it my new home. In the beginning of 1960 (my trip in 1959 was to assess the situation), I moved to the city and began my work. The move, which was based on the choice of the people of Tyre and on the recommendation of Sayyed Abdul Hussein Sharafeddin, was blessed by Sayyed Borujerdi,[63] who was the Grand Ayatollah at the time, and Sayyed Muhsin al-Hakim.[64] Both supported my endeavor. Tyre is the place where I began my work and where I wish to pursue it.

1.7 Religion in the Service of Life

In my religious studies, and later on in my religious work, I followed a principle that was maybe not new to Islam, but which was certainly novel

[61] The dates mentioned do not fully align, since Sharafeddin died in 1957. It is likely that Sadr received letters from Tyre residents who supported him in 1958, but that the more important invitations came later, around 1959, when he had his "trial visit" mentioned in the Chronology. He decided to take on the mantle of Sharafeddin in 1960.

[62] *Maktab-e Islam* was a magazine/journal, established by Ayatollah Shariatmadari in 1958, and the first "modern" publication of the Qom Seminary. Sadr published several texts on Islamic economics; see Part II.

[63] Hussein Borujerdi (1875–1961) was the Grand Ayatollah and leading Shi'i marja' who expanded the Qom Seminary.

[64] Ayatollah Sayyed Muhsin al-Tabataba'i al-Hakim (1889–1970) was an Iraqi marja' in Najaf. Following the death of Hussein Borujerdi, he became the leading marja' of the Shi'i community in the world. Several members of the Hakim family were later murdered by Saddam Hussein, including his sons Mahdi, assassinated in Khartum on January 19, 1988, and Muhammed Baqer, killed along with around eighty other people in an al-Qaeda bombing in Najaf on August 29, 2003.

in religious practice: I believe that religion should be in the service of life, and that the afterlife, heaven, hell, divine judgment and everything that exists beyond this life are a result of our worldly actions. Contrary to what many people believe, religion is not simply a pathway for the afterlife. People should not become religious and strengthen their relationship with God only when they fall ill, become poor or are broken, defeated or nearing death. On the contrary, a person who is strong, virtuous, healthy and full of life is the best placed to benefit from religion, which organizes his life as well as his sense of self, and his relationships with his fellow humans, their world and God.

Religion should first and foremost be in the service of life. This principle is not new. It is mentioned in the Qur'an:

> We shall recompense the steadfast according to their noblest deeds. Be they men or women, to those that embrace the Faith and do what is right We will surely grant a happy life; We shall reward them according to their noblest deeds.[65]

> Believers, obey God and the Apostle when he calls you to that which gives you life. Know that God stands between man and his heart.[66]

Life is religion's first concern. I noticed that the prevalent tendency amid Shiʿi scholars was to guide people away from solipsism and mere dedication to prayer and worship at the mosque – this is a result of Shiʿi history, which is filled with tragedies, or of the oppression practiced by rulers in excluding Shiʿis, their Imams and scholars from politics. So, I tried to bring religion back into people's lives and sought its help in rectifying error and relieving pain. Of course, certain aspects of people's lives are affected by the state, but I have not yet managed to conceive of a state founded on the principles and values of Islam – which is anyway impossible in Lebanon.[67]

We were able to play a role in all public affairs outside politics controlled by the state. What helped us in this respect was the fact that the Lebanese state assumes only a small part of public affairs, with many

[65] Qur'an 16:97. [66] Qur'an 8:24.

[67] This statement indicates a dual conundrum in Sadr's political thought. He says that a uniform religious state is impossible to build in Lebanon (including an Islamic/Muslim state, in contradistinction to a Shiʿi state). The previous sentence, which reads more literally, "I have not yet managed to *build* a state founded on the principles and values of Islam," must be understood in the broader context of the century-long debate on the nature of an Islamic state.

social issues left to the people. Cultural and even health matters are, in large part, left to Lebanese communities and institutions. For example, when I was a teacher in the early 1960s, I was told that 64 percent of students were taught in private schools, while the Lebanese government provided education to only 36 percent. The same applies to hospitals, as most are private. This is due to a non-patriotic yet widespread tendency in Lebanon to support private, missionary, nongovernmental and unofficial institutions. There was fertile ground in the social, cultural and health domains for us to act and leave an impact on people's lives.

This is when I undertook several activities. I took charge of an association in Tyre called al-Birr wa-l-Ihsan[68] and changed its statutes, so that it could start looking after the affairs of the poor. We focused on the problem of begging and managed to put an end to a phenomenon rampant in Tyre. We also took care of the household affairs of the poor, child education and health and social conditions. We then tackled the root causes of poverty by offering vocational training. We also addressed women's concerns in the city and added to existing services of several institutions – including kindergartens, health centers, a nursing school; literacy, sewing and housekeeping centers and the like – which still exist today.

I also established a "girls' house"[69] and organized sports activities in Tyre. I held sports tournaments and gave trophies to the winners. I managed to bring back religion to people's lives, in word and deed, and to sway public opinion in that direction. Other communities often invited me to give lectures in churches and monasteries. I even remember that I was once invited to give a lecture at a nuns' convent, where men are usually not allowed. The head of the monastery told Boutros Dib,[70] the director general of the presidential palace, that the spirituality I shared with the nuns during that lecture was equivalent to years' worth of the spirituality with which we try to endow such institutions – not just Shiʿi institutions. What enabled me to do so was my profound belief that religion should be in the service of life. I was also invited to several other regions, and, in the process, I observed the situation of the Shiʿi

68 *Al-birr wa-l-ihsan*, dedication and charity. 69 *Bayt al-fatat*.

70 Boutros Dib (1922–99) held various academic and political positions, including the presidency of the Lebanese University, Lebanon's representative at UNESCO, director general of the presidential palace, ambassador to the Holy See and to France, and professor at several universities.

community in Lebanon in its various aspects. I noticed great room for improvement – a challenge beyond any one individual. It was then that I realized that other communities in Lebanon had central institutions of their own that served and helped their followers. So, I supported the idea of a Supreme Islamic Shiʿi Council (SISC).[71] Our hard work came to fruition in May 1969, if I recall correctly, with the establishment of the SISC. I then moved from Tyre to Beirut and began working through that institution.

1.8 Religious Role

In general, the role I choose is based on the belief that religious energy[72] must be in the service of humankind. We must educate people, elevate their status and free them from the shackles of oppression. This is perhaps what one might view as my "political role."[73] I must reiterate here, in all honesty, that just as the role of religion cannot be restricted to people's death, poverty or illness, the very concept of faith in God cannot be separated from faith in humanity.

There are numerous Qur'anic verses stating that faith in God cannot coexist with a disregard of the plight of the oppressed. Faith, in the Islamic or religious sense, carries two dimensions: the first is celestial, and the second is worldly, reflecting conviction in both God and in human responsibility. Taking an interest in people's affairs and conditions is part of the Islamic faith.

Therefore, just as I considered myself responsible for people's social, health and cultural affairs as part of my religious role, I also believed that my religious faith and role compelled me to attenuate people's suffering. Shiʿis, as well as people from many other different communities in Lebanon, suffer from sectarian constraints, feudal oppression, political corruption, Israeli aggression and many other tragedies and misfortunes. This is true particularly for the young generation. One could even go as

[71] The Supreme Islamic Shiʿi Council (al-Majlis al-Islami al-Shiʿi al-Aʿla) was established by law, giving it the imprimatur of officialdom, in 1967. It took two further years for it be fully active.

[72] *Quwwa* (literally, "power").

[73] The original text includes the following mention: "what you referred to in your fourth question." The reference confirms that the Imam delivered this text in response to a list of questions by the interviewer, with prepared written notes that have survived (facsimile samples can be found in the 2019 Arabic edition; see n. 2).

far as saying that despite Lebanon's prosperity and relatively advanced quality of life, the majority of its citizens face severe oppression. The very existence of this oppression calls for people to revolt against it. Our work consists of fighting oppression in all its forms. This is perhaps the political role I am said to play.

I try not to refer to that role as "political" and to keep it within the framework of my religious work. But if fighting oppression is political, then so be it. Of course, the presence of Israel is a form of oppression against the entire region, the Palestinian people and even nearby regions. We must fight it. But how? That question, in my view, is political and must be answered by experts, rulers, members of the military and politicians. They are the ones who must determine how Israel should be fought. Backwardness in Lebanon, and the deprivation in border regions and in the Beirut suburbs that we call "the belt of misery" – both regions are effectively "slums" and another form of oppression that must be fought. This is a core aspect of our religious role. But how? This is also a question that I leave [again] to experts, as they are the ones who must work and devise solutions to these problems. I still believe that my interest in people's affairs and in fighting oppression, backwardness and deprivation are part of my religious role in Lebanon.

1.9 Shiʿis and the Arab World: Cooperation and Confrontation

We know of course that developments across the Arab world are interlinked and inseparable. It is necessary for Lebanon to have relations with the wider Arab world, as it is bound to interact with it in one way or another.

However, we must highlight the fact that, throughout history, Shiʿis faced war on the battlefield as well as in the public sphere. They have been horribly misrepresented in the Islamic and Arab worlds as an ideological[74] minority. Now that an official Shiʿi institution has been established in Lebanon, it has become imperative to clarify to the Arab world what Shiʿism stands for, not for preaching purposes[75] – as I do not believe in preaching – but rather to rectify relationships and prove to the

[74] Again, Sadr uses an Arabized version of the French *idéologie*.

[75] *Tabshir*, proselytism.

Arab world that Shiʿis are committed pan-Arabists and devoted Muslims, far from the image of Shiʿism portrayed by historian Ahmad Amin as "a refuge for all those who wish to dismantle Islam."[76] It is for this reason that we have reached out to the Arab world: to portray the true image of Shiʿism. In light of these interactions with the Arab world, and from the heart of Lebanon, we have set off on the path of public work in Lebanon and in the Arab world as a whole within the remit of our religious role.

1.10 The Supreme Islamic Shiʿi Council

The establishment of the Supreme Islamic Shiʿi Council was an essential step for the Shiʿi community to ensure balance and equality in Lebanon. Lebanon, it is said, is a mosaic of sixteen different communities. Each religious community manages its own religious affairs, its relationships with co-religionists living abroad, its relationships with other communities and several social issues. While these areas are regulated or in the process of being regulated in all other communities, they were neglected or dysfunctional in the Shiʿi community. This included Shiʿis' religious affairs, religious observance days, their scholars, mosques, religious education curricula, religious education on radio, television and newspapers, endowments and many other aspects. Before the Supreme Islamic Shiʿi Council began to manage these affairs, the only religious institutions that existed for the Shiʿi community were the sharia courts, which managed personal legal affairs and oversaw the implementation of personal status provisions.[77]

[76] Ahmad Amin (1878–1954) was a leading Egyptian scholar of Islam and a prolific author. On Amin in English, see Makoto Mizutani, *Liberalism in 20th Century Egyptian Thought: The Ideologies of Ahmad Amin and Husayn Amin* (London: I.B. Tauris, 2014). Amin was considered controversial in Shiʿi circles because he did not consider Shiʿism a mainstream tradition within Islam.

[77] The first state recognition of the Shiʿi community took the form of a decree by the French High Commissioner in Lebanon, Henri de Jouvenel, on January 27, 1926, which established a system of Jaʿfari family courts for intra-Shiʿi divorce and succession disputes. See Tamara Chalabi, *The Shiʿis of Jabal ʿAmil and the New Lebanon: Community and Nation-State, 1918–1942* (New York: Palgrave Macmillan, 2006), 122, 141; Chibli Mallat, *Democracy Redefined: Michel Chiha and the Lebanese Constitution* (Edinburgh: Edinburgh University Press, 2025), 285. The Lebanese legal system includes a separate set of laws and courts for each major religious community to adjudicate "personal status" disputes, mostly marriage, filiation and inheritance.

Second, there was also a need for an institution to manage the relationship between the Shiʿi community in Lebanon and Shiʿis around the world. This is crucial, as such relationships may either be in conflict or in harmony with national interests and aims.

Third, there was a need to manage the relationship of Shiʿis with other Muslims, whether positive, negative or otherwise. Someone needed to assume responsibility and take on this important role, as we are all citizens of the same country. Religion plays an enormous role in a person's life. If citizens are left unguided, their relationships with members of other communities become frayed. There are many examples in this regard: The relationship between Shiʿis and Christians took one form in Byblos,[78] another in the south[79] and yet another in the Bekaa.[80] This is unacceptable. These relationships should be managed in a responsible way, and that is the third role that the Supreme Islamic Shiʿi Council set out to fulfill.

Fourth, as I mentioned above, several social, cultural and health-related aspects had been dysfunctional, and the Supreme Islamic Shiʿi Council is meant to improve the living conditions of Shiʿis.

The fifth point is to coordinate efforts, as they often overlap. For example, there could be several similar associations in the same country, or several competing movements striving to achieve the same objectives. These efforts could be guided and better harnessed for the service of country and community.

Lastly, and perhaps most importantly, Lebanon's governing system is sectarian. This means that the state structure is divided among the various communities. The Shiʿi share is limited to nineteen out of

[78] Byblos or Jbeil is a coastal city north of Beirut. It is one of the oldest and longest inhabited cities in the world and a UNESCO World Heritage Site. The region's population is mainly Christian, with a sizeable Shiʿi minority.

[79] The southern part of Lebanon mainly comprises the South district (*muhafaza*) and the Nabatiyeh district. Its population is mainly Shiʿi, with a considerable number of Christians and Sunnis.

[80] The Bekaa (al-Biqaʿ) is the large plain situated between Mount Lebanon to the west and the Anti-Lebanon mountains to the east. It was considered in Roman times a granary of the empire and is Lebanon's largest agricultural area and its main source of local grains and produce. It is home to several important archaeological sites, such as the late Roman temples of Baalbek and the Umayyad city of Anjar. Its inhabitants are Christians, Shiʿis and Sunnis.

ninety-nine.[81] However, there is no authority to oversee implementation and ensure that this percentage is met in public appointments, the general budget, development projects or public policies – which is why the Supreme Islamic Shiʿi Council was founded.

As you can see, these five crucial roles were ignored, which is why the Shiʿi community was so disadvantaged. It was necessary to establish the Islamic Shiʿi Council, the most recent communal institution founded in Lebanon. Some might argue that the Shiʿi community has distanced itself from the nation by establishing the SISC. That is incorrect insofar the other communal institutions were already established: Dar al-Fatwa[82] manages all the affairs of the Sunni community, Mashyakhat al-ʿAql[83] manages all the affairs of the Druze community and there are also institutions for all the Christian communities.

1.11 Achievements of the Council

As a national institution, the Supreme Islamic Shiʿi Council assumes all these vital roles. But we must not forget that an institution cannot be effective without structure, human resources, cadres and the like. Consequently, the Council first began to undertake institutional work: studies, organization, managing endowment affairs, censuses and so on. Studies show that Shiʿi participation in the Lebanese state was marginal and that Shiʿis were denied their rights in public office, public employment, institutions, budgets and all state-related affairs. Shiʿi regions were also disadvantaged. South Lebanon suffered from social, political and security deprivation, exacerbated by recurrent Israeli aggressions. The Bekaa suffered from backwardness; there were no courts in the region, and clans were in charge of managing people's

[81] Reference here is, with an ironic overtone in Arabic, to the detailed apportionment of public jobs in the administration, and the proportion allowed to Shiʿis, leaving them at the time nineteen parliamentary seats among the ninety-nine seats in the National Assembly. The figure is taken from the census of 1932, which was the last one carried out officially in Lebanon and counted 155,035 Shiʿi residents out of 793,396, a proportion of ca. 19 percent.

[82] Dar al-Fatwa, established in 1922, is a government institution tasked with managing the affairs of the Sunni community.

[83] Mashyakhat al-ʿAql, or the Druze Communal Council, "administers the temporal, social and financial affairs as well as the religious interests of the community, represents them in matters related to its functions, and ensures the promotion of their rights" (Council website: http://mouwahidoundruze.gov.lb/).

affairs. Some areas had even established clan councils, as if they were living in the Middle Ages.[84] This backwardness needed to be addressed. When the Council's studies revealed the extent of the problem, the Council urged the state to act, as was stipulated in first article of the Council's statutes. In the Council's first year, Israel committed several acts of aggression against the south. When the Lebanese authorities failed to respond, we declared a general strike in 1970.[85] It was unprecedented: it covered all Lebanese regions – it included the airport, the [Beirut] port, hospitals, public and private institutions and departments. They all shut down in response to our call. As a result, Parliament issued a law establishing the Council for South Lebanon[86] and allowed farmers in the south to plant more tobacco,[87] and the government presented a law on weapons and a law on military service to Parliament. Naturally, some of these initiatives were nothing more than a placebo, but others came to fruition. For example, the Council of the South was established and built many schools, roads and electrical and water networks in the south, in addition to carrying out afforestation efforts.

1.12 Demands and Protests

When we first carried out our studies on the causes of this backwardness, we made peaceful demands with presentations to the president, the prime minister, relevant ministers and other officials. All our efforts were in vain. Our youth felt deprived, leaving them an easy target for radical political movements who start by voicing people's political and social demands and soon turn to economic and philosophical indoctrination. We noticed that a large portion of the Shiʿi youth was becoming indoctrinated. Marxism, as you know, is a social, political and economic school of thought, but it is also based on the philosophy of dialectical materialism,[88] in other words, atheism. We had a

[84] Sadr uses the term "Middle Ages" loosely, as is still common colloquially, to refer to backwardness.

[85] May 26, 1970.

[86] Majlis al-Janub, or the Council of the South, was established as a governmental institution for the development of the region.

[87] South Lebanon has long been famous for its tobacco plantations, which provided jobs for large numbers of people in agriculture, manufacturing and commerce.

[88] Musa Sadr uses the French *matérialisme dialectique*.

responsibility to stop the spread of this philosophy in Lebanon. We started to sense that the situation called for a different form of action, so that deprived Shi'i youths stopped feeling that the Supreme Islamic Shi'i Council favored an oppressive system over their interests. So, we began voicing our demands in a different way.

In early 1974, we called for a meeting of the cabinet to demand that Shi'i ministers – there were four at the time in the cabinet of Prime Minister Takieddine el-Solh[89] – resign if the Shi'i community was not granted its rights. We gave them a four-month ultimatum, and then extended it to six. When the six months ended, we saw that the Shi'i ministers valued their position in power more than the rights of their fellow Shi'is, just as they had always done, and we had to escalate by staging protests. The first protest we organized was in the 'Amiliyya Educational Complex[90] on the occasion of Ashura,[91] followed by a large protest in the town of Bednayel[92] in the Bekaa on Muharram 25,[93] on the occasion of the martyrdom of Imam Zayn al-Abidin.[94] Later, we held a massive protest in Baalbek[95] on the *arba'in*[96] of Imam Hussein, followed by Tyre's great protest, in which nearly 150,000 people participated. I do not remember the exact date, but it was also on a day of religious commemoration.[97]

During these protests, we repeated that both Islam and faith in God require people to stand by the oppressed and the vulnerable. We refused to accept continued deprivation, and we swore not to rest as long as there remained deprived Shi'is or non-Shi'is in Lebanon, and as long as there were still deprived regions in Lebanon, Shi'i or not. We took this oath in Baalbek, and it was the foundation upon which we launched the

89 Takieddine el-Solh (1908–88) held several positions, including MP for the Bekaa, interior minister and finance minister. He was prime minister in 1973–74.

90 January 31, 1974.

91 The Day of Ashura is marked by Shi'is around the world to mourn the martyrdom of Imam Hussein, son of Imam Ali and grandson of the Prophet Muhammad, in the Battle of Karbala in 680.

92 Bednayel is a town in the Baalbek district.

93 February 17, 1974.

94 The fourth Shi'i Imam, Imam Zayn al-Abidin (b. 658) led a quietist life in Medina after surviving the Battle of Karbala. He was reputedly poisoned in 712.

95 March 17, 1974.

96 *Arba'in* (literally, "forty") is the religious commemoration of the martyrdom of Imam Hussein. It occurs forty days after Ashura.

97 It was held on May 5, 1974, coinciding with the commemoration day of Zahra, the Prophet Muhammad's daughter.

Movement of the Deprived.[98] This movement sought to give substance to the Supreme Islamic Shiʿi Council and to other institutions – that is, it sought to transform the deprived and dispossessed and those concerned with their affairs from a static force surrendered to oppression into a dynamic one. This is a legitimate national movement.

1.13 Between Two Movements: The Deprived and the Intellectuals

When we launched Amal, the Movement of the Deprived, in our protests and gatherings, we freed people from apathy.[99] These were people living their lives in mosques, markets and villages, completely detached from social concerns – and we brought them together within a political movement. This movement needed to be organized so as not to be exploited by those who rejected it and sought to tear it down. We also did not want people to say, "You took an oath that you failed to fulfill," so we established the Movement of the Deprived.

As mentioned in the Amal charter, the movement focusses on three categories of people:

- those who are presently dispossessed;
- those who are deprived of their social, political, financial and other rights in public affairs;
- those who are concerned about their future.

There are also people who are not deprived at present, but who feel that this country will dispossess their children in the future, and therefore believe it is necessary to establish a system that will guarantee a fair future for them. Any person who empathizes with the dispossessed and takes an interest in national affairs and the reality of deprivation in the country would support this movement.

[98] Harakat al-Mahrumin (Movement of the Deprived) was formed in March 1974 as a mass protest movement. Amal (Afwaj al-Muqawama al-Lubnaniyya, "Units of the Lebanese Resistance," with the Arabic acronym meaning "hope") was formed in 1975, originally as a political movement, but it evolved into a political-cum-military organization led, after the disappearance of Sadr, by Nabih Berri, Speaker of the Lebanese Parliament, since 1992.

[99] *Hiyad*, "neutrality" – the word was commonly use in Lebanese politics in the 1970s and remains a trope in Lebanon denoting the will of several Lebanese groups to keep away from regional interference.

Broadly speaking, the Movement of the Deprived is not religious; it is evidently a political, social and nonsectarian movement. Perhaps, today, most of its members come from the Shiʿi community, given my religious and political position in Lebanon, but there are also non-Shiʿis and even non-Muslims among the movement's cadres and ranks. You may remember that enormous nationwide efforts were made after the Tyre protest.

Originally, we had planned a large protest in Beirut, to be followed, if they [the government] didn't agree our terms, by civil disobedience that would upend the stagnant situation, starting with bringing down the government[100] or even the state[101] itself. However, we realized there was a widespread distribution of arms – this was 1974 – and so a big buildup of weapons across Lebanon.[102] We were bound to clash with Lebanon's Christians had we escalated our actions, and we have always opposed sectarian and civil war. We believe that social issues should be advanced through democratic, rather than armed, struggle, in Lebanon in any case.

We began to communicate, in the Lebanese Nadwa,[103] with a group of intellectuals from different communities. That is how the movement of the intellectuals was born. One hundred and ninety intellectuals signed a

[100] *Hukuma*, meaning here the cabinet or council of ministers.

[101] *Dawla*, meaning here the political regime.

[102] Lebanon's descent into chaos was atmospherically described by journalist Jonathan Randall: "I awoke before dawn one Saturday [in October 1975] to the sound of battle down in the tree-lined streets of my neighborhood, called Kantari. The Phalangists had been probing in nearby streets – less, I figured to protect the upper-class Christian residents, who traditionally looked down their noses at the Gemayels' [in 1975 Bachir Gemayel commanded the militia of the Phalange, or Kataeb, Party, founded by his father, Pierre Gemayel, in 1936] Boy Scout antics, than to seize the gold in the Central Bank vaults some eight hundred feet farther west, in Moslem territory . . . [the next day] my apartment door burst open and a dozen armed men rushed in. Much to my relief they were from a breakaway offshoot of the Communist Party run by bright young Christians and manned, like so many of the West Beirut militias, with poor Shia Moslems. Amid the chaos these intruders at least represented authority – and a human, if threatening presence." Jonathan Randall, *The Tragedy of Lebanon: Christian Warlords, Israeli Adventurers and American Bunglers* (London: Hogarth, 1990 [1983]), 67–69. Also looking back, David Hirst highlighted the run-up to 1975 as "a process of non-state militarization": his *Beware of Small States: Lebanon, Battleground of the Middle East* (London: Faber and Faber, 2010) succinctly charts the descent into violence at 98–113, including the role of regional states and the war's immediate impact on "ordinary" Lebanese. Randall and Hirst have contributed remarkable books in English about the Lebanon war.

[103] The Lebanese Nadwa (al-Nadwa al-Lubnaniyya), known in French as Le Cénacle Libanais, was created by Michel Asmar in 1946. It mainly held lectures, and Sadr read several lectures in the Cénacle. See also Chapter 4, n. 5.

statement declaring their support for the movement, followed by a General Assembly meeting. We established the General Secretariat for Committed Thought in the Service of the Deprived,[104] whose members were mostly Christian. The Movement of the Deprived is not religious. It is political, social and anti-sectarian. The first article of its statutes stresses the importance of having faith in God, as we believe that faith is the starting point and the driving force for most believers. Faith also guides people in their attitudes and behavior; many movements drift away from the straight path in exceptional and critical times. This is no different to what happened during Lebanon's crisis,[105] as many people committed heinous acts by targeting and taking vengeance on the innocent out of sectarian fear. The Movement of the Deprived never took part in such acts, because its objectives and actions are based on faith in God. One's actions should always be consistent with one's objectives.

Today, the Movement of the Deprived is a powerful force, and I believe that it will play a positive, effective and active role in improving Lebanon's situation in the future. As for the Supreme Islamic Shiʿi Council, it has established its place on the Lebanese scene because it has given Shiʿis a seat at the national table. Ever since independence, Lebanon's affairs have been managed through a Maronite–Sunni dialogue, with this Maronite–Sunni axis making choices on behalf of all other Lebanese communities. Shiʿis now have a say in this dialogue; they have become a power that negotiates, is negotiated with, poses questions and discusses.

One of our partisans in the Movement for Committed Thought in the Service of the Deprived, Father Yuwakim Mubarak,[106] considers that Lebanon has witnessed three historical eras:

1. the Druze era, when Lebanon was unified and Greater Lebanon was established during the time of Fakhreddine and his compatriots;
2. the Maronite era, when Lebanon began to have relations with the west; and
3. the Shiʿi era, during which society is being built through the Movement of the Deprived.

[104] In Arabic, al-Amana al-ʿAmma li-l-Fikr al-Multazim fi Khidmat al-Mahrumin.

[105] This again refers to the first period of wars in Lebanon in 1975–76.

[106] Joachim (Yuwakim) Mubarak (1924–95) was a Lebanese priest and scholar devoted to Islamic–Christian dialogue. A close friend to Sadr, he is the author of several scholarly works, including the five-volume *Pentalogie Islamo-Chrétienne* (Beirut: Cénacle Publications, 1972–73).

The first era was political, the second cultural and the third social. The first era established an entity, the second a civilization[107] and the third is building a society from within.

That is why I believe that the Movement of the Deprived has a future, given Lebanon's tragic experiences, as most right-wing and left-wing parties were involved in unjustifiable acts, while our movement was not.

1.14 Peace and War

The Lebanese war was wrong and futile; political parties took part in it without regard to dire consequences. Our movement, meanwhile, always called for peace, even when it was forced to arm itself to defend neighborhoods.

Both right-wing and left-wing parties took vengeance on the innocent and were involved in sniping, mutilation and sectarian killing. I used to tell people, "Anyone who fires at Deir al-Ahmar, Shlifa or al-Qaʿ[108] would be firing at my mihrab, at my minbar,[109] and at my house." At the time, the Communist Party and other secular parties in the Bekaa were carrying slogans such as, "Glory to Islam," "God Is Great" and "Islam Is in Danger," and they were urging people to fight Christians.

This experience will help the movement play an effective future role in Lebanon. It will also help in Lebanon's shift from communalism to democracy.

Popular and politically nonsectarian movements with faith in God have a massive role to play, and we hope our movement can contribute in one way or another.

1.15 War on Feudalism

Our position with regard to feudalism and leftism: We are opposed to feudalism, because it results in social injustice. It is a form of social backwardness, and we in our charter reject backwardness and injustice.

[107] *Hadara*. [108] Christian villages in the Bekaa valley.

[109] The mihrab is the central niche in a mosque that indicates the qibla (direction of prayer toward the Kaaba in Mecca). To the right (as seen from the congregation) of the mihrab usually stands the minbar, the raised platform from which the prayer leader, or imam, addresses those congregated. There is a rough equivalence of the mihrab with the altar and pulpit in a church. The mihrab is semicircular, like the apse in a church. For its etymology, s.v. "mihrab," *Encyclopaedia of Islam, Second Edition* (Leiden: Brill, 2012).

Feudalism, internally, is comparable to colonialism externally. It carries on economic investments[110] that are not compatible with Lebanese society nor with our current era.

This is a very broad topic. Our battle against feudalism has its ups and downs, and it includes pauses based on political circumstances that pose a threat to our nation, but we oppose feudalism in general.

1.16 Lebanese Political Parties and Change

As for leftism, we believe that it is a force of change, and we think of ourselves as a force of change too. However, we have had a bitter experience with the Lebanese left, particularly the Communist Party, the Communist Action Party[111] and other Lebanese and Palestinian Marxist parties, which have become the modern, more advanced form of feudalism. They have modern feudal lords. They are groups of people who advance political slogans but never practice what they preach. They carried sectarian slogans during the Lebanese war, they were murdering people based on their identity cards[112] or responding to such acts by doing the same. These are despicable, thuggish practices. We also suffered in our alliance with them, as they did not uphold their commitments and stabbed us in the back in times of hardship.[113]

Communism, as a school of political thought, is based on Marxist philosophy and reasoning, which is a philosophy of materialism that we can never come to terms with. We can, however, agree with certain aspects of dialectical reasoning, because it is not necessarily atheistic. It is

110 *Istithmar*, investment. Sadr probably refers to the negative side of economic activities, including usurious practices and exploitative investment.

111 The Communist Action Party (Munazzamat al-ʿAmal al-Shuyuʿi) was a Marxist–Leninist political party whose main supporters in the 1970s were Shiʿis. The rise of communism among the more deprived sectors of society both in Lebanon and in Iraq is discussed in Mallat, *Renewal*, 7–15.

112 It was common in the Lebanon war for militia to check people's identity cards with a view to kidnapping or killing their holders when they belonged to a different religion. This particularly heinous practice was known in Arabic as *al-qatl ʿala al-huwiyya* (killing on basis of one's identity card). Human Rights Watch reported in 2017 that around 17,000 people were "disappeared" in the 1975–90 war. Bassam Khawaja, "Still No Justice for Thousands of 'Disappeared' in Lebanon's Civil War," Human Rights Watch, August 30, 2017, http://bit.ly/3M30uql.

113 In the early months of the war, a brief alliance between Amal and the left was formed among groups opposed to broad Christian right-wing factions, including ethnic cleansing of Shiʿi neighborhoods like Nabaa in east Beirut.

a way of thinking that is neither closer to, nor more distant from, religion than Aristotle's way of thinking. Dialectical reasoning can be used in several areas, and our region is not free from contradictions, nor from the contrast between substance and form, or the synthesis that exists to solve the conflict between thesis and antithesis. We are not far from Hegel's dialectic.[114]

However, we can never accept philosophical materialism – a belief in nothing other than matter – and historical materialism. As a result, we do not agree with communists and some leftist parties, neither strategically nor ideologically. Even our temporary alignment with them is difficult to maintain. That said, we are close to leftist thought in general, because it is a force of change, and we hope that Lebanon can change for the better.

1.17 What Is Secularism? What Is Sectarianism?

Secularism has two original meanings: authority emanating from the law, [as opposed to authority] from religion, from God; and laws taken from [outside] religious sources.

In Lebanon, due to the presence of sixteen different communities, it is not possible for any religion or community to impose its beliefs on the government. Moreover, Israel is a racist state based on religion.[115] This creates strong reactions in the region. Any support for religion helps strengthen Israel's foundations. At the level of state structure, we reject absolutely a religious approach and we welcome secularism.

Lebanese laws are secular.[116] Laws should ideally be based on common denominators between Islam and Christianity; they should be aligned with the shared values of Islam and Christianity, so that no law is issued that contradicts religious behavior or ideology. But in practice, today, Lebanese laws are secular.

At present, secularism can be seen from two angles in Lebanon: The first is related to the system of government, which is communal. This means that the structure of the state is divided among the various communities. For example, the president is a Maronite, the parliamentary

[114] Sadr uses in this passage several French words: *matérialisme*, *dialectique*, *thèse*, *antithèse*, *synthèse*.

[115] Literally, "religious thinking."

[116] By this, Sadr means that most laws in Lebanon are national and apply to all regardless of religious communities, except for "personal status" (family-related) laws.

speaker is a Shiʿi, the prime minister is Sunni, the deputy speaker and deputy prime minister are Greek Orthodox and so on. The majority of people in Lebanon believe that political sectarianism must be abolished, and we in the Movement of the Deprived and in the Supreme Islamic Shiʿi Council believe so. The Council's General Assembly has called for abolishing political sectarianism. We believe that while the system may have been established to ensure justice and fairness between communities, this did not happen in practice. A calculated conspiracy took place between feudal lords [to perpetuate the system].

Political sectarianism clearly impedes competence and undermines institutions. For instance, it is not possible to increase the number of soldiers in the army because not enough Christians are joining the ranks. The same applies to the Lebanese University and other institutions. Political sectarianism plagues Lebanon, and that is why we believe that it should be abolished.

The second angle from which secularism is viewed is personal status law. Should we unify personal status provisions and secularize them, or should we keep the current, communal personal status legislation? So far, we have been supportive of the personal status laws, because we believe that the presence of all these different communities in Lebanon is a gift from God, and that Lebanon's cultural message must be a model for coexistence among different communities. These are the kinds of experiences that humanity will need in abundance in the future, as continents and countries draw closer together. If we abolish the communal personal status laws, which regulate birth and death in people's lives (governing marriage, and so birth, and inheritance, and so death); if we sever people's ties with such particulars in their lives and secularize all laws – we fear that citizens might lose their sense of communal identity. We do not want that to happen; we want Lebanon to be a place where all the different communities coexist and cooperate. We want it to be a miniature model of the world as a whole.

There are, however, others who call for the abolition of the personal status laws and who support complete secularization. This needs to be agreed between all the Lebanese people. We often say that, when it comes to social and political causes, one must not fight but rather accept the opinion of the majority and try to achieve the required change through democratic struggle. I also believe it is possible to design a unified law that takes into consideration the religious obligations of and unifies personal status provisions for all communities without secularization. This can be done by setting a general format and adopting a common formula that allows contracting parties to vary the clauses of their contracts. Contracts are law between the parties. Let anyone belonging to any community include contractual clauses they deem necessary. For example, Muslims can set certain conditions to bring the unified personal status law closer to their own; likewise, Christians can set certain conditions to align the unified law with their beliefs. Such a law would enable the establishment of a unified court system, with unified outcomes for all of cases. This could be a solution, and we will propose it in dialogue meetings to be held in the near future.

1.18 Religion, Institutions and Politics

On how to develop political institutions, intensive efforts are being made at the Supreme Islamic Shiʿi Council, where submitted proposals and a plan of action include abolishing political sectarianism by establishing one electoral district covering all Lebanon, and other measures inspired from experience around the world. This may be agreed upon and adopted by the state and all political institutions. But the main question is: How can religious institutions be developed?

Religious institutions can benefit from modern methods of organization, research and work – these methods help develop all institutions, not just religious ones. But while religious institutions can benefit from modern experience, they can achieve the most by staying true to their raison d'être – that is, they should not simply become institutions with interests, benefits, endowments and members constantly trying to defend their position and thinking that the people should serve them. When this happens, they would be losing touch with their religious raison d'être.

If institutions maintain their dynamism, and do not lose their mission to help people – or to use a more accurate expression, they do not become an "institution" that has lost its dynamism in religious matters – then religious institutions will not think only about their well-being but about serving people. Only then would they stand by the dispossessed, the oppressed, those in need and those facing hardship and distress; only then would they support the people and contribute to improving their status and living conditions.

When religion and religious institutions are put in the service of the people, they are no longer exposed to the risk of segregation, division, sectarianism, fundamentalism and discrimination, because people are the ultimate purpose of God's religion and should be at the heart of all religious institutions.

That is why religious institutions in general must not be detached from the people or seek selfish benefits. They must try not to employ many people or seek to better their situation.[117] It would be wrong for a religious institution to think that maintaining a stable budget or establishing endowments to secure funding for itself would be beneficial. These funds would expose the institution to a risk of inertia. Religious institutions can develop by returning to their roots, to the early days of religious movements. If we look back at history, we can see that religious movements were in their beginnings active, participatory, creative, dynamic, helpful and capable of improvement; they produced a wide array of currents, and therefore established a new civilization and advanced history. By contrast, movements that abandon religion lose these traits and become institutionalized. As such, religious institutions can benefit from modern advances to develop, provided they remain rooted in their pure origins and maintain their grassroots. Once that is achieved, religion will be able to overcome all the challenges of our time. If modern social ideologies, when they are first launched, are able to meet present-day needs, religion can certainly do so when it is coupled with conscious thinking and modern reasoning.

This applies to all religious institutions. Specifically for Shiʿi religious institutions, we must reiterate that innovative interpretation (ijtihad) is permissible in Shiʿi fiqh, and the vast results of the work of Shiʿi scholars are readily available. This allows us to adopt ideas and solutions that offer ways to face the challenges of our time, helping additionally to develop our institutions and preserve their grassroots nature. I often mention the example of how we can develop zakat[118] to meet present-day needs, by transferring zakat funds to the National Social Security Fund or by updating employment contracts. Given that ijtihad is part of Shiʿi religious reasoning, the personal status laws can easily develop to include marriage and divorce provisions that are aligned with the needs of men

[117] This statement probably means that religious institutions should not replace the state welfare system, nor should they employ people whom they do not need to function.

[118] Usually rendered in English as "alms." The Arabic verb *zaka*, "to thrive," carries a notion of "purification," in that the act of giving alms purifies the wealth that remains/purifies the giver. Zakat is one of the "five pillars" of Islam.

and women today, freeing them from the oppression that often exists due to a rigid system or [conservative] officials.

1.19 Relations with Iranian Political and Religious Currents

As mentioned, I was born in Iran, and I spent the first years of my youth there.[119] I was twenty-six when I left. During that period, like any other citizen, I had my preferences, opinions and dreams. It was during the time of the Mosaddegh[120] movement, which sought to nationalize the petroleum industry. The very idea of nationalization and of resisting colonial economic and political ambitions began in Iran through the movement of Mosaddegh and his companions. This movement was then carried over to the Suez Canal, which was also nationalized, ushering in an era of liberation after independence in the Middle East in general. Like many other young people, I was very supportive of Mosaddegh's movement. Mosaddegh headed a political party called the National Front, which brought together a group of young people and political leaders immersed in Islamic religious culture. Through their efforts, several Muslim students' movements were established. Mosaddegh's National Front included a group of political leaders and parties, among which was a national Islamic organization formed in the wake of a conference that was held to establish connections and relations between Muslim scholars, engineers and the like. It was a progressive Islamic movement. Among its members were engineer Bazargan, Mahmoud Taleghani, Dr. Sahabi, engineer Sanjabi[121] and several other committed

[119] Obviously, this section predates the 1979 Iranian Revolution and helps set the interview around the end of the first phase of the civil war in the first months of 1977.

[120] Mohammad Mosaddegh (1882–1967) was prime minister of Iran from 1951 to 1953. For many Iranians a symbol of resistance to foreign domination, his government was overthrown in the 1953 coup d'état reestablishing the Pahlavi dictatorship, a pivotal moment in Iran's history whose assessment remains controversial. For various analyses, see Ervand Abrahamian, *The Coup: 1953, the CIA, and the Roots of Modern US–Iran Relations* (New York: New Press, 2013); Darioush Bayandor, *Iran and the CIA: The Fall of Mosaddeq Revisited* (London: Palgrave Macmillan, 2010); Homa Katouzian, *Musaddiq and the Struggle for Power in Iran*, rev. ed. (London: I.B. Tauris, 1999).

[121] Mehdi Bazargan (1907–95) was a deputy minister and the first Iranian head of the National Iranian Oil Company under Mossadegh. In 1961, Bazargan founded the Freedom Movement of Iran (Nahzat-e Azadi-e Iran) and was the first prime minister appointed by Ayatollah Khumaini after the 1979 Iranian Revolution. Mahmoud Taleghani (1911–79) was an Iranian theologian and senior Shiʿi scholar opposed to

national figures, who played a major role in Mosaddegh's uprising and the development of his [movement]. I was very supportive of them at the time.

When I left Iran and assumed my responsibilities in Lebanon, I fell behind on developments in the political and religious currents in Iran, as I was preoccupied with my local duties and ongoing problems in Lebanon. Some of my friends and family, however, stayed in Iran and naturally found themselves having to choose between different currents – including the official [state-sponsored] right-wing party[122] – and, consequently, they were at risk of being submerged in the dominant atmosphere. This exposed them to danger, especially those among them who traveled to Europe. They could not be part of the struggle, because, at the time, the left and the communists monopolized social activism. I did not want my friends to fall under this influence. Instead, we established a progressive militant current, which, I dare say, was also a revolutionary Islamic current.

Nowadays, there is an Islamic progressive movement, led by the Muslim Students' Organization in Europe, Iran, the United States, Canada and elsewhere.[123] Whenever I am in Europe, I show my support for this organization, give lectures and courses to its members and contribute to their research. Their political and religious behavior is exemplary. I see this organization as a natural ally of the Movement of the Deprived. I insist that our movement is not sectarian, but it is founded on faith in God. The same applies to the student movement.

Besides, I do not have any role in the political fights in Iran. As with our relationship with the government, we act in terms of Lebanon's best

the rule of Shah Mohammad Reza Pahlavi. He was Tehran's first Friday prayer imam after the Iranian Revolution. Yadollah Sahabi (1902–2002), a writer, university professor and member of parliament, played a major role in the 1951 nationalization of oil. Karim Sanjabi (1904–95) was an Iranian politician and member of Mosaddegh's National Front of Iran who served as education minister under Mossadegh in 1952. Bazargan, Sahabi and Sanjabi played leading roles in the 1979 revolution but fell out with Khumaini soon afterward.

122 In March 1975, Mohammad Reza Pahlavi created the Resurgence Party (Hizb-e Rastakhiz) as the only accepted political party. Prior to that, there had been two: the National Party (Hizb-e Melliyun), replaced in 1963 by the New Iran Party (Hizb-e Iran Novin), and the People's Party (Hizb-e Mardom), which were known as the "yes" and "yes sir" parties. See Ervand Abrahamian, *Iran between Two Revolutions* (Princeton, NJ: Princeton University Press, 1983), 420, 440–46.

123 Sadr uses MSO, the English acronym.

interest. At first, I had a good relationship with the Iranian government. At a later stage, Iranian intelligence services seemed to become uneasy about my activities, so I responded in a press conference. This caused some tension. But when the situation in Lebanon began to deteriorate, I attempted to put this relationship back on the right track, given the massive influence of the Iranian government in the region. I believe that good relations with Iran could help to shield the south and Lebanon as a whole against these dangers. My intention is by no means to stir tension with the Iranian government; on the contrary, I am trying to maintain a good relationship with all regional governments. It is best to avoid side battles so as to focus on ending [Lebanese] suffering and addressing the concerns of Shiʿis in Lebanon.

1.20 A Vision for Lebanon

I am often asked about my vision for the future, the future of Shiʿis, of Lebanon, of the south and of the Arab world. People ask me whether I am hopeful or what I think is yet to come. My usual answer is that I am not a spectator to express optimism or pessimism, or even to express a vision. I believe that each individual should play their part in building the future. If we leave the regional situation to unfold without intervention, the future will no doubt be dark, because our region has been afflicted with two calamities. One is a dangerous enemy, and the other is a severe illness.

The first problem is Israel. As we all know, Israel is an expansionist state. This makes it a threat to its neighbors. Israel is a modern, advanced and industrial nation, which means that it seeks to colonize the region in modern ways to find new markets, and this makes it even more dangerous. Israel also has expertise in intelligence, espionage and [fomenting] conspiracies, which enables it to manipulate regimes and manufacture tensions in the region. It sees these efforts as an investment in settling the region. This poses a threat to the Arab world and to Lebanon, specifically south Lebanon and its Shiʿi population.

The second danger is the region's vast wealth, which has sharpened the global conflict to dominate the region. The world powers in conflict over this region by no means behave fairly, taking a limited share and leaving the rest for the region's people; they are colonizing powers greedily fighting for resources. They have a constant interest in the Middle East, and this has caused immense problems and suffering.

These two realities are a danger to the Arab world, and this spills over to Lebanon, to the south, to the Shiʿi community and to other parts of the country, which is a major focal point in the region. In the face of these global ambitions, and given the presence of Israel, it is necessary to act reasonably and on a comprehensive scale. In the coming months, one should act with focus, precision and planning. Even in the past, if a country had such immense wealth it would have been the subject of colonial ambitions, and this has become truer in our current era.

This is the general picture, but there is another angle from which to view the situation, which is that despite these two calamities [Israel and misuse of oil wealth] in the region, Arab regimes have failed to think progressively and to address the problems and difficulties of their people. There are severe conflicts within the Arab world itself. Every two Arab countries have had their share of explosive disputes. This applies to Morocco, Mauritania and Algeria; Tunisia and Libya; Libya and Egypt; Egypt and Syria, although during the [recent] crisis, their relationship has improved;[124] Sudan and Libya; Iraq and Syria; and so on.

Without a doubt, the Arab world's innumerable problems result from backwardness. To protect the Arab world's interests, there must be unity, which is the Arab world's only weapon. With unity, Arabs can resolve all their problems, which can all be traced back to underdevelopment. Arabs are as rich in their minds as in their resources. The Arab mind is capable of informing, speaking and organizing, but it is not being properly put to use. Gradually the [educated] wave will rise – there is a growing trend in the region to make use of the power of the mind.

I am certain that the Arab world will see more progress; the Arab workforce will become more skilled, the Arab mind will become more discerning and Arab leaders will be able to truly lead their nations. We are encountering more ideas and calls for thinking and planning, and we are seeing more robust capacities and aptitudes. This trend – toward an enhanced use of reason and thought – is like a wind blowing

[124] When Egyptian president Sadat broke his alliance with Syrian president Assad in the middle of the 1973 October War, tension developed between the two previously allied countries, but it subsided at the time of the interview of Sadr, as Egypt and Syria came to a common agreement over Lebanon in the fall of 1976 that stopped the fighting by spreading an Arab deterrent force (which consecrated in practice Syrian military domination over the country). Several other disputes mentioned by Sadr have endured.

over the whole Arab world. We will no longer have regions that are rich in resources but poor in the skills needed to manage these resources; such a reality would be completely out of touch. In any case, that is what we are striving for.

As for Lebanon's future, I say that Lebanon's very existence is a threat to Israel, and that is why the country is suffering so much. Lebanon is the first target in Israel's war on the Arab world, and that is because of the coexistence of its various communities. Lebanon is living proof that it is possible to build a nation in the Middle East. Israel claims it is impossible to build nations that include people from different religions, either in the Arab world or anywhere else. That is why Lebanon's existence is a threat to Israel. The country has suffered greatly and has been the subject of Israeli conspiracies, from the last two-year [war] until this very day.[125] But the world must know that if Lebanon collapses, the situation will spill over to the rest of the Arab world. In Syria, for example, there are approximately one million Christians, one million Alawis, a sizeable community of Ismailis and a large number of Sunnis.[126] That is why Syria will no doubt be affected by the situation

125 This again suggests that the interview which forms the basis of the text was completed in 1977, during the lull that followed the two-year civil war (1975–76) and the resumed hostilities in early 1978.

126 Sadr is one of many Shiʿi scholars who issued fatwas in the 1970s about the Alawis' "denominational/doctrinal unity" (*al-wahda al-madhhabiyya*) with Shiʿism, which was useful for Hafez al-Assad as the Syrian constitution required the president to be a Muslim. This was just after the Syrian National Assembly inserted a clause in the 1972 constitution that the head of state be a Muslim; see Patrick Seale, *Asad: The Struggle for the Middle East*, rev. ed. (Berkeley: University of California Press, 1995), 173; Ajami, *The Vanished Imam*, 174. The Alawis, or Nusayris, are mainly present in Syria, southern Turkey and northern Lebanon. For a brief account of their beliefs, see Hanna Batatu, *Syria's Peasantry, the Descendants of Its Lesser Rural Notables, and Their Politics* (Princeton, NJ: Princeton University Press, 1999), 17–20. For a more recent discussion of the Alawis' role, see Michael Kerr and Craig Larkin, eds., *The Alawis of Syria: War, Faith and Politics in the Levant* (London: Hurst & Company, 2015). Ismailis form a community that believes, like the Twelver Shiʿis, in the first six Imams, but have adopted a different seventh Imam, Ismaʿil b. Jafar. Their development in history has also differed considerably from that of other Shiʿis, and modern Ismailism follows the leadership of the Aga Khan. Sadr does not mention the Zaydis, also Shiʿis, who differ from the Twelver by having chosen Zayd b. Ali (d. 740) as the fifth and ultimate Imam, instead of his brother, Muhammad al-Baqer (d. 733), whose progeny continues until the twelfth Imam, who went into occultation. Zaydis are a much smaller Shiʿi group than the Twelvers and are based in the northern part of Yemen and in adjacent territories in Saudi Arabia. Their theology and legal teaching differ considerably from those of the Twelvers, as does their clerical structure. Zaydi Imams ruled North Yemen until the 1962 revolution. Many

in Lebanon, and we are already seeing the first signs of the collapse [between the two countries] with the rising tensions. In Egypt, there are three to six million Copts,[127] who are affected by the troubles in Lebanon. Credible sources tell me that there is already tension there, and that the Copts have been deeply affected by the situation. They even conveyed to the United Nations the fact that despite their large numbers in Egypt, they are denied their rights. This also poses a threat to Egypt. Not only that, but the repercussions of the explosion would also reach Africa, Europe and the entire world.

Zionism is challenging the world and testing the waters in Lebanon. If it succeeds, this will also overwhelm the United States. This reality must be expressed and defended the world over. The present words [of confrontation with the United States] express it plainly.

I believe that the future of Lebanon and that of the entire world are intertwined. And since the world is not yet willing to succumb to Zionism and to sectarian strife in general, it will come together to preserve Lebanon's unity. If Lebanon overcomes internal sectarian division, it will remain, as it has always been, a miniature model of the world, with a bright future no doubt.

1.21 The South: Surrender or Challenge?

There remains the problem of the south, this tormented and victimized region of Lebanon. It faces the hardest destiny – I don't say the most dangerous one – for the south also awaits the destiny of Lebanon.

The reason for that is clear as day: Israel is preventing the deployment of the Arab Deterrent Force,[128] and therefore impeding the

Yemeni Zaydis are known in modern times as Huthis, a group which struck an alliance with Shi'i Iran.

[127] The Copts are Christians mainly in Egypt numbering between four and twelve million (figures are disputed in the absence of an official census) who follow the Patriarch of Alexandria. For a recent, accessible discussion of their beliefs and outlook, see Gerard Russell, *Heirs to Forgotten Kingdoms: Journeys into the Disappearing Religions of the Middle East* (New York: Simon & Schuster, 2014), 216–60.

[128] The Arab Deterrent Force (Quwwat al-Rad' al-'Arabiyya) referred to by Sadr was an Arab League peacekeeping force, consisting of 25,000 Syrian troops and 5,000 from other Arab countries, established by the Cairo summit of October 25–26, 1976, at the request of the Lebanese authorities and sent to Lebanon to deter the re-emergence of the conflict, remove heavy weapons from militias and maintain the ceasefire. It was deployed across the country, with the exception of the south, following an Israeli veto.

Arab-anchored peace. There is also the fact that armed Palestinians are present in the south and will remain there regardless of whether or not peace is achieved. There will be no peace in the next three years, at the very least. Imagine an armed group being present in a region for three years without state oversight . . .[129] What would that lead to? It would lead to dire and severe consequences, especially with the splintering of the Palestinian resistance into a rejectionist front, a peace front and a moderate one (keeping in mind that the majority of Palestinians are moderate). This is further exacerbated by the fact that interference by Arab countries has led to a situation in which each Arab country has its own organization within the Palestinian resistance. The lack of security in the south will unfortunately prevent any progress or development in the next three years.

As for the threats to the south, I do not believe that Israel is likely to invade the south, because the world in general, and the United States more specifically, are safeguarding the south and recognize Lebanon's southern borders as international borders.[130] This does not stem from their love for Lebanon and its people, but the fact is that any instability on Israel's northern borders, and so Lebanon's southern borders, will lead to renewed violence in the region and to the collapse of the power balance, undermining stability in the entire region. By supporting the Palestinian–Syrian rapprochement and by creating an environment of Arab solidarity and internal peace in Lebanon, we will try to save the south or to contribute, however modestly, to minimizing suffering and hardships there.

The fate of the south will have a pivotal impact on the future of Shiʿis. I think that tensions in the south will ultimately prove beneficial for Shiʿis. If you look at the map of Shiʿi presence, you will notice how broad it is compared to Israel. Shiʿi presence extends from South Lebanon to the West Bekaa, which connects the south to the Bekaa

See Dilip Hiro, *Lebanon, Fire and Embers: A History of the Lebanese Civil War* (London: Weidenfeld and Nicolson, 1993), 44–46.

[129] It is not clear why Sadr mentions three years. It is probably just an indication of his skepticism to see matters improve in the short term.

[130] In the course of 1976, the Israelis established a line of exclusion inside South Lebanon, a few miles into the country, to keep Palestinian military presence outside the strip delineated. It invaded the south in March 1978, a few weeks before Sadr's disappearance, and again in 1982, occupying Beirut. It is noteworthy that Sadr appears nuanced on the approach of the United States, which has since been standing far more uncritically on the side of successive Israeli governments.

valley, and spans the length of the Bekaa. The majority of Shiʿis are concentrated in these areas, with some communities around Beirut[131] and in North Lebanon. No matter what Lebanon's political future is, this Shiʿi community will be faced with the Israeli challenge, which is first and foremost a cultural one. When a Shiʿi sees the Israeli youth or Israeli villages, weapons or society face to face, they have two – and only two – courses of action, whether through their state or their community, or by themselves [individually]: they can either surrender to the challenge or rise up to meet it. Surrender means being subordinated to Israel and becoming mere instruments of this new, major power in the region. This would lead to corruption and defeat. Most Shiʿis will never accept this fate. No one will be able to convince a people that they are failing and sinking in the depths of corruption. Therefore, in the twenty-five years to come, Shiʿis have no other option but to rise to the challenge. This challenge is first and foremost cultural, which means that we must develop our villages to rival Israeli villages; we must develop our youth to rival the Israeli youth; and we must develop our weapons and our thinking to rival those of Israel. The path to get there will be long and arduous, but we must complete it nonetheless. As a result, after, or during, the upcoming quarter of a century, the Shiʿi community will become the vanguard of Muslims and Arabs, and it will assume its historic role in guiding Arabs and Muslims toward progress and civilization against the very presence of Israel.

I am personally optimistic about the future of the Shiʿi community, and, God willing, I will dedicate every fiber of my being toward ensuring its well-being.

[131] The Shiʿi demographic presence in Beirut developed over the years as a result of both the continued troubles on the border with Israel and the search for jobs far more widely available in the capital.

Part I
Humanism in Islam

Theology and Philosophy

2

Islam's Stewardship of Human Meanings and Values

The concept of "humanism" appears simple and straightforward,[1] but in practice it has proved elusive, with schools of thought differing over how to define it or identify its various dimensions.[2] Many intellectuals active in civil society, or leaders of social movements and activities, claim the welfare of humanity is the driving force behind their ideas and efforts, and love of man their ultimate motivation.

To overcome the vagueness and opaqueness that envelops the concept of humanism, without becoming entangled in verbal and logical contortions, we must look at the reality of man, his truth and his existence. From the noun "human" we turn to examine the more abstract notions derived from "human" – "humanism" and "humanity" – and their meaning, the values associated with them and their effectiveness and strength.

To begin with, man is a special creature, a created being who differs from other created beings in that he possesses freedom of choice: his actions emanate from reflection and will, even if to a relative extent. Secondly, he is largely influenced by nature and the elements of the universe surrounding him. Thirdly, he is a social creature who interacts intensively with other members of his species. Fourthly, he is fundamentally a creature of God, the creator of the universe and of life, with all that this multidimensional relationship entails in its repercussions on him and on all his other relationships.

These are the four chapters of the book of man.

[1] This chapter was presented at the Sixth Conference of the Islamic Studies Academy at the Azhar, March 30, 1971. See the Chronology under 1971.

[2] For Sadr's humanism, see Section I.1.

Human values, therefore, are the original roots instilled in the human clay so that a human being can grow, through his own effort, in a comprehensive and integrated way where no single aspect of his existence develops at the expense of another, and none of the roots becomes rigid, brittle and immovable so as to inhibit the continual movement of man toward improvement and perfection. These human values are lines tracing the path toward the comprehensive perfection of man and emanate from his soul and existence. It is God's hue and His nature, from which He fashioned the seeds and propensities of human nature at the instance of creation, which then are transformed as man follows the straight route to effective meaning and values.

2.1 Other Views

If we deny the first aspect of man's existence [free will], thereby giving credence to his being a phenomenon like any other in nature, and if we interpret his decisions and actions as natural and inevitable phenomena;

or if we separate him from other natural beings, and we consider him to be fashioned, in both body and soul, separately from the material world in which he lives and in this way subject him to ordained fate;

or if we consider him just as an individual, with the sole foundation of a society merely as a collection of individuals;

or when we ignore his attachment to God;

[in all these cases] we are limiting the scope of man in the realm of the eternal and immortal, and we are denying his connection to the formation, role and fate of all other creatures.

When we espouse one of the four views set out above, we find ourselves confronted with a different human being and a different concept of humanity.

We can find in French existentialism an urgent desire to adopt the first view [denying free will]. In the Greek and Oriental Peripatetic philosophers, we find an inclination toward the second view [that human beings are separate from the material world and subject to fate].

In the Jewish tradition and some followers of anarchism we see an inclination to thoughts resembling the third view [man as simply an individual, and society simply a collection of individuals]. The fourth view is seen among materialists in general, and in the Western philosophers who resisted scholastics and neutralized all influence of metaphysics on physical entities. This fourth group comprises most contemporary social scientists and philosophers.[3]

2.2 Islam and Humanity

The Qur'an affirms complete harmony between religion and humanity:

> Therefore, stand firm in your devotion to the true Faith, the upright Faith which God created for mankind to embrace. God's Creation cannot be changed. This surely the right faith, although most men may not know it.[4]

The hadiths also express the harmony of Islam with human nature through the dictum "every born creature is born in nature."[5]

If we observe that the concept of "Islam" implies submission to God, meaning that everything and everyone taking their true place in God's creation is Muslim,[6] then the position determined by God for the creation of man is what He has designed for him to realize, at one and the same time, in his humanity and his Islam. Consequently, man in his real place is associated and bound up with the Creator and with other humans with all other natural creatures: man's "Islam" *is* his humanity.

The following Qur'anic verses clarify this truth:

> Say: "We believe in God and that which has been revealed to us; in what was revealed to Abraham, Ishmael, Isaac, Jacob, and the tribes; to Moses and Jesus and the other prophets by their Lord. We make no distinction among any of them, and to Him we submit."

3 French existentialists, as represented by Jean-Paul Sartre (*Being and Nothingness*, first published in 1943), would generally be taken to argue that human choices shape human "existence." Oriental Peripatetic philosophers, following Aristotle, stressed the importance of nature and the human need to understand it. While anarchism can be portrayed as excessively "individualistic," it is hard to see how this might apply to "the Jewish tradition [literally, school]" or what Musa Sadr means by "Jewish tradition." By "materialists" in general, Sadr seems to be thinking both of self-professed "materialists" like Karl Marx and of twentieth-century Anglo-Saxon philosophers who explicitly rejected "metaphysics," like A. J. Ayer, *Language, Truth and Logic* (London: Gollancz, 1936).

4 Qur'an 30:30.

5 Hadith reported by various tradents, e.g., on www.dorar.net/hadith/sharh/11472. The rest of the hadith makes it clearer by explaining that "his two parents make him Jewish, or Christian, or a Mazdaite" (*fa-abawahu yuhawwidanihi wa-yunassiranihi wa-yumajjisanihi*).

6 It is unclear whether Musa Sadr is here referring to *islam* in the sense of acceptance of the One God, or to the specific religion of Islam.

> If they accept your faith, they shall be rightly guided; if they reject it, they shall surely be in schism. Against them God is your all-sufficient defender. He hears all and knows all.
>
> We take on God's own dye. And who has a better dye than God's? Him will we worship.[7]

2.3 Drawing the Details

Although humanity and its values are integrally linked to mankind, man himself cannot define those values, for several reasons.

First, the perceptions and feelings of individuals and of communities are influenced by their culture and their specific circumstances, and by their concrete, material interests. Second, both individuals and communities are in a continual process of improvement, and therefore they are continually incomplete and incapable of perceiving fully the potential wider dimensions of human existence, dimensions they strive to reach. If a person wishes to set forth the specifics of humanism or the key constituents of humanity he or she would do so in relative terms, and this would lead to a plurality of concepts of humanity, with goals based on illusion and fantasy.

As for God, creator of mankind, creator of the universe and of life, His station is suited to the delineation of the detail of the dimensions of humanity, in an integrated, complete whole. This is why religion is necessarily transcendent, absolute and metaphysical.

In order to reaffirm the validity of this approach and justify its adoption by Islamic scholars, we reassert the well-known principles that "legal obligations are the expression of rational obligations," and that "what reason determines is also determined by the law (*shar'*)."[8] That is when there is a rule. Here is the fundamental point we wish to make in this study, namely, that Islam is humanism in its meanings and its values, and that humanism is Islam.

7 Qur'an 2:136–38.

8 These two principles belong to the genre of *qawa'id fiqhiyya* (legal rules or maxims). These are generally aphorisms encapsulating general principles of the law in its most abstract sense, akin to Roman legal maxims. These two rules cited by Sadr privilege the place of reason vis-à-vis law, expressing their convergence. This is particularly true for Shi'i jurisprudence, whose leading scholars consider "reason" ('aql) to be a central source of law.

2.4 The Humanism of Faith

The foundation of Islamic faith is belief in the one God who possesses the attributes of the "most gracious names"[9] and the sublime qualities; "He begot none, nor was He begotten."[10]

This belief, firstly, cleanses the human being from total submission (worship) to all objects natural, or from submission to any other person, however high her standing: man's existence is not defined materially.

Secondly, this belief mobilizes all the individual's capacities to achieve his single, most elevated goal. It protects individuals from deviance, degradation and loss, and from giving way to polytheism or idolatry. It protects the human being's life and activities from being crushed or fragmented.

Thirdly, this sets man in the direction of an infinite objective and sketches an abiding path for his ambition, something he can pursue over the long term, from the cradle to the grave – and beyond the grave. For death does not stop the movement of man toward perfection. Rather, work continues with the blessing of "a good child, books of learning and flowing charity," as the hadith puts it.[11] Improvement and rewards increase when man has embarked on the right part, and if someone after his departure pursues its benefits until the Day of Judgment.[12]

Fourthly, it places constant human striving for perfection far away from clashes and conflict with others, since the attributes of the infinite and the nonmaterial world essentially drive, and effectively govern, a human being's activities and his offerings to others.

Fifthly, it unites the capabilities of the community and coordinates its members as if in a team race, warding off the danger of common idolatry that would divide and fracture society, shattering the power and agency of its members: "Do not divide your religion into sects, each exulting in its own doctrines."[13]

Sixthly, the meaning of "He begot none, nor was He begotten" excludes the subjective element from the social gains. People are equal like the teeth of a comb, and each man shall be judged only be his labors. "He only has what he labored for."[14]

[9] Qur'an 20:8. [10] Qur'an 112:3.

[11] Majlisī, *Biḥār al-anwār*, 2nd ed. (Beirut: al-Wafā', 1983), 2:22–23.

[12] This probably refers to trusts (waqfs) in perpetuity. See Chapter 10, n. 33.

[13] Qur'an 30:32.

[14] Qur'an 53:39–41 (translation modified). The reference to the equality of human beings likened to "the teeth of a comb" comes from a hadith used by both Shi'is and Sunnis;

In this connection, we also consider the impact of faith in the Day of Resurrection, in divine justice, accountability and the vision of the human being and whatever issues relate to him in terms of good or evil, even just "an atom's worth."[15] I affirm here that the impact of this faith on human values reflects also the following traits:

First: the exalted place of man, rendering him responsible for all his works and actions – large or small, secret or overt – and for all of his spoken expressions and all that he hides within himself. Responsibility rests with his own soul and what he does to others. The way he is so honored is a great matter for humankind.

Second: faith reassures him that hidden or openly displayed efforts do not go to waste, and affirms that his loyal striving is welcomed – even if not rewarded for reasons beyond his will: "He who leaves his dwelling to fight for God and His Apostle and is then overtaken by death shall be recompensed by God."[16] And he who by error does not reach his goal will also be rewarded, in accordance with the Muslim scholars' formulation.[17]

Third: from the second reflection we deduce that belief in resurrection can facilitate man's stewardship in changing society for the better, as well as changing himself. The believer strives to do this without attending to the opinions of those invested in the status quo: he desires to please God and chooses the most fulfilling reward.

Fourth: we must not overlook repentance in generating human effort and in overcoming despair and fear of depression.

2.5 Humanist Culture in Islam

The general concepts proposed by Islam for forming an original, primary culture for the Muslim – and for creating a comprehensive view of man,

see, e.g., https://dorar.net/h/a299eb2d7392665bf974bf861846e797?sims=1. It is used often by Sadr and like-minded social Muslim reformists.

[15] "On that day mankind will come in broken bands to be shown their labors. Whoever does an atom's weight of good shall see it, and whoever does an atom's weight of evil shall see it also" (Qur'an 99:6–8).

[16] "He that leaves his home in the cause of God shall find many a refuge in the land and great abundance. He who leaves his dwelling to fight for God and His Apostle and is then overtaken by death shall be recompensed by God. Surely God is forgiving and merciful" (Qur'an 4:100).

[17] This refers to a well-known hadith about the efforts of scholars being rewarded even when they fail.

the universe and life – are rooted in human values and their preservation.

When we follow Islam's views of man, life, the universe, society and so forth – matters not taken up by scientific practice and empirical investigation but remaining for the most part in the realm of theory – we can see the depth of their humanity.

Mankind in the Qur'an is honored and accorded preferential status over much of creation, for man is fashioned "in a most noble image;"[18] he is among the most excellent of created beings, crafted by God's hand to be God's deputy on earth; God taught him the "names" and imparted His own breath and spirit to him; commanded the angels to prostrate themselves before him; fashioned for his benefit the sun, moon, stars, night and day. Man is the only being honored with knowledge and wisdom, and by the ability to master the forces of the universe and all other beings. Fundamentally and intrinsically good, man has been shown good and evil,[19] and inspired by sin and piety,[20] so as to choose between them. This is a second distinction that sets him apart from all other beings and ranks him higher than angels.

As for death, illness and disasters, Islam's view of these is unique and humane. Death is an adornment of life: it is "a line traced round Adam's neck like the beauty of a girl's necklace,"[21] for it is a test of man and an opportunity for God to see how well he has acquitted himself.[22]

It is the entrance to the forgiving Lord for whom there is only sustained and enduring good, and not the end of the work of a human being.[23] For it is possible for a human to overcome death and remain cared for by the Lord, to be delighted with whatever God provides and to spread the good word beyond his death to those who have remained

[18] "We created man in a most noble image" (Qur'an 95:4).

[19] "Have We not given him two eyes, a tongue and two lips, and shown him the two paths?" Qur'an 90:8–10.

[20] "By the heaven and Him that built it; by the earth and Him that spread it; by the soul and Him that molded it and inspired it with knowledge of sin and piety; blessed shall be the man who has kept it pure, and ruined he that has corrupted it!" Qur'an 91:5–10.

[21] This comes from a speech of Imam Hussein; see Majlisī, *Biḥār al-anwār*, 44:366.

[22] "He created death and life that He might put you to the proof and find out which of you acquitted himself best. He is the Mighty, the Forgiving One" (Qur'an 67:2).

[23] "That which you have been given is but the fleeting pleasure of this life. Better and more enduring is God's recompense to those who believe and put their trust in Him" (Qur'an 42:36).

outside the fold; in this way the human can immortalize his works and preserve his activities.

As for disease and tribulations, impoverishment and loss of wealth, lives and benefits – they all constitute a test, contributing to the development of the human's abilities and training him to patiently endure, while at the same time alerting him to his true being and his belonging to God, to whom he must return.[24]

On the other hand, such calamities and diseases are like natural disasters that lead people to investigate their causes and to seek to control or minimize their effects; adversity is, therefore, tantamount to a divine school that elevates human knowledge.

Islam considers that the future belongs to the righteous, and victory to the friends of God.

"But it was Our will to favor those who were oppressed in the land and to make them leaders among men, to bestow on them a noble heritage."[25] This vision produces optimism, confidence in success and release.

The universe is a great mihrab[26] in which all things prostrate, bowing in praise and prayer to God: everything in the universe glorifies Him and prays to Him; everything in it is organized with a measure set for everything.[27] Such is the vision reflected in human actions and activities, in a powerful, positive and effective manner.

2.6 Human Society in Islam

The image that Islam proposes of the community of believers is one of the most important givens of Islamic culture, and one of the most influential in the care given to human values. Islam views society as one body; a single great human being, with no conflict, no factions and no classes. It is composed of individuals of different competencies and energy, but who are all sympathetic and cooperative, exchanging services

[24] This paragraph refers to Qur'an 2:155–56. "We shall test your steadfastness with fear and famine, with loss of life and property and crops. Give good news to those who endure with fortitude; who in adversity say, 'We belong to God, and to Him we shall return.'"

[25] Qur'an 28:5.

[26] The mihrab is the central niche in a mosque indicating Mecca's direction for prayer.

[27] "God will surely bring about what He decrees. God has set a measure for all things" (Qur'an 65:3).

with one another so that each finds completion and fulfillment through what he gains from others and what he contributes to others.

Society is formed by man and for man, it is man writ large and not simply one aspect of his existence – [man should be seen] neither purely as an individual nor as a collective. Were it otherwise, it [the image of man] would be simply a powerful means of exerting pressure on one side for the benefit of the other. This would lead to the misrepresentation of the truth of man and distortion of his true face.

Society in the view of Islam consists of the human being, all human beings and all types of human beings. No individual is par excellence, no class is preferred,[28] no element less valuable than others, no class without class.[29] There is no majority without a minority, and vice versa – all is only for the sake of human beings.

This society [in the Islamic conception] is formed for each and every human being; it is not a society that develops some aspects of human existence at the expense of others, neither individuality alone nor the collective alone; it does not develop body without spirit, nor vice versa: for there is no monasticism in Islam. This society is for every human being; it fosters all the abilities of every individual and offers opportunities for each and every positive energy latent in each and every individual.

The differentiation of peoples in the world community, in the view of Islam, exists only for them to become acquainted with one another, as they engage in exchange and cooperation that may culminate in human integration globally, along lines similar to individuals within a single society. Human loyalty to one's immediate surroundings should not be coupled with feelings of superiority or with racism. The nation, the people and the family are not idols to worship, and they cannot be developed, served or elevated at the expense of others.

Wealth in Islamic society, as in all other things owned by man, does not own man and must not control him: it is a trust (*amana*)[30] from God

[28] Musa Sadr is possibly referring here to the Marxian notion that the proletariat, or industrial working class, has the unique capacity to end class-based society and create a classless, communist society. While his point about "majority" and "minority" is one of logic, he might also be thinking of the need for minorities to retain rights even in well-functioning democracies.

[29] It is here unclear whether Musa Sadr is making the point that logically there cannot be a class without there being at least one other class or referring (as elsewhere, see Chapter 7) to the Marxist notion of the proletariat as a class acting to create a classless society.

[30] On "trust" (*amana*) and Musa Sadr's use of the concept, see Chapter 10, n. 33; Chapter 12, n. 10.

given over to man's hands for safekeeping. The basis is therefore man, not the money or any instrument, so that we can say that human energy lies first and foremost in the three elements of production.

Work can contribute to profits without loss, but the instrument does not have this option. Work, for which fixed interest (*riba*, "usury") is prohibited, can also secure monetary compensation [as in wages] without need for [the worker to own] capital.

Islamic rulings in the field of social economy are replete with humanism. As a consequence, the Qur'an expressed the riches of life of this world as temptation (*fitna*). Money must not overwhelm the human being, nor should the state become a state for the rich.

On the level of authority and power, Islam has rejected arbitrary authority of any person over another person, as well as inherited authority of any person over another other than in the case of minors. The only authority is that of God, or the authority that emanates from man's obligations, his bonds and his trustees, and this is conditional on the contracts being valid in terms of freedom, maturity of reason and knowledge.

Such a community is fertile ground for maintaining and developing human values.

2.7 Ethics in Islam

Ethics constitute the most elevated and the ultimate aspect of religious teachings. It is an essential part of religious development. Islamic morality is noted for powerfully fighting those factors that undermine the link between humans and other creatures and the interaction with their fellows. Such factors include cowardice, cruelty, arrogance, isolation – and vanity, which is a sense of self-sufficiency that prevents receiving and benefiting from others – as well as vanity and haughtiness, which obstruct the divine flow and hinder others from benefiting from the person. In a comprehensive review, Islamic ethics in fact constitute the cornerstone of human values – as well as the path to acquire and maintain them.

2.8 Islamic Rules Preserve Values

Islam does not ignore human needs or call anyone to disregard and combat them; it does not encourage monasticism in any of its various forms. Islam views the means of satisfying these needs as being "God's grace" or "a blessing from God" and it considers that fulfilling such needs with righteous intent is tantamount to the worship of God in good faith.

In addition, Islam has established limits in order to preserve various important aspects of man's existence and to maintain his capabilities and efficiency: all that has been created on earth has been given to man and Islam has rejected those who have "forbidden you to wear the decent clothes or to eat the good things which God has provided for His servants."[31]

On the other hand, we can attribute the classification of these needs, and approaches to satisfying them, along the lines of permitted (halal) and forbidden (haram), to "the Sufism of Islam," since man does not proceed with the fulfillment of his desires until he is certain of God's satisfaction, thereby avoiding setting himself adrift with desires that are merely rooted in the material world surrounding him.

This type of Sufism differs from the more well-known ascetic type of Sufism, which is based on ignoring desires deliberately in a quest for purity and perfection of the soul. Rather, desire is a transcendental need for man. What he can impose on himself by fulfilling his desires keeps him from a total dependency on his surroundings.

Man is required to be active, not passive, in his environment; he should be an effective and influential leader, and this cannot be achieved when he is swept away by his [unfulfilled] desires, or adrift in them.

What is unique and exceptional about Islam's rulings with regard to the haram and halal, apart from their contents and the reasons for actions defined under one of these two categories, is that they are expressed in terms of good, beneficial, delightful in opposition to bad, wicked, deleterious.

It is difficult in this brief presentation to review the Islamic rules and study their effects on maintaining human values, so we will conclude by mentioning some other significant points.

Rules on the extent and rigor of prescribed duties and obligations of religious worship, as well as prohibitions, are determined by a person's

[31] "Say, 'Who has forbidden you to wear the decent clothes or to eat the good things which God has provided for His servants?' Say, 'These are for the enjoyment of the faithful in the life of this world [though shared by others]; but they shall be theirs alone on the Day of Resurrection.' Thus do We make plain Our revelations to men of knowledge" (Qur'an 7:32).

potential and the need to keep her within a sphere of comfort and ease. If hardship and embarrassment are experienced in following these precepts, they may be waived just as harm must be prevented and injury compensated in daily transactions.[32]

The intervention of certain factors or of states of ignorance, coercion, necessity, oblivion and forgetfulness can each engender a waiver, or lifting, of responsibility and nullify the obligation of commitment.

As a consequence, work takes on the character of worship and convivial sociability, with performance of duties within the family and society acquiring the rank and status of worship, keeping them with sanctity and humanity. Relations between individuals and groups in all cases must be humane. This is emphasized and highlighted by the rules governing warfare.[33]

These, then, are examples and headings summarizing the attention Islam gives to human values and concepts. I present them to this gathering in humility, noting that every title presented here is in fact a chapter of a blessed register. The continuity between the values of Islam and those of humanism requires enlarging the present investigation to be part of an encyclopedic approach to Islamic sciences. I only hope that this humble presentation of my findings be acceptable to God, the codifier of the law, creator of man, and to your good selves. I humbly seek your forbearance.

[32] Sadr appears here to refer to rules over fasting being waived for travelers if they lead to physical distress, and to the unlawful side of commercial transactions involving interest.

[33] Sadr refers to the laws of war in Islam, which feature several modern rules of engagement such as sparing noncombatants, women and children.

3

Islam and Human Dignity

As we examine human dignity in Islam – a theme I believe to be a cornerstone of Islam's view of human beings and fundamental to its view of humankind – it may be useful to summarize the consequences of this principle and so illustrate its profound influence on realizing Islam's mission.[1]

The first steps in a person's upbringing, on their path to fulfillment and excellence in all spheres, should enable them to gain self-awareness of their human dignity. Failing that, they will not attend to themselves and are unlikely to undertake any activity aimed at improving their situation. Without such self-awareness, they forego their inner life both in the present and as they look forward. They even forego the past.

In such a state there is little scope of convincing a person of the benefits of working to improve their affairs and the various aspects of their outlook, and scant chance they will move forward to something better. Such a person will remain listless and indifferent, fixed in their ways – preferring to continue in their present mode of existence rather than shoulder the burden of change and take the initiative to overcome inertia, to strive, to become truly active and to gain agency in life.

We do not disregard self-love, the firm instinct in a person that instills energy to defend and protect the self and bring benefits to it. However, we say that this instinct is developed to the extent that human consciousness is raised: it works for the good when it encounters goodness appropriate to it, and where it shields and protects itself from what undermines its own goodness and elevation.

[1] Lecture delivered at the American University of Beirut, February 8, 1967.

Self-love is the human being's driving force, but it is a sense of dignity that determines *maqam*[2] – the person's status or reputation – and that sets or sketches out the broad paths of his or her life journey and designates the fine goals they choose to pursue, goals through which they can distinguish foes from allies and devise effective ways to defend themselves.

We do not deny that standards of human life can sometimes be raised by pressure and coercion – but we do not believe such an approach is at all suitable for achieving humankind's greater perfection. Coercion carries many negative consequences, including psychological damage and inadequate results, leading to an individualistic society rather than one where people display a sense of community. Such an approach should be avoided.

So let us leave this aspect of study to the educational psychologists, and let us begin our survey of Islam and dignity of humankind or the human person.

3.1 The Human Being Is the Deputy of God on Earth

Islam considers the human being to be the deputy of God on earth. Humans have been taught all the "names" of God, and God's angels prostrate themselves in honoring humankind.

> When your Lord said to the angels: "I am placing on the earth one that shall rule as My deputy," they replied: "Will You put there one that will do evil and shed blood, when we have for so long sung Your praises and sanctified Your name?"
>
> He said: "I know what you know not."
>
> He taught Adam the names of all things and then set them before the angels, saying: "Tell Me the names of these, if what you say be true."
>
> "Glory be to You," they replied, "we have no knowledge except that which You have given us. You alone are all-knowing and wise."
>
> Then said He: "Adam, tell them their names." And when Adam had named them, He said: "Did I not tell you that I know all the secrets

[2] *Maqam* is literally a "place" or "station."

> of the heavens and the earth, and know all that you reveal and all that you conceal?"
>
> And when We said to the angels: "Prostrate yourself before Adam," they all prostrated themselves except Satan, who in his pride refused and became an unbeliever.[3]

The concept of successor,[4] or deputy, underlines the independence of human beings and their freedom of action on this earth. But the paths set forth for humankind to follow, the guidelines that humans have been given, these are God's recommendations, or exhortations, for His deputy.

God teaches His attributes or "names" to Adam as the qualities that all those enjoying the faculty of reason would do well to return to, time and again. Simultaneously, God reaffirms to His angels that they must recognize their ultimate incapacity and powerlessness, and that He alone knows the unseen, of both heaven and earth.

This teaching and affirmation [that God alone knows the unseen] reflects the extraordinary potential of the human mind, its ability to know all earthly matters and comprehend the interacting forces within the scope of the human being's rule and deputyship. It is this potential that was placed in his hands and at his disposition, for his life's work and mission.

The prostration of the angels, an elite among beings, confirms the subservience and submission of all beings to humankind, and their reverence for humans. The import of this will become clearer later. The Qur'anic verses cited above convey and epitomize a sense of God honoring human beings. The freedom to dispose independently, and to enjoy the extensive potential to take independent initiatives, when combined with the submission of all other general orders of beings to humankind, constitute the three key dispensations conveyed in these verses: freedom, knowledge and the relationship to prophecy.

3.2 Humans and Free Will: Freedom of Choice

Angels know well that having independent freedom of action requires humans to have both an acute awareness of evil and the ability to do evil.

[3] Qur'an 2:30–34.
[4] *Khalifa*, variously translated as "vice-regent," "deputy," "caliph" or "successor."

It is this that motivates the angels to say that "humans will corrupt the earth and spill blood." Being vulnerable to this danger does not diminish the stature or dignity of human beings. It renders them all the more notable and prominent, by highlighting the nature of human independence and freedom of action in the world.

Iblis[5] (referred to as "Satan" in the Qur'an) is the only angel who refused to bow in humility to Adam and who instead displayed arrogance toward him. For this he was banished from God's heavenly kingdom, and he will face just punishment on the Day of Resurrection:

> The angels all prostrated themselves except Satan, who was too proud, for he was an unbeliever.
>
> "Satan," said He, "why do you not bow to him whom My own hands have made? Are you too proud, or do you deem yourself superior?"
>
> Satan replied: "I am nobler than he. You created me from fire, but him from clay."
>
> "Begone, you are accursed!" said He. "My curse shall remain on you until the Day of Reckoning."
>
> He replied: "Reprieve me, Lord, till the Day of Resurrection."
>
> He said: "Reprieved you shall be till the Appointed Day."
>
> "I swear by Your glory," said Satan, "that I will seduce them all except Your faithful servants."
>
> He replied: "Learn the truth, then (and I speak nothing but the truth): I will surely fill hell with all your offspring and with your followers all."[6]

This Iblis, who became an accursed[7] devil after refusing to bow down to Adam, commands an army of evildoers operating in the lives of humans, and brings this raging struggle to paroxysm – both in the individual soul and in the world at large. The victors in the battle, those sincere in their worship of God, are the fruits of the universe, for whom it was created as the arena for exercising their deputyship and its realm. Men and women are fashioned by the hand of God, and instilled with His spirit:

[5] Iblis is a proper name, roughly equivalent to Lucifer in the Christian tradition.
[6] Qur'an 38:73–85. [7] *Rajim.*

> Your Lord said to the angels: "I am creating man from clay. When I have fashioned him and breathed My spirit into him, kneel down and prostrate yourself before him."[8]

Humans were created from earth by God's hands and the spirit blown into them is God's spirit. This explains the characteristics found in the human being, which extend in their scope from the land to the sky; it also shows the dignity instilled in humankind: God considers human beings to be a pinnacle of existence, a climax of creation.

> We created man in a most noble image and in the end, We shall reduce him to the lowest of the low: except the believers who do good works, for theirs shall be a boundless recompense.[9]

> We first created man from an essence of clay: then placed him, a living germ, in a secure enclosure. The germ We made a clot of blood, and the clot a lump of flesh. This We fashioned into bones, then clothed the bones with flesh, bringing forth another creation. Blessed be God, the noblest of creators.[10]

3.3 Islam's Invitation to Knowledge

God singled out human beings, among all creation and amid all created beings, with a distinctive capacity to become endowed with God's own ethics, and for this reason they were created free, and empowered with the gift of acquiring scientific knowledge and wisdom. Islam is at pains, in many places in the Qur'an and the Sunna of the Prophet, to emphasize these points, and to elevate the morale and self-esteem of human beings; to bring them to feel that they are held in a uniquely honored station, favored above the rest of the creation. Following the hadith "Adopt the ethics of God."[11] And in the Qur'an, "We have bestowed blessings on Adam's children and guided them by land and sea. We have provided them with wholesome things and exalted them above many of Our creatures."[12]

The Qur'an then proclaims that whatever is found on or around earth was created for humankind, for its use and benefit.

[8] Qur'an 38:71–72. [9] Qur'an 95:4–6. [10] Qur'an 23:12–14.

[11] "Takhallaqu bi-akhlaq Allah"; hadith related, e.g., in Majlisī, *Biḥār al-anwār*, 58:129.

[12] Qur'an 17:70.

> He created for you all that the earth contains.[13]

> He has pressed the night and the day, and the sun and the moon, into your service: the stars also serve you by His leave.[14]

Islamic teachings affirm that God is close to the human being, nearer to him than to any other thing or being. Humans feel this closeness and proximity and draw nearer God to find His strength and power.

> We created man. We know the prompting of his soul, and are closer to him than his jugular vein.[15]

> If My servants question you about Me, tell them that I am near. I answer the prayer of the supplicant when he calls to Me; therefore let them answer My call and put their trust in Me, that they may be rightly guided.[16]

> Believers, obey God and the Apostle when he calls you to that which gives you life. Know that God stands between man and his heart, and that in His presence you shall all be assembled.[17]

The Prophet tells us that "the heart of the believer is the throne of God the merciful."[18]

The emphasis is on God's proximity to humans, which serves to elevate their morale and spirit, transporting them beyond fear, anxiety and sorrow, and distancing them safely from moral vices that arise from weakness, fear and greed – such as dishonesty, hypocrisy and greed.

Proximity to God facilitates spiritual enrichment and the incorporation of His moral values in the human soul. In the Qur'an, a person is portrayed as the "equivalent" of, or "equal" to, the entire universe, as he or she reflects the august, sublime and supremely knowledgeable creator. In the words of the hadith, she is called an "equal match for the horizons," encapsulating the entire universe:

> We will show them Our signs in all the regions of the earth and in their own souls, until they clearly see that this is the truth.[19]

[13] Qur'an 2:29. [14] Qur'an 16:12. [15] Qur'an 50:16. [16] Qur'an 2:186.
[17] Qur'an 8:24.
[18] "Qalb al-mu'min 'arsh al-rahman"; hadith related, e.g., in Majlisī, *Biḥār al-anwār*, 5:39.
[19] Qur'an 41:53.

The poetry of Ali b. Abi Talib expresses it strongly:

> I claim that you are a small planet;
> inside you the whole universe is enfolded.
> You are an open book
> whose letters reveal the hidden.[20]

The trust that the entire universe could not carry, humans were able to bear:

> We offered Our trust to the heavens, to the earth and to the mountains, but they refused the burden and were afraid to receive it. Man undertook to bear it, but he has proved a sinner and a fool.
>
> God will surely punish the hypocrites and the idolaters, both men and women; but to believing men and to believing women He shall show mercy. God is forgiving and merciful.[21]

However one wishes to interpret the meaning of "trust" or "covenant" (amana) – religiously, epistemologically, socio-politically or simply as responsibility – in all cases human distinctiveness and greatness lie in their taking the trust in hand in bearing the covenant.[22] To be in such a position is a celebration of humankind and humanity's place and status.

3.4 The Place of Prophecy

We observe the status of prophecy as that of the divine message, of friendship with God and communication with Him; it is the place of selection, of love.[23] It is the place of God's word, somewhere designated only for humans, and the most honored status that any creature can reach.

> God has surely been gracious to the faithful in sending them an apostle of their own to declare to them His revelations.[24]

[20] The *diwan* (collection of poetry) of the first Imam, Ali b. Abi Talib (d. 661), can be found on www.aldiwan.net/. These two lines are available at www.aldiwan.net/poem31063 .html.

[21] Qur'an 33:72–73.

[22] On "trust" (amana) and Musa Sadr's use of the concept, see Chapter 10, n. 33; Chapter 12, n. 10.

[23] The adjectives here evoke "names" associated with prophets: Abraham is called Khalil Allah, the "friend of God"; Moses is called Kalim Allah, "communicator with God"; Muhammad is called Mustafa, "selected by God"; and Jesus is called Habib Allah, "God's love."

[24] Qur'an 3:164.

> If We had made him an angel, We would have given him the semblance of a man, and would have added to their confusion.[25]

Several verses of the Qur'an similarly denote the singling out of the distinctive rank that God accords to His prophets and messengers. This should suffice as an indication of humankind's nobility, and as evidence of the honored position of man in Islam.

Let us now turn to some details in the teachings to maintain and protect human dignity in some – indeed all – dimensions of human existence. This is because Islam probes humankind and human existence in detail. In making and in elaborating its core precepts, Islam bases itself upon honoring the human, and considers this a major objective of religion, a central purpose of the message of the faith.

What follows is a summary of these teachings.

3.4.1 God's Creation

Religion in brief is the nature of God as reflected in the way He created humans.[26] Religion is the true expression of this nature; it reveals the human as clear, untainted, uninfluenced by misleading factors:

> Therefore, stand firm in your devotion to the true Faith, the upright Faith that God created for mankind to embrace. God's creation cannot be changed. This is surely the right faith, although most men may not know it.[27]

A hadith offers an interpretation of the verse: "Every human is born with [God's] nature."[28] Religion, according to these teachings, is itself human nature. But men and women by themselves cannot express this, for they are influenced by the circumstances that surround and agitate their lives, giving a particular color to each person's feelings of self and sense of their own nature.

It is appropriate that human nature should be expressed on a different level or station, one that is not subject to matters external to the human

[25] Qur'an 6:8. [26] *Fitra* has meanings of creation, birth, nature or instinct.

[27] Qur'an 30:30.

[28] "Inna kulla mawlud yulad ʿala al-fitra," Kulaynī, *al-Kāfī* (Tehran: Dār al-Kutub al-Islāmiyya, 2000), 2:668. Hadith also available in the Sunni collection of al-Bukhārī, *al-Ṣaḥīḥ* (Beirut: Dār Ṭawq al-Najāt, 2001), 2:104. The Arabic here rendered as "nature" is fitra.

being – that it should be expressed at a level above all other influences, a level that has created all these influencing factors. This is the station of God, who codified religion, and who finds in human nature His own law (sharia) and message.

3.4.2 The Preservation of the Self and of Others

Islam has accorded respect to the lives of human beings by considering that whoever saves a soul saves the whole of humankind, and that whoever deliberately kills a person kills all human beings and is punished in hellfire.

> That was why We laid it down for the Israelites that whoever killed a human being, except as punishment for murder or other villainy in the land, shall be regarded as having killed all mankind; and that whoever saved a human life shall be regarded as having saved all mankind.[29]

In Islamic teachings, killing a person includes also destroying an embryo. Nor has Islam permitted an individual to commit suicide on grounds that his life is his own property. God categorically forbids such doing away with life: "Do not kill yourselves. God is merciful to you."[30]

God made killing a wrong that must be compensated with amends to the blood relatives or the next of kin. This aspect of Islamic law is nowadays widely accepted.[31] Islam attaches extreme importance, one might even say exaggerated importance, to preserving the lives of others, and it warns those who ignore the concerns of the poor and orphans, because such neglect may bring about the death of a poor person from destitution or disability.

> Give generously for the cause of God and do not with your own hands cast yourself into destruction.[32]

> Whatever alms you shall give shall rebound to your own advantage ... you shall not be wronged.[33]

In a hadith on the verse "Let those who are solicitous about the welfare of their young children after their own death take care not to

[29] Qur'an 5:32. [30] Qur'an 4:29.
[31] In classical law, reference is to *diya* ("blood money"), paid to the next of kin by the murderer; in modern law, Sadr means civil compensation for the family of the victim.
[32] Qur'an 2:195. [33] Qur'an 2:272.

wrong orphans. Let them fear God and speak for justice,"[34] Imam Sadeq has this comment: "To take care of a Muslim family, to clothe and feed them, is more loved by God than undertaking seventy pilgrimages."[35]

3.4.3 The Liberation of the Essence

Islam purified the status of the human being, forbidding him from worshipping idols, from worshipping human beings, indeed from worshipping any person or thing. It considered humans too elevated to worship any but God, or to submit to any being. In many of Islam's teachings, we find warnings against, and prohibition of, seeking fulfillment of any need without [recognizing the ultimate source as] God.

3.4.4 The Sanctity of the Word

There are several teachings calling for us to dignify words pronounced by human beings just as much as honoring humans themselves – such words are seen as opening the gateway to all that is good and as shields against evil . . . "Believers, fear God and speak the truth. He will bless your works and forgive you your sins."[36]

"Speaking the truth" has been interpreted variously to rule out lying, slander, false accusation, obscenity, indecency, abomination, sarcasm, even extremism. As for the actions of witnesses and their testimony, they are given special attention by Islam: witnesses have a special duty to give evidence, for it is by their means that claims are considered, rights achieved and punishments meted out. But evidence can be accepted only from a person who is fair and just. False testimony has always been considered a major sin, with anyone duly found guilty deserving great punishment.

Any commitment, including any verbal commitment, is honored in Islam: "You are accountable for all that you promise."[37] Mutual commitments such as those expressed in contracts must be adhered to. Violating them is prohibited.

> Believers, be true to your obligations.[38]

[34] Qur'an 4:9.
[35] Imam Ja'far al-Sadeq (d. 765); hadith related in Kulaynī, *al-Kāfī*, 2:195.
[36] Qur'an 33:70–71. [37] Qur'an 17:34. [38] Qur'an 5:1.

> For how can you take it back when you have lain with each other and entered into a firm contract?[39]

An oral promise commands and demands respect. This is expressed in the hadith "the believer's promise is his religion."[40] Complying with oral commitments that establish a contract is obligatory, as in the hadith "Muslims honor their obligations, except for a condition that prohibits doing good or one that allows evil."[41] Obligations make contractual transactions an expression of social commitment, thereby both reinforcing social needs and enriching the commitments.

The spoken word, the spoken utterance, is so respected in Islam that it is accepted as a gateway into religion. To achieve affiliation with Islam, nothing more is required than to recite the doctrine of the unity of God and the prophecy of Muhammad – denying the value of such recited recognition is prohibited: "Do not say to those who offer you peace, 'You are not believers' – seeking the chance booty of this world."[42]

Islam gives the same weight to the written word and to the spoken utterance. Islam's severe insistence on holding humans fully accountable for every word they utter can be found in the Qur'anic reference to commitments recorded by "noble recorders."[43] This affirmation is itself a form of protection, and a form of honoring the human. The words spoken by reliable persons, trusted notaries, are taken as a record, above and against all others. The concern to record and document the words of the human reflects the deep attention to, and for, his fate. It recognizes his honored status: "Each word he utters shall be noted down by a vigilant guardian."[44] "Surely there are guardians watching over you, noble recorders who know of all your actions."[45]

3.4.5 Happiness and Behavior

Islam's teachings have accorded human work[46] specific attention and a place of high respect. When it comes to true personal happiness or

[39] Qur'an 4:21. [40] Imam Ali's hadith; related, e.g., in Majlisī, *Biḥār al-anwār*, 65:311.
[41] Kulaynī, *al-Kāfī*, 5:169. [42] Qur'an 4:94.
[43] "Surely there are guardians watching over you, noble recorders who know of all your actions" (Qur'an 82:10–12). In a modern context, this would refer to notaries, but more generally to trusted and reliable people writing down oral exchanges.
[44] Qur'an 50:18. [45] Qur'an 82:10–12.
[46] *'Amal* is "work" in a general sense encompassing effort, behavior, commitment, actions.

misery, Islam rejects external factors, and sees work as the only consideration – it is man's path to either joy or misery.

> By the soul and Him that molded it and inspired it with knowledge of sin and piety; blessed shall be the man who has kept it pure, and ruined he that has corrupted it![47]

> Each soul is the hostage of its own deeds.[48]

The Qur'an affirms as erroneous the idea held by some peoples that they alone were the children of God, loved by Him and loving Him. This idea is a central underlying cause for division and fragmentation between societies. For it contradicts true unity, the true unity of God and His creation, and it rules out the recognition and appreciation of human actions:

> If you claim that of all men you alone are God's friends, then you should wish for death, if what you say be true. But because of what their hands have done, they will never wish for death. God knows the wrongdoers.[49]

The Prophet Muhammad advanced this principle to its utmost when he addressed his daughter Fatima: "O Fatima, work on your soul, for there is nothing more valuable that God has provided you than your own self."[50]

In the domain of human societies and their formation, their presentation and image, their organization, levels and problems, Islam places all responsibility at the doorstep of the human being alone, of humankind alone. It is humans who create societies, and it is through their labor that plans are drawn up and responsibilities and tasks allocated – just as it is humans who cause problems and create difficulties.

> God does not change a people's lot unless they change what is in their hearts.[51]

> Corruption has become rife on land and sea in consequence of man's misdeeds. [He has ordained it] so that they may taste the fruit of their own works and mend their ways.[52]

[47] Qur'an 91:7–10. [48] Qur'an 74:38. [49] Qur'an 62:6–7.
[50] al-Nīsābūrī (d. 1014), *al-Jāmiʿ al-ṣaḥīḥ* (Beirut: Dār al-Fikr, 2009), 1:133.
[51] Qur'an 13:11. [52] Qur'an 30:41.

And in the hadith: "The way you behave is the way you will be ruled upon."[53]

The work of human beings is the only force capable of formulating history and advancing it. No other force can take history forward, and there is no role for any conceivable factor external to the effort of human beings in shaping society and in establishing its main characteristics. These are all the work of the human. Based on his knowledge, his ignorance or his negligence, the work of the human takes its course. He chooses a path, he sets a direction, and the result is what he chooses for society.

History's development, commonly called "historical determinism,"[54] is in fact nothing other than the interaction between the human and the universe: the human being, in accordance with his needs and desires, seeks to understand the world in which he lives. He then reads a line, and learns, and he allows this reading to influence his life, heighten his awareness, raise his way of living, and so he transforms the features of his environment. And then, he reads another line . . .

This is why the only hero on history's stage is the individual, for she formulates, develops and propels history, even as she herself moves forward in continual interaction with the universe. The individual's work, and nothing but her work, is the source of all development. Can one find a greater honor or more exalted status than this?

In economics, Islam, for the first time in history, came to consider human labor as an element of overarching importance. Islam declares it to be unlawful, even sinful, to divest the worker of the fruits of his labor. It seeks to insure and protect the person usurped by the usurper, as much as it does for the victim of theft, or the worker deprived of his wage, and considers the one who so deprives him of his rights to be unworthy of the fragrance of paradise.[55]

If in addition we observe in Islamic law the corpus of Islam's teachings on the practical application of jurisprudence, we find evidence that work is the first of the three factors of production – labor, machines, capital.

[53] al-Muttaqī al-Hindī (d. 1567), *Kanz al-ʿummāl fī sunan al-aqwāl wa-l-afʿāl*, ed. Bakrī Hayyānī and Ṣafwat al-Saqwa (Beirut: Muʾassasat al-Risāla, 1989), 6:189.

[54] *Jabr al-tarikh*. Sadr is here emphasizing the importance of free will against the arguments of determinists, whether religious (like Calvinists) or not (like many Marxists).

[55] This "socialist" reading of labor and its fruits as belonging exclusively to the laborer is common to the generation of Sadr. See Chapters 7–8.

Such findings might appear strange, but this is the reality, as I will briefly explain:

1. Islam categorically prohibits riba, which is guaranteed profit on capital, shielding it from any loss.[56]
2. If capital is used by a person other than its owner in a contract known in Islamic law as *mudaraba*,[57] profits are divided on an agreed upon basis between the worker and the owner of the capital. The laborer in a partnership is shielded from loss, with any losses borne by the owner of the capital.
3. Islam does not permit any share of profit to be allocated to the owners of any tools. This is clear in the jurists' discussion of agriculture and irrigation partnerships. Only a fixed fee for hiring tools or equipment is allowed.[58]
4. Compensation for work can be done either by paying the laborer a wage, or by including the laborer in a mudaraba partnership.

From such principles we can conclude that labor in Islamic jurisprudence has three distinctive prerogatives: a fixed wage; a share in profits; and protection from loss.[59]

As for capital and tools, each is distinguished by a single prerogative. Capital shares in profits without any guarantee or any fixed return. The owners of tools receive a fixed fee without any share in profits.

[56] Riba is generally translated as "interest" or "usury." While the prohibition of riba is uncontested within the Islamic tradition, the application of the concept has been vigorously debated, especially with the rise of modern "Islamic banking," including within courts. For the issues raised by the illustrative 1991 decision of the Pakistan Federal Sharia Court, see Mallat, *Introduction to Middle Eastern Law*, 338–45.

[57] Mudaraba, which translates as partnership for profit and loss (similar to the *commenda* in medieval European law), is a commercial venture in which investor and trader share the profits in the venture, but only the investor normally bears the burden of loss. See the extensive treatment of the contract in Muḥammad Bāqer al-Ṣadr, *al-Bank al-lā ribawī fī al-Islām* [The interest-free bank in Islam] (Beirut: Dār al-Taʿāruf, 1983), first published in Kuwait in 1969.

[58] *Muzaraʿa* is a contract in classical law, still practiced in some countries, joining owner and tiller of land in a partnership in which they share the profits. *Musaqat* involves a similar arrangement with irrigated land. For an adaptation of the two contracts from a modern economic perspective, Sadr could rely on Muḥammad Bāqer al-Ṣadr, *Iqtiṣādunā* [Our economic system] (Beirut: Dār al-Taʿāruf, 1984), first published in Najaf in two volumes in 1959 and 1961.

[59] The laborer has either a fixed wage, or a share in profits, but is always protected from loss.

This brief presentation may be sufficient to convey Islam's perspective on human labor, and the degree of dignity assigned from its beginnings to the human being, long before any modern developments.

3.5 Islam and Work

Islam views work and its effects as a form of maintaining belief, as well as being a result of belief. This confirms Islam's immense concern for human labor: "Evil was the end of those who did evil, because they had disbelieved God's revelations and derided them."[60]

Responsibility for actions, be it large or small, serves to reaffirm the person's elevated place, a place afforded him by his work, and a place that establishes or provides for the impact of his good works, even the smallest of these, in the world – notwithstanding whether the person is aware of these impacts:

> Whoever does an atom's weight of good shall see it, and whoever does an atom's weight of evil shall see it also.[61]

> You shall engage in no affair, you shall recite no verse from the Qur'an, you shall commit no act, but We will witness it. Not an atom's weight in earth or heaven escapes your Lord, nor is there any object smaller or greater, but is recorded in a glorious book.[62]

This responsibility is a strong guarantee of the value of human work; it serves to prevent humans' labor being wasted, being diverted from a positive, productive and useful course.

Maintenance of the sanctity of work is brought to mind by expressions relating to virtues and vices, permitted and forbidden things – halal and haram. An emphasis on work is intended to honor humankind and to free it from stain, desecration and degeneracy. We find in Qur'anic verses as well as in the sacred life of the Prophet an expression of forbidden things that illuminates this interpretation:

> Believers, wine and games of chance, idols and divining arrows are abominations devised by Satan. Avoid them, so that you may prosper.[63]

It is appropriate here for us to insist that there is a purpose in relying on the principle in religion of following what is permitted and rejecting

[60] Qur'an 30:10. [61] Qur'an 99:7–8. [62] Qur'an 10:61. [63] Qur'an 5:90.

what is forbidden. This is to protect the human being from dissolution and loss in the material world around him, let alone in the respect for basic interests in his obligations, in what is lawful for him, away from the prohibitions that undermine him.

If a human being simply attempts to fulfill the needs of his body, or if he allows himself to be swept away by his emotions, without restraint or hesitation, he will remain shaped by the world around him, rather than him influencing that world. Such a human being cannot be a leader of the universe or a deputy of God on earth. He ends up instead dissolved, lost, in it.

Attention to the permitted and the prohibited protects human autonomy, elevates the human being above dissolution and strengthens him against the risk of loss. It is not enough for a need to be fulfilled. It should be a lawful, permitted need.

Respecting the boundaries between good and bad does not mean ignoring a human being's reality or his actual needs. It does not see in combating the soul and weakening the body anything other than a strength for the spiritual world, for there is no contradiction between body and soul. These are principles, along with others, that Sufi groups adhere to.

I should add here Islam's appreciation of cleanliness and its role as part of the faith. Hundreds of hadiths on the need to remain clean derive from Islamic teachings. Hygiene and cleanliness are pillars of human dignity.

3.6 Opinion and Beliefs

a. Opinion and beliefs are both the fruit of human thinking. They are the product of this most noble aspect of human existence. Islam honors them with pride of place and seeks to uphold and preserve a person's freedom in respect to them. It leaves true comprehension of doctrine to thought and to the rational effort of interpretation – leaving it to the person herself, and even going further: Islam holds that any doctrine not founded upon carefully thought-through principles is not worthy of consideration. There is no excuse [for not holding such a well-founded doctrine] unless a person has failed to establish its validity after having exhausted the effort of his thinking and intellect. "There shall be no compulsion in religion."[64]

[64] Qur'an 2:256.

b. Purity of intention is considered the core and the soul of belief: "To each person according to her intention."[65] And yet a person is not to be punished on the basis of her intentions and thoughts alone, as she needs to follow up with deeds and words. In the hadith, "God relieved His people of the burden of nine things ... among them the obsession to think about creation and jealousy of God for what humans have not themselves conceived."[66]
c. Among the most beautiful aspects of Islam in the way it highlights and preserves the honor of humankind and its diverse pursuits is concern for effort, even when wasted. The capacities a person may exert for achieving good are many and so varied! She struggles, spends her wealth, time, services, energies, depletes her life force, yet she does not achieve her desired results because of accidents or obstacles that block her plans, which may fall by the wayside, forgotten by history, for reasons for which she cannot be held responsible. How much energy and talent are expended yet rendered fruitless due to mistakes and errors that impede successful and productive outcomes? These wasted efforts – and other sensitive and painful considerations that may obstruct implementation and realization of the doctrine's sacred mission without ever coming to light – are all valued in Islam, and therefore in Islam's purview they are preserved rather than wasted or disowned: "He that leaves his dwelling to fight for God and His Apostle and is then overtaken by death shall be recompensed by God. Surely God is forgiving and merciful."[67]

Or, as in a well-known rule in Islamic law, "she who makes an effort and succeeds receives a double reward, and she who fails still receives her [single] reward."[68]

Islam pursues the effort to honor and dignify human beings in the face of decadence, delinquency and degeneracy. It proposes the creation of a humane, humanistic society that is suited to the reality lived by human beings and takes into account all aspects of their existence in an

[65] Ṭūsī, *Amālī* (Qom: Mu'assasat al-Baṭhā', 1993), 618; Bukhārī, *al-Ṣaḥīḥ*, 6:2.
[66] Kulaynī, *al-Kāfī*, 2:463; Ibn Mājah, *Sunan*, ed. Muḥammad Fu'ād 'Abd al-Bāqī (Beirut: Dār Iḥyā' al-Kutub al-'Arabiyya, 1952), 6:659.
[67] Qur'an 4:100.
[68] This rule (*qa'ida*) appears often in connection with the work of scholars, especially jurists, and originates in a hadith common to Sunnis and Shi'is; see the original formulation, e.g., at https://dorar.net/hadith/sharh/64014.

environment enabling the growth and development of individuals' talents and capacities. The human being is the reason why society is created. That is why it is necessary to look at the reality of the human being and to plan accordingly.

Society should not be "individualistic."[69] Such a society denies an essential aspect of human existence, namely, the social side of life. In an individualistic society, traits spring from the negative and latent tendencies of egoism, from what the Qur'an calls a passionate soul that is "prone to evil."[70] Egoism grows in individuals when there is no protection or balance, no judicious arrangement of priorities – bringing a clash between the egoisms of conflicting individuals, meaning the powerful dominate and the weak are oppressed. Eventually the weak become so exploited they are merely tools for the strong, and society loses an important part of its own capacity. The powerful themselves become tools or instruments advancing their own egoism.

Laws enacted in this situation reflect the status quo and not what must be done to protect and preserve the individual's humanity and her soul. Society that takes shape under such circumstances is cast in the mold of unequal struggle, as the weak are controlled and dominated by the powerful, with self-interest trumping all.

Nor should human society be "socialist,"[71] for a society structured along such lines ignores two key aspects of human existence: freedom, and independence of action. Instead, the individual is seen only as part of the group in the same way he is just a small part of nature. Here the interests of the group take priority and plans are made based solely upon them. Consequently, the shape society takes in its organization reflects spontaneously upon individuals, who may lose their original sense of selfhood and character.

Human beings' diverse natural gifts cannot grow in such a situation, as society is itself weakened and loses the strengths and capacities of its individual members. Given the interaction between society and the individual, each affects the other, leading to tensions that disrupt social development and producing continuous turbulence, with harmful consequences in people's lives.

[69] Musa Sadr here uses the French word *individualiste*. [70] See Qur'an 12:53.
[71] Musa Sadr uses the French *socialiste*.

3.7 The Individual and the Formation of Society

The society that Islam proposes and favors is one that accords recognition to the individual in all her personal and social aspects.

To clarify this, we draw attention to the innate presence[72] of the good within the human, along with, at the same time, the appeal of evil – and the ensuing psychological struggle that results from human freedom and independence. We then stress that positive and good human actions are those that do not oppose or clash with the rights of others and are harmonious with those of society. This is given expression by Islam when it offers instruction for the mandate of the heart and the sound soul. Acts or works that clash with the rights of others are desires of the passionate "soul that is prone to evil"[73] – as the religious precept puts it.

No doubt categorizing actions into these two types entails outlining individuals' rights, which are part of the proposed social order and which derive from universal principles that should be upheld to maintain the correct relationships between individuals. From this short explanation, we conceive of the individual's freedom as proceeding along a parallel track to the freedom of other individuals, and of the interests of individuals as being in harmony with society's interests.

On the other hand, we can conserve and maintain all the positive energies of the individual without these leading to overstepping boundaries and violating the rights of others, or to a conflict between individuals or between classes, scrambling to diminish others' sacred rights.

> Vie with each other to earn the forgiveness of your Lord.[74]
>
> Vie with each other in good works.[75]

When the diverse efforts of individuals meet each other's efforts positively, greater cooperation, mutual support and solidarity – in all their different dimensions – are achieved.

Among Islamic teachings based on honoring humankind is the recognition of the comprehensiveness of human needs. Islam recognizes them all and considers that God blessed them as gifts and issued precepts to regulate desires arising from these needs. God recognizes that the effort to fulfill these needs in legitimate ways is a form of worship. Commerce, agriculture, construction and toiling to generate permissible life

[72] Fitra (see nn. 26, 28). [73] Another reference to Qur'an 12:53 (see n. 70).
[74] Qur'an 3:133. [75] Qur'an 5:48.

sustenance all constitute a virtuous struggle or jihad. Mastery in work is likewise a form of worship, as is marriage – and whoever failed to acknowledge this the Prophet of Islam considered not one of his own. In his advice to Abu Dharr al-Ghifari, the Prophet established the principle that a Muslim can be in a state of permanent worship, even when he eats or sleeps.[76] Islam is not content to let human needs be neglected or ignored. The hadith considers those who spend all their time in prayer and neglect efforts to earn a living shall remain without an answer from God to their demands, for He prefers those who strive [and work on] themselves.[77]

3.8 Islam and Society

We find in these precepts extensive efforts to maintain a felicitous balance and coordination of all aspects of human existence, so that no single aspect overwhelms or violates others.

The most prominent among these efforts and teachings is what Islam teaches about women, and in particular the need to prevent a woman's gender from dominating all other dimensions of her existence. For this reason, she is prohibited from acting just to titillate or seduce, so that her humanity is not dissolved in her feminine charms. She should neither be viewed, nor should she view herself, through this lens alone – for doing so would deprive her of fundamental aspects of her existence and diminish her human potential.

One of the brightest pearls in the necklace of Islam's teachings is the appeal to honor others. Every Muslim must respect others in their person, in their property and in their reputation and dignity. It is forbidden in Islam to violate [the rights of] others by word or deed.

Islam begins the attempt to care for and maintain the individual even before his birth, for it enjoins a man seeking marriage to choose a fitting mother for his progeny, as in the hadith "Choose carefully (the mother) for your child."[78] Islam sustains this concern throughout pregnancy, labor and birth, early childhood, and ascending phases of education.

[76] Abu Dharr al-Ghifari, a close companion of the Prophet, is often cited in early Shiʿi literature. Abu Dharr was one of the first of five people to recognize the prophecy of Muhammad. He is associated with the argument that Muslims should not accumulate wealth beyond personal needs.

[77] See, e.g., Kulaynī, *al-Kāfī*, 2:511.

[78] Ibid., 5:332; Nīsābūrī, *al-Jāmiʿ al-ṣaḥīḥ*, 2:168.

We can discover hundreds of principles and guidelines in these areas, all of them founded on the core principle of honoring humankind.

Some consider that Islam in the Qur'an or in the hadith attempts sometimes to diminish the value of the human being, as in verses that assert that humankind originated from dust, or clay, or dirty water, or a drop of sperm: "He is created from an ejaculated fluid that issues from between the loins and the ribs."[79] And we read in the hadith comments about human beings as humble things who all end in death, as well as other such expressions of denigration.[80]

In fact, Islam seeks to protect the individual from the peril of deviation and self-delusion – particularly in moments of victory. "Indeed, man transgresses in thinking himself his own master."[81] Obsessed with wealth, their children, or glory, human beings fall into potentially devastating psychological peril.

To treat this pathology, Islam provides guidance in a variety of expressions and phrases. This is to make it clear that to honor the human in humankind is to make him balanced and sound, to help him strive for the excellence wished upon him, even though he was created by the will of God from the same elements as all other creatures. Dignity is a trust whose source is God, and God grants it to a person without permitting her to use this trust to deceive others. Everything that the human may possess is a trust from God. Human beings must fulfill the delivery of this trust in sincerity and with dedication.

> Give in alms that which He has made your inheritance.[82]

79 Qur'an 86:6–7. English translations vary due to different interpretations of the Arabic, with some holding that *al-sulb* ("backbone," "loins") refers to the man, and *al-tara'ib* ("ribs") to the place where a necklace sits on a woman's chest.

80 Ibn Abī al-Ḥadīd, *Sharḥ Nahj al-balāgha* (Cairo: Ḥalabī, 1960), 452; Ibn Shayba, *al-Kitāb al-muṣannaf fī al-aḥādīth wa-l-āthār* (Riyadh: al-Rushd, 1988), hadith no. 34362.

81 Qur'an 96:6–7. 82 Qur'an 57:7.

4

Islam

Authenticity, Spirituality, Development

Within this series of lectures I have been assigned the broad topic of Islam as one source contributing to culture in Lebanon.[1] Doing real justice to the diversity, expansiveness and inclusiveness of Lebanon's culture would itself add cultural and historical breadth to the many dimensions of Islam as a subject.

Investigating the impact of Islam on Lebanon's culture takes us back to the earliest days of its spread in this region: from the first Islamic governments and dynasties established in Damascus and elsewhere, to the seventh-century passage through Mount Lebanon of the respected companion of the Prophet, Abu Dharr al-Ghifari,[2] and onward to our present day through the interaction of the population in all of these regions with Islam's message and mission.

Lebanon's religious scholars contributed to the expansion of the culture and civilization of Islam, conveying it to the entire world by means of their huge production of books and treatises in south

[1] Lecture delivered at the American University of Beirut, July 23, 1966. "Islam: Authenticity, Spirituality, Development" was one of twenty-three lectures in a series, given by various people, organized by Salwa Nassar, head of the physics department at the American University of Beirut. Nassar, who died aged fifty-four in 1967, was the first Lebanese woman to achieve a PhD in physics and wrote on creativity in higher education as well as more technical scientific matters; see her obituary "Salwa Nassar, College Head, Dies after Long Illness," *Physics Today*, September 1, 1967, https://physicstoday.scitation.org/doi/10.1063/1.3034465. Among other speakers were Yusuf Yazbek, leading Lebanese communist, Father George Khodr, Orthodox priest and subsequently bishop, Michel Asmar, founder of the Lebanese Cénacle (see n. 5), and Kamal Jumblatt, the leader of the Progressive Socialist Party (assassinated in 1977).

[2] On Abu Dharr al-Ghifari, an early companion of the Prophet, see Chapter 3, n. 76.

Lebanon's Jabal Amil, Baalbek, Beirut and Tripoli. I must also note the interaction of the Arabic language, generally, with Islamic texts and teachings – especially the Qur'an. You can see that all this exceeds what can be covered in one lecture. The challenge is all the more daunting given the reputation of this world-renowned institution of higher education, and the knowledge and achievements of those present.

I found it perplexing to choose one aspect of the topic to address today, which led to some delay in presenting my lecture. I opted eventually to address the overall title of the lecture series in a flexible and broad fashion, so as to focus on Islam itself, rather than to attempt to cover all its diverse and varied influences on our Lebanese culture.

While grappling with all these dilemmas [on how to approach the lecture], the encounter of Western and Eastern ideas and opinions in Lebanon helped motivate me. For here in Lebanon there are ideas and views on everything, including Islam, and some of these, through their lack of precision, blur essential aspects of Islam. Such exchanges have received great attention from eminent scholars such as Massé, Lammens, Dermenghem and Massignon.[3]

Please accept my apology, especially as I am straying from my area of expertise [in religious studies]. I hope that my efforts and modest presentation will meet the challenge.

4.1 Research Methods in Religion

I mentioned that the rich encounters of perspectives and ideas, as well as these scholars' studies, have served to blur essential precepts of Islam, but in no way do I wish to belittle these extraordinary scholars, who

[3] Henri Massé (1886–1969) was Professor of Persian at the École Nationale des Langues Orientales Vivantes, Paris, from 1927 to 1958. He is the author of a reference book on Islam, *L'Islam*, 5th ed. (Paris: Armand Colin, 1948). Henri Lammens (1862–1937) was born in Ghent and settled in Lebanon, where he taught at the Saint Joseph University of Beirut. A Jesuit, he was interested in Islamic philosophy and history, traveled widely in the Levant, and thought positively of the French role while also sympathetic to the notion of a "Greater Syria." He was a prolific writer on early Islam, and the author of *La Syrie, précis historique*, 2 vols. (Beirut: Imprimerie Catholique, 1921). Emile Dermenghem (1892–1971) was a French scholar and archivist, author of several books on the Prophet, including *La vie de Mahomet* (Paris: Plon, 1920 [new ed. Alger: Charlot, 1950]) and *Mahomet et la tradition islamique* (Paris: Le Seuil, 1955). Louis Massignon (1883–1962) was a French Catholic who paved the way for the positive approach to Islam expressed at the Second Vatican Council (1962–65). His most famous book is on the Sufi scholar executed for his views, al-Hallaj (d. 922), *La passion de Hallâj*, 4 vols. (Paris: Gallimard, 1975).

devoted their lives to the study of the East and of Islam, or to detract from the value of their extensive and profound efforts – or from their service to world civilization. Rather I wish to affirm that religious principles, spiritual truths and systems of belief cannot be expressed purely and simply in simple phrases and terms, nor can they be studied merely by perusing a few books and articles on the subject. Each science, each tradition, has its specific terminology, the true significance of which cannot be mastered without vast study of the particular field of knowledge, and, indeed, without thorough practice in the area. This is certainly the case with the general and specific truths expressed by jurists in their terminology.

When it comes to religious concepts and thought, we have to remember that they draw on a chain of spiritual concepts, moral life and historic events transmitted through stories and biographies across generations, and that they are therefore linked with a history of beliefs and religious ethics, including what has been passed down by the companions of the founders or "heroes" of these ideas.

This special process, which resembles to a large degree the role of personalities and figures in art and literature, makes it challenging to study religious principles and ideas in any depth, and to be able to offer any judgment. The scholar must review the whole picture in every diverse aspect, within the historical context, while at the same time keeping in mind current events and texts to talk with the living adherents and conceptualizers of these principles and clarify points of similarity and ambiguity – making possible far deeper exploration of the ideas.

I believe that a review of the chapters on terms and definitions used in the works of Islamic jurisprudence[4] will confirm what I have said. And I would agree that the most effective approach to studying such principles and ideas is the approach adopted in this lecture series, and by the Lebanon Cénacle in their efforts to assign the task to specialists and request the utmost objectivity.[5]

[4] *Usul al-fiqh* (literally, "the roots of jurisprudence") is the Islamic theory or philosophy of law. Depending on context, we have translated both *usul* and *fiqh* (the corpus of Islamic jurists' writings on law) as jurisprudence.

[5] The Cénacle (1946–84) was a discussion forum established by Michel Asmar (1914–84), with participants from different sects and with varying political allegiances or views, that explored notions of "Lebanon" and Lebanese identity. See Nadim Shehadi, *The Idea of Lebanon: Economy and State in the Cénacle Libanais 1946–54* (Oxford: Oxford Centre for Lebanese Studies, 1987). A Cénacle collection was edited by Ghassan Tueni (1926–2012),

The points I attempt to cover in this lecture are these:

1. the authenticity, originality and essential nature of Islam;
2. spirituality in Islam, its relative strength and weakness; and
3. Islam's concern for social welfare, above and beyond [abstract] belief and morality, and its focus on meeting the challenges of development.

4.2 Authenticity

With regard to the authenticity of Islam, I wish to refer to the works of Orientalists and other more recent scholars who affirm that Islam drew upon the beliefs of the other faiths and expressions of divinity that were widespread before Islam's emergence and remained so when the Prophet Muhammad traveled with trade caravans around the Arab world.[6] Islam also was influenced by pagan beliefs and customs prevalent in the Arabian Peninsula as well as in Persia and Byzantium, both of which had commercial and political links with the Arabs of Mecca. Sumerian and Sabaean customs and traditions also had an impact on Islamic rituals of worship and customs.[7] Avoiding an unnecessarily long exposition, I prefer to limit my remarks here. There is no need to cite specific texts by these scholars.

4.2.1 Islam's View of Other Religions

Before assessing the validity of these scholars' claims, we should consider Islam's stated position on the divinely revealed religions. The Qur'an

also a speaker at the forum and publisher of the leading Lebanese Arabic daily *al-Nahar*, in a book published by Dar al-Nahar, which includes a selection of lectures in French and in Arabic, *Les années "Cénacle"* (Beirut: Dār al-Nahār, 1997). Musa al-Sadr's contribution to the Cénacle in 1964, "al-Islām wa-thaqāfāt al-qarn al-ʿishrīn" [Islam and twentieth-century culture], is at 463–72.

6 Muhammad spent much of his childhood tending goats for his uncle Abu Lahab. "But his uncle took him sometimes on his travels and on one occasion when Muhammad was nine, or according to others twelve, they went with a merchant caravan as far as Syria." Lings, *Muhammad*, 29. The later role of trade routes in the spread of Islam is examined by Richard Bulliet, *Islam: The View from the Edge* (New York: Columbia University Press, 1994).

7 Sumer, in what was later called southern Mesopotamia and is now Iraq, was one of the first human civilizations, lasting from the sixth to the second millennium BC. The Sabaeans, people of the Kingdom of Saba (ca. 1200 BC–AD 275) in southern Arabia, are mentioned in both the Bible and the Qur'an.

announces that Muhammad's message is the final link in the chain of divinely inspired religions, that Muhammad is the "seal of the prophets,"[8] that he believes in them and their prophecies and that he attests to their being prophets of the Lord.

> Say: "I am no prodigy among the apostles."[9]
>
> The Apostle believes in what has been revealed to him by his Lord, and so do the faithful. They all believe in God and His angels, His scriptures and His apostles: We discriminate against none of His apostles.[10]

The Qur'an also affirms that God's religion is one and the Qur'an calls it *Islam*, asserting that all prophets have followed a God-given approach and religious precepts: "He has ordained for you the faith which He enjoined on Noah, and which We have revealed to you; which We enjoined on Abraham, Moses and Jesus saying: 'Observe the Faith and do not divide yourself into factions.'"[11]

The Qur'an trusts and relies in many verses on the transmission of beliefs, judgments and parables from earlier divine revelations. Logically, then, there is nothing suprising or objectionable in there being a similarity between the beliefs, prescriptions, judgments and morals of Islam and those of other divinely revealed faiths.

4.2.2 The Distinctive Feature of Islam

Notwithstanding these remarks, we say that Islam has a distinctive character throughout its teachings and practices, taking on its own identity and essence, thereby distinguishing itself from other religions and systems of belief.

The scholar of various Islamic fields can discover this character with great clarity in all Islam's teachings and practices, namely, what is given expression as *tawhid* or "unity," "union," "oneness." Islam is known as the "religion of tawhid." The word *islam* in the Qur'anic sense is surrender to God,[12] the Lord of the worlds, "when every soul in the

[8] *Khatim al-anbiya'* is usually translated as "seal of the prophets." The tradition means the last of all prophets sent by God.

[9] Qur'an 46:9. [10] Qur'an 2:285. [11] Qur'an 42:13.

[12] Arabic has no capital letters. We use here *islam* (lowercase in English), which has a common root (the Arabic letters *sin-lam-mim*) with *salam* (peace), in contradistinction

heavens and the earth has submitted to Him, willingly or by compulsion. To Him shall they return."[13]

Islam, then, is to join and merge with the trajectory of everything that is in the heavens and on earth, to attain unity with that path and all that it encompasses, a unity of principle, of destination, and a source of eternal and everlasting sustenance.

In addition, Islam, according to Qur'anic interpretation,[14] is the willful prostration of man in glorification of God, and his/her prayer in the quest of the unitary procession of created beings that is, in all its parts together, prostrating in unison, glorifying and praying to the one God, and facing the sole mihrab[15] of the universe.

> Do you not see that those in the heavens and the earth, the sun and moon and the stars, the mountains and the trees, the beasts and countless men – all do homage to God?[16]
>
> All that is in the heavens and the earth gives glory to God. His is the sovereignty, and His all praise. He has power over all things.[17]
>
> The thunder sounds His praises.[18]
>
> The seven heavens, the earth and all who dwell in them give glory to Him. All creatures celebrate His praises. Yet you cannot understand their praises.[19]
>
> Do you not see how God is praised by those in the heavens and those on earth? The very birds praise Him as they wing their way. He notes the prayers and praises of all His creatures; God has knowledge of all their actions.[20]

Society is therefore, in the Islamic conception, like a single body, as in the hadith "if one part is suffering all the other parts become afflicted,

with *Islam* (uppercase, the "new" religion). While for a Muslim, the difference may not exist, or may be a fine one, a Christian or a theist may accept islam as "surrender" to God without embracing Islam. Colin Turner, *Islam without Allah? The Rise of Religious Externalism in Safavid Iran* (London: Curzon, 2000), explores this issue when examining the early Safavid period in Iran.

13 Qur'an 3:83.

14 *Tafsir* is often rendered as "exegesis," referring to informed interpretation of the Qur'an as an Islamic genre.

15 The prayer niche in the mosque (mihrab), facing the direction of the Kaaba, is used here metaphorically.

16 Qur'an 22:18. 17 Qur'an 64:1. 18 Qur'an 13:13. 19 Qur'an 17:44.

20 Qur'an 24:41.

feverish and watchful."[21] Similarly, Islam views man as a single and complete being, with body and soul comprehensively integrated.

In the domain of faith and creed, God is "the first and the last, the visible and the unseen";[22] the starting and ending point, "We belong to God, and to Him we shall return."[23]

The end destination, the goal, is the one God – in observing Islam's way (*sayr*), in devotion (*ʿibada*) and struggle (jihad): "They were enjoined only to serve God and to worship none but Him";[24] "God's religion shall reign supreme."[25]

In Islam we find a clear attempt to establish social, financial, civic and moral systems on a shared foundation that brings individuals together, such that each one is part of the whole rather than an isolated unit – to use an expression from the discipline of logic.

The Qur'an gives guidelines on matters of resources, on honoring commitments, on the understanding that resources are "shared" and added to the whole, consecrating this teaching and affirming this rule [of unity]. Islamic art reflects this distinctive feature through the curvature or geometry of the arabesque, a single variegated and multifaceted line.[26] In sum, the distinctive feature of Islam is unity in belief, jurisprudence, art and exegesis.

We can now return to look in detail at some of the statements of Professor Henri Massé, the French Orientalist.[27] This will allow us to see with greater clarity the essential authenticity of Islam.

4.2.3 God

God is the Sole, the Unique, the One, Supremely Unitary. "Nothing can be compared with Him."[28] "His are the most gracious names."[29] He sets ideals and the attributes of perfection, and rises above all defects,

[21] A well-known hadith in both the Sunni and Shiʿi traditions, related by Bukhari (d. 870) and other famous hadith tradents; see, e.g., https://dorar.net/hadith/sharh/4340.

[22] Qur'an 57:3. [23] Qur'an 2:156. [24] Qur'an 98:5. [25] Qur'an 8:39.

[26] "Arabesque" is a French term derived from Italian, where it was first used in the sixteenth century, meaning literally "in Arab style." Describing a tradition in Islamic art and architecture, Blair and Bloom write: "The arabesque has infinite correspondence, meaning that the design can be extended infinitely in any direction. The structure of the arabesque gives sufficient information so that the viewer can extend the design in his or her imagination." Sheila Blair and Jonathan Bloom, "Art and Architecture: Themes and Variations," in Esposito, *The Oxford History of Islam*, 215–67.

[27] On Massé, see n. 3. [28] Qur'an 42:11. [29] Qur'an 20:8.

shortfalls or needs, for He is the Eternal. "He begot none, nor was He begotten."[30] He is devoid of any specific affiliation or association with any thing, person or phenomenon.

The world in its entirety, and humanity with all its individuals, in all its events – they are all equal before Him, the Creator, who is eternally active in creating: there can be no existence or sustenance for created things and for creation as a whole without His will and without His action. He is the knower of the unseen and the seen, for whom not even the smallest weight of an atom can hope to remain unobserved.

The scholar [Massé] sees that this belief in God as absolute perfection, which is made clear in the interpretation of "God" in Islamic texts, has implications for how we nurture and bring up human beings – making "God" far from an abstract idea, or just an image in the heart or in religious rituals.

Thinking of God as profoundly abstract, free from ambiguity, beyond a specific connection to any matter, removes individualistic sanctity from all things, and so it detaches the human being from any intellectual, rational, emotional, practical or social constraint. This renders the human being, the "servant of God,"[31] a free agent who takes on the affairs of life without impediment or restraint. God's wholeness thereby reflects on the entire universe and on human beings in particular, who are seen in their best image, perspective and order.

The notion of the "ever-present God,"[32] as the Qur'anic expression has it, provides the link between pure divine abstraction and God's being "closer to him [man] than his jugular vein,"[33] and with the earth's being "on the Day of Resurrection . . . in His grasp" and the heavens folded "in His right hand";[34] for while eyes cannot see Him, He can see the eyes.[35]

Yes, God is far from perceivable by minds and intellects: "Every time you delude yourselves into thinking you have distinguished Him in His

[30] Qur'an 112:3.

[31] *'Abd* is usually translated as "servant" or "slave" and is not in this religious sense peculiar to Muslims: Arab Christians used the phrase *'abd al-masih* ("servant of the Messiah") or *'abd yasu'* ("servant of Jesus").

[32] *Al-ihata bi-qayyumiyya*.

[33] "We created man. We know the promptings of his soul, and We are closer to him than his jugular vein" (Qur'an 50:16).

[34] "They underrate the might of God. But on the Day of Resurrection He will hold the entire earth in His grasp and fold up the heavens in His right hand" (Qur'an 39:67).

[35] "No mortal eyes can see Him, though He sees all eyes. He is benign and all-knowing" (Qur'an 6:103).

most subtle features, you have created nothing but your own delusion, and it will come back to haunt you."[36]

Nevertheless, "He is with you wherever you are,"[37] and "with everything beyond comparison, and beyond everything without exception."[38] Such understanding and awareness greatly reassure man, removing from him fear and loneliness, assigning him an agency and a responsibility that are inspiring – so that we can see the deep impact of thought on human life, meaning it is far from abstract.

> To God belongs the east and the west. Whichever way you turn, there is the face of God.[39]
>
> The believer's heart is the throne of the All-Merciful.[40]
>
> I am with the heartbroken.[41]
>
> Whoever visits an ill person has visited Me on My throne.[42]
>
> The generous man touches the hand of God at the instant of his charitable act.[43]

The scholar sees a new image of God in Islam, one that differs from the images in all other religions. If the Christian faith in God can be summarized with the expression "God is love," then the Islamic faith can be summarized as "God is truth," with all the meanings layered in the word "truth."

Later translators of the Qur'an have done well to retain the word "Allah" in their translations, rather than resort to the comparable expressions in other languages.[44]

36 Literally, "be pushed back to you." See Majlisī, *Biḥār al-anwār*, 66:293.

37 Qur'an 57:4.

38 This is a Shi'i hadith, with Sadr quoting *Nahj al-balagha*, in the poetical description by Imam Ali of God as standing literally beyond compare (*muqarana*) with all things created, yet standing with all things created without them being separate (*muzayala*) from Him. See Majlisī, *Biḥār al-anwār*, 4:247.

39 Qur'an 2:115.

40 Majlisī, *Biḥār al-anwār*, 55:39.

41 Ibid., 73:157. This hadith is not generally accepted by Sunnis.

42 Ibid., 78:225, with variations. This hadith appears in different expressions among Sunnis for the "visit of the ill" (*ziyarat al-marid*). See, e.g., https://bit.ly/4aoDsCd.

43 Sadr mentions that this is a *hadith qudsi* (sacred hadith), imparted to the Prophet directly from God (as opposed to a *hadith nabawi* [prophetic hadith], which is only the Prophet's), but we were not able to find the original text verbatim.

44 Musa Sadr is here emphasizing the oneness of God. Allah is used in Arabic by Christians and Muslims alike. Considering the audience of the present book, we still preferred the use of God over that of Allah.

4.2.4 The Angels

While they are as deeply rooted in time as the ancient religions, the conception of angels in Islam and in other religions differs from the one advanced by philosophers along the lines of Platonic ideals, or "lords of the species," or "lights of illumination."[45]

The subject of angels in Islam has been thoroughly discussed in books by scholars from the East and the West, and to assist their efforts they have drawn upon words of religious historians and theologians regarding various fabrications and myths, particularly those angels familiar to them such as Gabriel, Michael, Israfel and Azrael. Some of these great Orientalists were of the view that the idea of angels was a foreign import introduced to Islam, as shown by the angels' names having non-Arabic roots.

As we study the originality of Islamic thought about angels, let us recall Islam's affirmation of the other divinely revealed faiths – and all that they carried with them.

Muslim scholars of religious history, biographies, theology and jurisprudence are responsible for words they have uttered or written. But the sources of Islamic law are themselves not detailed regarding the belief in angels and concern themselves with the matter only in terms of education – which we shall examine presently. In the original sources of Islam there is no discussion of the essence of angels, their characteristics, or whether their nature is nonmaterial or material. Consequently, belief in these and other details is not considered part of [core] Islamic belief. Muslim believers need only believe that God's angels exist, just as they believe in God, His prophets and His books; and that God made the angels into messengers who praise and glorify their Lord, worshipping Him day and night.

45 "Lords of the species" for *arbab al-naw'*, "lights of illumination" for *al-anwar al-isfahbadiyya*. The philosophical references that Sadr refers to are hard to identify precisely, but they generally refer to the Platonic tradition in Islamic philosophy, which developed in particular with Suhrawardi (d. 1191) and the *ishraqi* tradition (school of illuminative philosophy), all the way to the great philosopher Sadr al-Din al-Shirazi (d. 1640), known as Mulla Sadra. See Henry Corbin, *Sohravardi et les Platoniciens de Perse*, vol. 2 of *En Islam iranien, aspects spirituels et philosophiques*, 4 vols. (Paris: Gallimard, 1972). The concept of *anwar isfahbadiyya* (*isfahbadi*, "light") appears in Mulla Sadra's magnum opus, *al-Ḥikma al-muta'āliya fī al-asfār al-'aqliyya al-arba'a* [Transcendent wisdom in the four journeys of the intellect], ed. Muḥammad Kāẓem Muṣṭafawī, 2nd ed. (Qom: Maktab al-I'lām al-Islāmī, 1999), 3:44, 147. The isfahbadi lights are those of the stars and planets. See Sadr's preface to Corbin's *Histoire de la philosophie islamique, des origines jusqu'à la mort d'Averroës* (Paris: Gallimard, 1964) in Chapter 5.

> Angels who never disobey God's command and who promptly do His bidding.[46]

Muslims believe in angels because they are mentioned and narrated in the Qur'an. As for the scientific dimension of the concept of angels, I know of no principle or religion, apart from Islam, that has examined it in the narratives of the prophets – with the exception of the first chapter of the Gospel according to Matthew, and in the Acts of the Apostles, both in a very brief manner.[47]

Several Qur'anic verses mention angels as "those who govern the affairs of this world."[48] These verses lend support to attributing to angels many of the major events that take place in this world and in the next.

> As for those who say: "Our Lord is God," and take the straight path to Him, the angels will descend to them, saying: "Have no fear and do not grieve. Rejoice in the paradise you have been promised. We are your guardians in this world and in the world to come."[49]

In sum, the idea is that the angels at God's command manage the seen and unseen forces of the universe, in obedience to God's will, which they implement in full and without delay. Anyone following the path of truth is accompanied by angels who assure him: "We are your guardians in this world and in the world to come." The follower of the path is not alone on his way to truth; the powers of the universe, deployed in the hands of the angels, assist and support him, and relieve him of fear.

The believer who follows the path of truth and justice does not feel isolation, loneliness or fear. He feels accompanied by the universe: the universe is by his side, shoring up his strength and powers. And he is therefore confident that he will be victorious: "know that God is his

[46] Qur'an 66:6.

[47] This is a reference to an angel appearing to Joseph (Matthew 1:18–25) foretelling the birth of Jesus, and to Herod's intentions of killing male babies (Matthew 1:18–20, 2:12–21). While more common in the Old Testament, angels appear rarely in the New Testament; for example, in telling shepherds where to find the newborn (Luke 2:8–14) and ministering to Jesus after his temptation by Satan (Matthew 4:11). There are several references to angels in the Acts of the Apostles, also known as the Book of Acts, which begins with angels appearing to the disciples at Christ's ascension to heaven to promise his return (1:10–11). In 5:17 of the Acts, an angel opens a prison door to allow the apostles to escape and continue their work. There is no explanation in the Bible of the nature of angels.

[48] Qur'an 79:5. [49] Qur'an 41:30–31.

protector, and Gabriel, and the righteous among the faithful. The angels too are his helpers."[50] And this feeling is essential to those carrying forward a divine revelation and mission, to those persons of principle who are attempting to establish and rebuild man and his society.

4.2.5 Satan

Discussion of Satan, the king of evils, is linked to that of the angels; as the Qur'an recounts, he was created with them, before Adam's creation. Like them he was obedient to God, glorifying Him and prostrating himself to Him. But Satan then rebelled in defiance when God commanded him to prostrate himself before Adam – in Satan's view a lesser, non-angelic being. He was then given until Judgment Day to wage a campaign to lead man astray, mustering all his evil powers to this end.

This interpretation of the created Satan is completely different from that given by the ancient Persians, for whom Ahriman, the creator of evils, is in eternal struggle with the god of good, Ahura Mazda.[51]

The interpretation of the created Satan differs completely from that of Ahriman as the source creator of all evil, in both principle and consequence: the psychological struggle that a believer undergoes with the two gods, one of good and one of evil, is monstrous, with the entire universe, his society and his very existence, fate, behavior and times all caught up in eternal conflict – he is a devastated human being, truly weak and vulnerable. Satan in Islam is unlike the concept of the angel of hell, or the leader or the god of the underworld found in some other interpretations.

The Islamic understanding of Satan is also quite distinct from the view that Satan is the great monotheist who refrained from prostrating himself to anyone but God. It is quite distinct from the view that Satan in this way became the head of the saints and of those who believe in the one God.

[50] Qur'an 66:4.

[51] Zoroastrianism, originating among Persians in antiquity, has changed as a religion over three millennia. It has limited texts, and there is uncertainty about even when its founder and eponym, Zoroaster, lived. There was an evolution from Stone Age pastoralists' fascination with water and fire to Zoroaster's belief, to quote a leading authority, that Ahura Mazda was the "the one uncreated God, existing eternally" and that there was "in the beginning, only one beneficent Being existing in the universe." Mary Boyce, *Zoroastrians: Their Religious Beliefs and Practices* (London: Routledge & Kegan Paul, 1979), 19–20. Musa Sadr's point is that there is no ambiguity in Islam: God created Satan as well as all else.

The authenticity of religious thought about Satan reaches its pinnacle in the Qur'an, from the perspective of education and religious upbringing. Satan's original name is Iblis, an angel very close to God who was banished from His closest circle because of his haughty and arrogant insubordination, which merited him the name "Satan."[52] His deviation from the path, his expulsion and his misery are all outcomes of his defiance of the commands of his Lord – they are not attributable to any wretched essential inner nature, nor do they result from a spontaneous or random act of expulsion and banishment from closeness to God.

On the other hand, Satan in essence represents the unified forces of evil that gather in opposition to the forces of good in the eternal struggle between truth and falsehood, whatever their nature or extent, or however they are described.

The most important educational consequences ensue from this idea of Satan and from his being given the task of seducing people and leading them astray, marshalling for that purpose his soldiers, among them the soul that is "prone to evil":[53] this all consolidates the principle that man must choose, that he should recognize that he is making a choice between good and evil and that he is not simply driven to play a role assigned him by the universe.

The Qur'an clarified this in a marvelous historical depiction of the process of creation, in verses 30–38 of "The Cow." These verses show God's will in providing the earth with a successor,[54] who is neither a guided tool nor a machine running automatically. He wished to create a being who acted freely, according to his own will.

Free and independent action and freedom of choice cannot be achieved by man absent his human inclination to either good or evil, or without there being in the world paths of good or evil he can choose. God created man with these characteristics, and then He taught him "the names of all things," so equipping him to learn the truths of existence and of the forces of the universe, and to master the task of learning about

[52] The original Hebrew term *satan*, a common noun meaning "accuser" or "adversary," was rendered into Greek as *diabolos*. Neither Hebrew nor Arabic, unlike modern English, uses a capital letter to signal a proper name; see Henry Ansgar Kelly, *Satan: A Biography* (Cambridge: Cambridge University Press, 2006), 2–3. The Arabic "name" *al-shaytan* means something like "the demon." Kelly attributes the notion that Satan "fell" due to arrogance and pride, an original sin, to the third-century Christian writer Origen of Alexandria.

[53] See Qur'an 12:53.

[54] *Khalifa*, now rendered *caliph* in English.

them by continuously seeking knowledge. He then commanded the angels to prostrate themselves before Adam, and they did so, obeying His order. Their subservience and submission to humankind necessitates compliance of the forces of the universe, all of which are in the hands of the angels. In this way Adam became the lord of the universe, the successor of God on earth. Iblis declined to prostrate himself to Adam and was banished from God's inner circle, and at his request was given until Judgment Day to attempt to tempt and seduce man, propagating evil and promoting its path, and reinforcing the malicious and misguided instincts of men.[55]

The universe is the arena in which one walks along a straight path, from which one may also be diverted, straying and becoming lost. Standing at a crossroads, man listens to the voice of God speaking to his rational faculty, in the language of reason, in the language of his conscience, the language of the prophets of God, and of other means of guidance. And he listens to the voice of Satan in the language of the "self that is inclined to evil,"[56] the voice of the elements of evil and corruption among men and others. Man listens to the two calls in his life and responds by free will to the call of good, or to the call of evil. We can see that Satan, in the Islamic conception, plays a prominent role in deepening the power of human choice.

> God sought to accomplish what He had ordained, so that, by a clear sign, he that was destined to perish might die, and he that was destined to live might survive.[57]

4.2.6 *The Prophet*

A prophet is one among the servants of God, and he shares with them the same conditions, needs and desires. Like them, he feels all that they feel in terms of psychological turmoil in the struggle between good and evil. But in his speech, actions and communion with other people, he adheres to and follows the course that is revealed to him, even when he is not responding to people's desires or satisfying them. He does not stray or deviate, does not speak simply out of passion and does not flatter people or seek to accommodate their whims. He weighs matters on scales that are not ones in common circulation.

[55] Musa Sadr is here continuing to draw on Qur'an 2:30–38.
[56] Another reference to Qur'an 12:53. [57] Qur'an 8:42.

A prophet is a servant of God, not an angel or a demigod: he lives, grows old, dies, is gathered[58] and held accountable for his deeds on the Day of Judgment. In this way he can be a good model for people, a leader not only for prayer, an imam, but a live source of support for people, who appreciate the reality in his mission and message as he opens to them the possibility of following his religious teachings.

There is much in the Qur'an concerning the lives of the prophets in general and the life of the Prophet Muhammad in particular supporting the above notion. Prophets have been criticized, encouraged, threatened, given advice and admonished for some of their actions. Yet the prophets enjoyed God's care, inspiration and guidance; in this way the prophet's words and his actions, his satisfaction with the work of others, became a life story and a good example for the community and nation.

In Islam, the distinguishing characteristic of the prophets is to be at one and the same time a servant and a messenger. The authenticity and originality of this idea is clear, and disproves the charge leveled by Bertrand Russell that the crucifixion of Jesus was an expression of class [struggle].[59] True, Islam, which has denied that Christ was crucified,[60] has affirmed that many prophets were killed for their calling: "Will you then scorn each apostle whose message does not suit your fancies, charging some with imposture and slaying others?"[61] The crucifixion of Christ is not denied in Islam because of his closeness to God or because of any influence of "gnosticism."[62] In Islam's view of Christ, the prophetic message is deeply human and does not remove human

58 There are many mentions in the Qur'an of "gathering" (*hashr*) and the "Day of Gathering" (*yawm al-hashr*), which is usually rendered in English as the "Day of Resurrection." For example, "Give glory to God on the appointed days. He that departs on the second day incurs no sin, nor does he who stays on longer, if he truly fears God. Have fear of God, then, and know that you shall all be gathered before Him" (Qur'an 2:203).

59 Bertrand Russell (1872–1970) wrote widely beyond metaphysics and logic, with many works on politics as well as his *History of Western Philosophy* (New York: Simon & Schuster, 1945). His *Practice and Theory of Bolshevism* (London: George Allen and Unwin, 1920) suggested that Bolshevism "combines the characteristics of the French Revolution with those of the rise of Islam" (5).

60 "They denied the truth and uttered a monstrous falsehood against Mary. They declared: 'We have put to death the Messiah, Jesus son of Mary, the apostle of God.' They did not kill him, nor did they crucify him, but they thought they did" (Qur'an 4:156–57).

61 Qur'an 2:87.

62 "Gnosticism" appears verbatim in Arabic, though, considering the reference to Russell, is possibly "agnosticism."

characteristics from the person who takes up the mission of communicating with God and of conveying His teachings in good faith and without distortion.

4.2.7 Judgment Day and the Resurrection

Belief in a Judgment Day and the resurrection is common to all religions and most schools of philosophy, but in Islam this belief is distinctive and original in the following aspects:

Firstly, reward after Judgment Day, in the resurrection, reflects the actions undertaken by man: "The day will surely come when each soul will be confronted with whatever good it did. As for its evil deeds, it will wish they were a long way off."[63]

This differs from punishment exacted in penal law, and from other interpretations of the afterlife, where recompense or sanction is a kind of response, good or bad, aimed at vengeance, discipline or reform. Whereas an act is distinct from the response to it in usual practice, in Islam the response in the hereafter to an act is that act itself, albeit in a form that is both proportional and eternal.

Secondly, on the Day of Resurrection the results of actions come to light; this is a time of discovering the truth of actions undertaken. An action's compensation and its just rewards are interconnected, and are bound up with the action at the very moment when it is undertaken, though they may not be visible at that time:

> Such is the promised day . . . Of this you had been heedless. But now We have removed your veil. Today your sight is keen.[64]

Thirdly, resurrection, in Islam, sees a person come forward, in body and soul, for judgment, and to receive the harvest of his or her life. The familiar debate among the Islamic philosophers in this context concerns the meaning of the "body that is resurrected"[65] rather than resurrection itself.

[63] Qur'an 3:30.

[64] "And when the agony of death justly takes him, they will say: 'This is the fate you endeavored to avoid.' And the Trumpet shall be sounded. Such is the promised day. Each soul shall come attended by one who will drive it on, and another to testify against it. One will say: 'Of this you have been heedless. But now we have removed your veil. Today your sight is keen'" (Qur'an 50:19–22).

[65] This is a reference to the debate, as occurs in Christianity, over whether resurrection involves the physical body.

Following these observations, scholars can clearly see the difference between resurrection in Islam, on the one hand, and such conceptions as the ancient Egyptian or pagan Arabian concepts of heaven and the return of the soul, or the magi's[66] notion of the victory of light over darkness.

Finally, the originality of Islam reaches its pinnacle in the field of parables and historical narration once we consider the extent of human culture across the world's regions and man's scientific and historical knowledge in the Prophet Muhammad's time, during the period of the revelation to him of the Qur'an: the Qur'an was not dependent on the scientific views prevailing in his times or the historical knowledge of peoples during that era. For example, the Qur'anic verses referring to the movements of the sun, moon, stars and earth were not in the least influenced by the Ptolemaic earth-centered model of the universe or its ideas. The verses that refer to the principle of creation, the formation of the earth, the expansion of the universe and so on all seem almost to comply with the most modern of scientific understandings and theories.

It is worth observing that the verses of the Qur'an relating to pharaonic history – particularly to the pharaoh contemporary to the prophet Joseph, who is known as "the honored one,"[67] and to the drowning and recovery of the body of the pharaoh at the time of the prophet Moses[68] – are verses that were not at all influenced by accounts prevalent at the time of Muhammad. Some of the information contained in these verses

[66] *Majus* in Arabic, corresponding to magi – Latin plural of magus. The word "magus" derives from Persian via the Greek – as the Zoroastrian priests of ancient Persia. Their role goes back beyond the Parthian and Sasanian periods (ending 642 CE), and before them the Seleucids (305 BC), to before Zoroastrianism became the state religion around 600 BC. Josef Wiesehöfer writes: "They played a part in royal investitures and burials and in the interpretation of dreams . . . What religious orientation they represented in what particular periods remains debatable." Josef Wiesehöfer, *Ancient Persia* (London: I.B. Tauris, 1996), 101. The word "magi" took on a pejorative sense in Christianity and is the root of the English word "magic." The Zoroastrian notions of light opposing dark and good opposing evil changed over time; see n. 51.

[67] *Al-'aziz*; see Qur'an 12:88.

[68] "We led the Israelites across the sea, and Pharaoh and his legions pursued them with wickedness and spite. But as he was drowning, Pharaoh cried: 'Now I believe no god exists except the God in whom the Israelites believe. To Him I give myself up.' 'Only now! But before this you were a rebel and a wrongdoer. We shall today save your body, so that you may become a sign for all posterity: for a great many of mankind do not heed Our signs'" (Qur'an 10:90–92).

was otherwise hidden to mankind before the discoveries concerning pharaonic history made possible by the work of Champollion.[69]

4.3 Spirituality in Islam

This topic has provoked a great deal of interest among critics and scholars concerned with religious matters, and I have read extensively and attended many such discussions, which generally do not go beyond stating that Islam intervenes in material concerns, calls for meeting aggression with a comparable aggression, or for meeting trickery with trickery, and concerns itself with marriage and emphasizes its importance. And they typically conclude that paradise in Islam is like a garden.

Some of these scholars ignore the boundless spirituality that manifests itself in Islamic beliefs regarding the Creator and His attributes and names, and in the place Islam accords to belief in the unseen,[70] making it the cornerstone of Islam in the Qur'an. Whatever the case, we have to discuss this in a cursory manner, following a note of introduction.

Established practice calls for categorizing things of the world in general, and the works of man, in particular, into material and spiritual. According to this distinction, we may be preoccupied with the material world, attending to matters such as eating, drinking, marriage, commerce and the like. Against this, we have prayer, worship, sacrifice, loyalty and devotion to thought and reflection, matters considered moral and spiritual in nature. The first category covers transient and ephemeral matters relating to the human body and man's immediate desires and needs; the second category serves more elevated, sublime inclinations, responding to the desires of man's soul and its capacities – where we find nonmaterial matters.

However, the truth is that this categorization lacks precision and accuracy. It suits neither philosophical interpretation nor religious teachings, and it cannot satisfy a believer's spirit of inquiry. For the "material," in philosophical interpretation, refers to any existing thing that has dimensions occupying space, including any moving or developing object

[69] Jean-François Champollion (1790–1832) was a pioneering French Egyptologist at the time when Napoleon's campaigns in Egypt (1798–1801) had sparked great interest in pharaonic civilization. Champollion was the first to decipher hieroglyphic scripts.

[70] *Al-iman bi-l-ghayb*, literally, "the belief in the realm of the unseen."

of a more complex nature, while the "abstract" [nonmaterial] is any entity without dimensions that as such needs no time, place or movement.

From this interpretation it follows that all movements issuing from man, or humankind, are material, including acts of worship, sacrifice, charity and thinking – they all derive from the movement of brain cells, themselves material. The philosopher cannot conceive of a separation of the body from the soul, or of actions issuing from one in isolation from the other, so that some acts can be called "material" and others "spiritual." Rather, the interaction of body and soul is such that for many philosophers they constitute a unitary construct. Sadr al-Din Shirazi's innovative idea was to consider the soul as an entity evolving from material toward spiritual presence.[71]

The true scale for weighing the spiritual rather than the material nature of an action undertaken by man is the act's motivation and goal. Many prayers, acts of charity and thoughts are at their core simply material; while many acts that are material, this-worldly, social or administrative reflect higher callings and ends, so these acts become holy acts of worship, through which the believer can make his entire life a prostration to God.

In addition, if we recognize that everything is God's creation and that everything in man's existence constitutes a reality and truth expressing divine will, then it would be very difficult to radically distinguish between one existing thing and another, or between one aspect or action and all other aspects and actions. It is impossible to discriminate and impose differences and distinction, unless man in his actions deviates from what God desires for him.

Looking at the spiritual dimension as such in Islam, we would state that Islam sanctifies all phenomena existing in the universe, considering them as both material and spiritual ways of prostrating and praising God. Even malevolent entities and harmful things are only relatively malevolent or harmful, such that within their proper place, or used appropriately, they become harmless and even benevolent.

Islam accords recognition to all aspects of the human being and his or her existence, all his or her desires and needs; Islam respects all of these.

[71] Again, Sadr al-Din Muhammad b. Ibrahim Shirazi (ca. 1571–1640), better known as Mulla Sadra, was a major philosopher under the Safavid Shah Abbas I, teaching at the seminary Madrasa-ye Khan in his home city of Shiraz, Iran. On Mulla Sadra, see n. 45 and accompanying text, and Index, s.v. "Mulla Sadra."

It then attempts to order and adjust man's relationships with others, his activities and his desires in order that he may play his part in the universe more effectively – namely, to act as a steward of God, or His successor on earth. In this way he can pursue a life that fully enables him to fulfill God's will and himself, enjoying his place in the universe. In this way, in the course of meeting a duty, every human act becomes an act of worship, and every movement becomes sacred.

We can see that Islam imparts the attribute of spirituality to all actions taken by man with sound motivation, so coloring all of existence with holiness. Rather than considering spirituality a weak presence in Islam, and considering that Islam concerns itself primarily with the material world, we should recognize the strength of this spiritual dimension. It is so strong that it gives everything a spiritual dimension.

The reason the Qur'an speaks, generally, of the spirit (*nafs*) rather than the soul (*ruh*) is perhaps to differentiate the spirit, which is concerned with addressing the needs of the body, from the soul. The soul is a specific abstract term for the absolute that manifests itself upon revelation and in the legal order. It accompanies the concept of angels in some Qur'anic verses.

Among the most delightful of Islamic teachings and principles are those that affirm that the good and beautiful things in God's creation are created by God for man, which rules out any attempt to forbid man from enjoying them and puts at fault anyone who tries to do so. Islamic teachings affirm this while at the same time warning that this enjoyment can lead to temptation. The greater one's blessings, the more wealth and honor increase, the more one's faith and piety must increase, lest man risk deviating from the straight path and giving himself up to distraction from his true self. As Imam Ali says: "Asceticism is not a matter of not possessing or partaking of something; it is a matter of not letting something possess you."[72]

It is in this light that we can understand paradise, the heavenly abode prepared by God for His devout servants, and it is in light of man's reality, the reality of creation, and the interpretation of the Day of Judgment and the hereafter, that reward is commensurate to man's works.

The Qur'an paints a picture of God's blessings in spiritual terms such as immortality; purity; serenity; absence of despair, boredom or lethargy;

[72] See, e.g., Muḥammad Ḥusayn Faḍlallāh (a leading Lebanese religious scholar, d. 2010), *Bayyināt* [Proofs], a collection of speeches, on his website, www.bayynat.org.lb/.

friendship; refraining from idle chatter and cursing; "only the greeting, 'Peace! Peace!'"[73] With all this, the Qur'an makes God's favor a far bigger and more marvelous blessing than the bliss of paradise. But His favor is reserved for the great souls who say, "O my God, I have not worshipped You out of fear of Your fire, or of Your heavenly paradise – I worship You because You are worthy of my devotion."[74]

As for meeting hostility or aggression with like for like, and without excess or intent to harm, this is part of the overall order of things, put in place to maintain society and safety, and to preserve man. We shall investigate this further in the last part of the lecture. I wish to mention one point here, namely, that Islam prefers forgiveness and considers it closer to piety and devotion, as long as it does not lead to the persistence of tyranny or resorting to injustice; anything else would mean that man had become a self-oppressor or one of the tyrants.

4.4 Social Matters

Islam's teachings are not confined to beliefs and moral guidance. They present a general system of life, including the individual's relations with others and with the state, administrative and international organizations, as well as personal status laws.[75]

Such detailed interventions into essential affairs of life may give rise to questioning of the rationale underlying these teachings – and whether it is feasible for a religious system or order, characterized by permanence and sanctity, to be instilled in an ever-changing society.

This I believe to be one of the most important points in this lecture. It is closely analyzed by books on Islam, and it has become an arena of questioning by many Muslims. To clarify the point, I will first ask this question: Do those who content themselves with belief and morality, or those who would wish religion to do so, believe it is possible to maintain faith and preserve good morals among those at work in the world without there being a plan based on faith and morals?

[73] "There they shall hear no idle talk, no sinful speech, but only the greeting, 'Peace! Peace!'" (Qur'an 56:25–26).

[74] Majlisī, *Biḥār al-anwār*, 41:14.

[75] Personal status law (*qanun al-ahwal al-shakhsiyya*), also known as family law, "covers marriage, separation, maintenance and alimony, custody over children, wills and *ab intestato* inheritance in the law of succession." Mallat, *Introduction to Middle Eastern Law*, 356.

Does man, as a single being and not as a plurality of beings, have the ability to isolate his soul from the impact of his body, or to prevent his body from interacting with his soul? Faith and morals are actions of the soul, and attributes of the soul – can they be distanced from the effects of actions undertaken by the body?

The answer is clearly no; the interaction between the aspects of a human being's existence is self-evident. For this reason, and to maintain faith and morality, a person must be committed to her actions, anchored to them with ties that sustain her faith and morality.

The Qur'an, like other sacred books, affirms this interaction and proclaims that bad deeds uproot faith from the heart: "Evil was the end of those who did evil, because they had disbelieved God's revelations and derided them."[76]

Is it reasonable that man should live in a society that contradicts the path he follows in his actions and is hostile to his faith and his morality, and not be influenced by that society?

The human being – in his very makeup and composition, in his life, needs, consciousness, thinking; in all aspects of this life – remains a social being who interacts with the society in which he lives. Can he isolate his faith, morality and personal actions from his interactions with society?

I think the answer to this question is equally clear. Islam affirms the need to create a society that is suited to faith, morality and good works, and proclaims openly: "No one who is full while his neighbor remains hungry has ever believed in God and the Day of Judgment, and I repeat: 'has ever believed.'"[77] To alert us to the contradiction that Islam sees between faith and a bad social situation the Qur'an asks: "Have you thought of him that denies the Last Judgment? It is he who turns away the orphan and has no urge to feed the destitute."[78]

On this basis we find that Islam, whose Prophet affirms that "I was sent to bring morality to completion,"[79] attempts to intervene in man's practical life, and in his social life. In the first, he [the Prophet] puts into place the principle of halal and haram – actions permitted and

76 Qur'an 30:10.

77 Hadith related by several tradents; see, e.g., https://dorar.net/hadith/sharh/135234.

78 Qur'an 107:1–3.

79 A Prophetic hadith also related by several tradents; see https://dorar.net/hadith/sharh/113995.

prohibited; in the second he institutes the broad legal framework that constitutes roughly half of Islamic teachings.

Let us now consider the difficulty of harmonizing laws and rules in a modern, constantly evolving society. To answer this, we need to consider three matters:

First: development in life and in human history is a matter of the interaction of man with the universe. Man, each and every day, increases his experience and furthers his knowledge, discovering new things about the universe. He then employs his new knowledge and puts into practice his new awareness, drawing benefit from his latest discovery of forces in the universe. In this way he develops his personal and social life and opens a new chapter in the long history of human development. Development is a matter of man reading a new line in the book of the universe, and then turning that new page to practice his new knowledge and enact the changes that result.

This is how we see development. There is nothing extraordinary underlying it, nothing extraneous that must be brought into the life of man from another world, into the world in which man lives. Development cannot be achieved from the outside; neither external sources nor some factor missing in human life are needed for change. There is nothing outside human life, outside the way we live, that facilitates our development; it comes from within.

Development is simply the interaction of man with the universe. We know that man and the universe were two elements on the scene of life from the dawn of creation; they have not been added to, nor diminished, in any way. They begin every page of life anew, with each fresh discovery that man makes about the universe as he interacts with it.

Second: religion in Islam is the law established by the creator of the universe and man, God almighty. The creator of the universe knows all aspects of its existence, its external features and internal workings, and knows also all aspects of the existence of man, all his needs and desires. God knows all, and so He established laws and rules for man to fully enjoy the universe and live a good and full life, just as an automobile manufacturer provides guidelines and instructions for the maintenance of a car and for the full use of its capacities: the manufacturer is an expert in how the car was manufactured, its detailed specifications and ways of making the fullest possible use of it.

Third: we say that God is the creator of the universe, and is fully cognizant of it; that He is the creator of man, and is all-knowing about man; and therefore that He set forth texts and guidance so that man could live in the universe a good and complete life with an exalted purpose.

In Islam's view, God also set forth law and guidance in words emanating from Him, namely, in the verses of the Qur'an. The Islamic faith believes that the meanings of the Qur'an are revealed in His very words. The word of God necessarily differs in essence and kind from the word of man, since man's ability to understand words spoken by human beings is constrained by the speaker's level of understanding, and this is a limitation that cannot be overcome. As the knowledge of the speaker increases, so increases also the scope for interpretation of his words and for a deeper exploration. Judges and attorneys can explore and investigate the meanings of legal texts in depths far beyond the comprehension and interpretation of laypeople.

Since the level of God's understanding is limitless, it is always possible to reconsider all the phases and levels of meaning of His words, and every time one digs deeper into His words one finds new meaning. In this sense, God's speech is similar to the secrets and truths of the universe – and in fact is itself part and parcel of the truths of the universe. Man discovers something new at every stage of his quest, just as every new page of the truth of man and the universe can provide man with new knowledge every day.

We can now return to the question we started with and say that man has interactions with the universe that form the basis for his development, and these interactions are ordered and regulated by God's sharia. Man's relations with the universe, too, have different teachings developed for each stage of his evolution and appropriate to the stage of human development or history in which men and women are living – teachings that regulate the constant linkages and interactions between humanity and the universe.

In sum, there are three factors on our stage, accompanying each other in reaching new stages of understanding and new truths: man, religion and the universe.

In this way, we are able to preserve the sanctity of religious systems belonging to mankind and to society, while at the same time providing scope for their development in a general framework that becomes clear to the scholar in his inquiry. As they develop and evolve, the teachings preserve their godliness, their power – and their potential to guide a leadership rooted in firm religious principles.

5

With Orientalist Philosopher Henry Corbin

5.1 Foreword

I first became acquainted[1] with the prominent French philosopher and professor at the Sorbonne Henry Corbin[2] by reading his excellent remarks in his comprehensive preface to Sheikh Shihab al-Din al-Suhrawardi's *Philosophy of Enlightenment* (*Falsafat al-ishraq*).[3]

I found him keen, passionate about Islamic philosophy, on which he spent over twenty-five years of his life. This made him familiar with its complexities, history and evolution.

Perhaps for the first time in the history of Orientalist scholarship, I found someone eager to study the philosophy of Sadr al-Din al-Shirazi,

[1] Musa Sadr wrote the present chapter as a preface to the Arabic translation of a major book by Henry Corbin, *Histoire de la philosophie islamique* (Paris: Gallimard, 1964). Corbin's work was translated by Nasir Mruwwe and Hasan Qubaysi as *Tārīkh al-falsafa al-islāmiyya* [History of Islamic philosophy] (Beirut: ʿUwaydāt Press, 1966). Sadr's text was also published in the journal *al-ʿIrfan*, "Maʿ al-Professor Corbin" [With Professor Corbin], vol. 54, in two parts (part 1 in July–August 1966, part 2 in September 1966), with an additional, short preface dated June 1, 1966. We begin here with the latter preface, which gives useful context to the chapter.

[2] Henry Corbin (d. 1978) was a major scholar of Islamic philosophy, especially in its Persian tradition, and the author of a four-volume masterpiece, *En Islam iranien* (vols. 1 and 2 in 1971, vols. 3 and 4 in 1973). A bibliography of Corbin is available as "Bibliographie complète de l'œuvre de Henry Corbin," www.amiscorbin.com/bibliographie/.

[3] There are several studies by Corbin on Suhrawardi (d. 1191) written before 1966, including the full volume 2 of *En Islam iranien*, entitled, *Sohrawardî et les Platoniciens de Perse*, and several lectures that are summarized or published in full in the *Annuaire de l'École pratique des hautes études, Section des sciences religieuses*, where Corbin taught. See "Bibliographie complète de l'œuvre de Henry Corbin," entries in 1955 to 1957, 1959 to 1961. An early publication is "Les motifs zoroastriens dans la philosophie de Sohrawardî," *Publications de la Société d'Iranologie* 3 (1946), texts in French (p. 57) and Persian (p. 64).

the author of *al-Hikma al-muta'aliya*, and the leader of the Islamic philosophical renaissance. Corbin wrote a priceless essay on him.[4]

He then met with my mentor Muhammad Husayn al-Tabataba'i, the prominent scholar of our time and the author of *Tafsir al-mizan*.[5] I found in Corbin's questions and Sayyed al-Tabataba'i's answers, which were compiled by the journal *Maktab-e Tashayyu'*, a depth of knowledge and a level of thinking that far surpass those of his Orientalist colleagues, as well as a devotion to his work that compels the reader's admiration.[6]

Corbin wrote magnificent works in collaboration with young Islamic philosopher Dr. Hossein Nasr. Whoever knows Dr. Nasr and his erudition in Islamic culture and the civilization produced by this nation throughout the ages, whoever knows Dr. Nasr and knows his respect for Professor Corbin, can only stand in awe before these great scholars.[7]

The Author, Professor Corbin, has also written remarkable articles and notes about several philosophical books, including his "commentaries" on Sadr al-Din al-Shirazi (Mulla Sadra);[8] his preface to *The Wisdom of*

[4] This refers to Henry Corbin, "Maqâm-e Mollâ Sadrâ Shîrâzî dar falsafa-ye Iran" [The place of Mulla Sadra Shirazi in Iranian philosophy], trans. S. H. Nasr, *Revue de la Faculté des Lettres de l'Université de Téhéran* 12 (1963): 1–34, translated from the French original, "La place de Mollâ Sadrâ (m. 1050/1640) dans la philosophie iranienne," *Studia Islamica* 18 (1963): 81–113.

[5] Muhammad Husayn al-Tabataba'i (d. 1981), a prominent Iranian/Shi'i philosopher, published between 1954 and 1972 an eclectic and mostly esoteric Arabic commentary on the Qur'an in twenty-seven volumes, *al-Mīzān fī tafsīr al-Qur'ān* (Beirut: Mu'assasat al-A'lamī, 1954–72). On Tabataba'i, see Hamid Algar, "'Allāma Sayyid Muḥammad Ḥusayn Ṭabāṭabā'ī: Philosopher, Exegete, and Gnostic," *Journal of Islamic Studies* 17, no. 3 (2006): 326–51.

[6] These texts were compiled in Muḥammad Ḥusayn Ṭabāṭabā'ī and Henry Corbin, *Shī'a: Majmū'ah-i muzākarat ba Profesur Hanri Kurbin* [Shi'ism: An assemblage of recollections with Professor Henry Corbin], ed. Hādī Khusrawshāhī (Qom: Mu'assasat-i Bustān-i Kitāb, 1960).

[7] Born in 1933, Seyyed Hossein Nasr is a prolific author on Shi'ism and on Islamic philosophy, including *Islamic Philosophy from Its Origin to the Present* (Albany NY, SUNY Press, 2006). He also wrote the prefaces to each of the following books by Tabataba'i published in English: *Shi'ite Islam*, trans. Seyyed Hossein Nasr (Albany, NY: SUNY Press, 1975); *A Shi'ite Anthology*, trans. William Chittick (Albany, NY: SUNY Press, 1978); *The Qur'an in Islam*, trans. Assadullah Yate (Tehran: Haeri Trust, 1987 [original Persian, 1974, first English edition, 1984]). On the relationship between Nasr, Corbin and Tabataba'i, see Algar, "'Allāma Ṭabāṭabā'ī," 341, 344–45, 348n71.

[8] Henry Corbin, "Eschatologie et réincarnation chez les Ishrâqîyûn (Sohrawardî et Mollâ Ṣadrâ)," *Annuaire de l'École pratique des hautes études, Section des sciences religieuses* (1961–62): 73–79. Whenever "Author" (capitalized) appears in this chapter, Sadr is referring to Corbin.

Illumination (*Hikmat al-ishraq*) by Shaykh Shihab al-Din al-Suhrawardi;[9] his preface to *Twin Wisdoms* (*Jami' al-hikmatayn*) by the Fatimi and Alawi philosopher Nasir Khusraw;[10] *Unveiling the Concealed* (*Kashf al-mahjub*) by Abu Ya'qub al-Sijistani; as well as Khusraw's interpretation of a philosophical poem by Abu Haytham al-Jurjani.[11]

All that is well and good. But when my dear brother Nasir Ahmad Mruwwe presented me with a copy of Corbin's *History of Islamic Philosophy*, I was amazed by his extensive efforts and his dedication to Islamic philosophy.

I still recall my pleasure when Nasir told me that he and his colleague, Husayn Qubaisi, had undertaken to translate this book and that the 'Uwaydat Press would print the translation to add yet another excellent book to its rich collection.

I have carefully studied this book, particularly the sections on philosophy, Sufism and the opinions on Twelver Shi'ism. Since the book addresses some of the key tenets of our doctrine, I believe it necessary to offer a few notes and observations to the reader of the Arabic version. I do not find it sufficient to express appreciation of the Author's contribution without clarifying where we stand.

Mr. Ahmad 'Uwaydat has kindly welcomed this initiative, and I have written these few lines as a preface for Henry Corbin's *History of Islamic Philosophy*, where I discuss the main tenets ascribed to Twelver Shi'ism in the work. I am now submitting this preface to *al-'Irfan* so that our enlightened readers may discuss it and offer their opinions and observations.[12]

5.2 Preface

This book opens to Western thinkers a new window to appreciate Oriental culture and discover the riches of its religious philosophical and mystical (Sufi) corpus.

[9] Henry Corbin, "Le Kitâb al-Hikmat al-'Arshîya de Mollâ Ṣadrâ Shîrâzî," *Annuaire de l'École pratique des hautes études, Section des sciences religieuses* 85 (1976–77): 269–74.

[10] Nasir-e Khosraw, *Le Livre Réunissant les Deux Sagesses (Kitâb-e jâmi' al-hikmatain) ou Harmonie de la Philosophie Grecque et de la Théosophie Ismaélienne* (Tehran/Paris: Adrien-Maisonneuve, 1953), 147 (French), 450 (Persian).

[11] Abu Ya'qub Sejestani, *Le Dévoilement des Choses Cachées (Kashf al-Mahjûb)* [Persian text with an introduction by H. Corbin, 1–25] (Tehran/Paris: Adrien-Maisonneuve, 1949), 25 (French), 115 (Persian).

[12] On *al-'Irfan*, which was established by Ahmad 'Aref al-Zein (d. 1960) in Sidon in 1909, see Mallat, *Aspects*, 9–15.

Professor Henry Corbin has made persistent efforts in writing this important work. It compels the reader's respect and admiration. He has surpassed any other single individual's capacity to treat the subject. Several studies and references he cites can only be found in the works of learned scholars and in manuscripts dispersed across the Islamic Orient, and in private and public libraries across the world.

Despite the difficulty of accessing such complex works, the Author navigates them with endless patience and composure to analyze, translate, arrange and present them to readers. His efforts surpass all available research, and he offers services to world culture far more valuable than those of many founding figures in this field.

The Arabic-reading audience will, in turn, find great intellectual pleasure in reading the translated version of the book. The reader will feel rightly proud of what his nation and the Orient have produced, and he will regret our ignorance of, and disregard for, a great civilization and cultural heritage, a disregard so marked that we have become like a mere mirror reflecting Western thought and intellectual production, as we forget that this corpus is the continuation of the founders of a monumental civilization and its cultural output in history.

The translation of this book is in itself an important contribution to Arab thought, commensurate with the challenges faced by the two remarkable translators and their efforts to find the original texts and the sources of these texts with the benefit of a more accomplished translation.

* * *

This weighty book contains fundamental analyses that accommodate scholarly criticism and deserve to be discussed seriously. The Author should be commended for raising questions that many have been reluctant to address.

His research is primarily based on books by scholars, philosophers and Sufis traced back to their authors. Our main reservation is that the opinions of these writers have been overgeneralized in the portrayal of their core faith and doctrine. Just as we cannot consider that the views of Pierre Teilhard de Chardin are those of the entire Catholic Church, so too we cannot hold the Hanafi school accountable for what is written in

The Bezels of Wisdom (*Fusus al-hikam*) by Muhyiddin b. ʿArabi, one of the most prominent Sufi masters in the Orient.[13]

In this preface, I try to clarify some views and opinions on the principles of jurisprudence, exegesis and doctrine,[14] which are part of our school of thought and our religion.[15] My purpose is not to discredit the Author or question the legitimacy of his sources. Thought is a spring that cannot be exhausted. It keeps on giving for eternity. All thinkers are accountable for their views and take pride in them. The cultural edifice rises with them all.

5.3 Exoteric and Esoteric

Among the most important points that the Author makes in this book is the distinction between the exoteric (*zahir*) and the esoteric (*batin*) aspects of religious teachings and religion in general, and the symbolism of the Qur'an. Corbin discusses extensively this duality as the basis of his analyses and conclusions. His understanding of Shiʿism is based on this duality and on the interpretation of the meaning behind the concept of *walaya* (guardianship),[16] the Imamate and the Hidden

[13] The vitalist philosophy of Jesuit priest Pierre Teilhard de Chardin (d. 1955) was very much in vogue in Lebanon in the 1950s and 1960s, probably known to Sadr from his colleagues in the Cénacle seminar (see Chapter 4, n. 5), in particular René Habachi (d. 2003), "Teilhard de Chardin et le drame du XXe siècle. Le génie de l'évolution," *Les Conférences du Cénacle 1*, Beirut, 1956; Habachi, "Teilhard de Chardin. Science, philosophie et foi," *Les Conférences du Cénacle 6*, Beirut, 1956. Muhyi al-Din b. ʿArabi (d. 1240) is a major classical figure of Sufism, and the author of a multivolume summa of esoteric journeys and "illuminations" known as *al-Futuhat al-makkiyya* (The Meccan revelations), as well as the *Fusus* mentioned by Musa al-Sadr. Henry Corbin was also a specialist of Ibn ʿArabi; see his *L'Imagination créatrice dans le soufisme d'Ibn ʿArabi* (Paris: Flammarion, 1958).

[14] The corresponding Arabic words are *usul*, *tafsir* and *ʿaqida*. *Usul* translates as jurisprudence in its English sense, close to a philosophy or theory of law. *Tafsir* is exegesis, in particular of the Qur'an, and *ʿaqida* is faith, doctrine. All three are full genres in the Muslim legal tradition, usul and tafsir in particular.

[15] A school of thought is *madhhab*, a polysemous word that, in this context, means both a particular school of law and tradition, here the Jaʿfari Shiʿi legal tradition.

[16] Corbin writes *walaya* (in French), with /a/, *fatha*, after the /w/, in contrast with the more accurate *wilaya* (with an /i/, *kasra*). In Persian, *wilaya* is pronounced *velaya* (as in *velayat-e faqih*, the later Khumaini concept of "the rule of the jurist"), with the /e/ oral inflection of the *kasra*. Because *walaya* prevails in all Corbin's works, we have preferred to keep his rendering in this chapter. It is unlikely that Sadr adhered to Corbin's use. For the reader not familiar with either Arabic or Persian, the fatha and kasra are inflection vowels that are not always written.

Imam.[17] The Author also addresses the problem of the suspension of revelation and the persistence of religious human life beyond this suspension.[18]

Scholars analyzing Islamic teachings and interpreting the Qur'an rarely adopt the symbolic approach or rely on its exoteric and esoteric aspects. The most common traditional approach is that of their varying perception and understanding.

I will give an example from our daily life to clarify this idea to the reader. The flower is seen by the child as a beautiful toy, by the patient or the traveler as a kind gesture, by the artist or painter as a subject matter for his work and by the natural scientist as an object with marvelous petals filled with active cells and meanings that others cannot behold.

These different interpretations are all true and valid. Rather than seeing them as contradictory, I prefer to perceive them as degrees and stages of reality. When we realize that, we understand the fundamental principle that underpins our research.

The truth – any truth – has multiple aspects and different implications, some of which are plain, while others are concealed. As it progresses further in its quest for truth and knowledge, human science discovers these aspects and implications, gradually picking them up, like petals, one by one.

Yet words differ from material truth. Their interpretation is restricted by two limitations:

The first limitation is the significance of the word and its connotation, in both plain and metaphorical meaning. Words can only be interpreted within the limits of their content and significance. If we go beyond the

[17] The Imamate is the belief of Shiʿis in twelve leaders of the tradition, hence *ithna ʿashari* (Twelver) Shiʿis. They are the Imams, with a capital I following Corbin, to distinguish them from an imam, leader of the prayer, or leader generally in the Sunni tradition. The Twelve Imams start with Ali (d. 661) and end with the going into hiding of the last Imam, Muhammad al-Mahdi, in 941, which is known as the Greater Occultation (*al-ghayba al-kubra*), in contradistinction with the lesser occultation between 874 and 941, when the Hidden Imam acted through a series of agents to protect him and the community from persecution.

[18] The Twelve Imams are believed by their followers to carry the message of the Prophet, including through their own hadith. Muhammad al-Mahdi's occultation in 941, when his fourth and last agent died, starts "the suspension of the revelation" mentioned by Sadr until the return of the Mahdi to save the world at the end of time.

limits, the word becomes a symbol, and its material significance takes on a figurative dimension.

The second limitation is the speaker's degree of knowledge and the intention in their words. We cannot interpret a person's words beyond her meaning of it and the truth she conveys. The higher the person's degree of knowledge and culture, the more meaning her words take on, and the more connotations of the word are unveiled. Scholars interpreting statutes and covenants have agreed on an absolute principle: they consider that the authors of these texts possess a degree of expertise and culture so advanced that they, as interpreters, need to go deep into the meanings of their words and display high proficiency in their interpretation.

There is always a limit that scholars and those who interpret words and texts cannot ignore, which is the degree of culture, knowledge and context of the original authors.

Divine speech cannot be hemmed in by the second limitation. God's knowledge knows no limit: "He has encompassed all knowledge" (Taha, 98).[19] Those listening to divine speech can interpret it in innumerable ways, with meanings relating to any aspect of reality and any field of knowledge. The only condition is that the interpreter does not go beyond the signified (*madlul*)[20] dimension of the word and that her interpretation does not exceed the content and implications of divine speech, whether in its plain or metaphorical meanings.

The word of God is an objective truth; it is the very incarnation of truth. It has several significations that conjure up several stages of interpretation, with every one of these significations intended by God to serve as truth for the listener and a path for the believer.

When we consider this characteristic of God's words [as carrying several meanings], we apply it to the Prophet's words, which are not spoken in vain, provided they are conveyed to us without distortion or [with a wrong] interpretation by the transmitter.

The scholars who study the Qu'ran's exegetes, their analyses of verses and of the Prophet's practices are in a similar situation. They understand that previous interpretations and analyses probe the meaning of sacred words with great depth. They find in Qur'anic verses or in hadiths, in

[19] References to Qur'anic verses appear in the main text of Sadr.

[20] The translation uses the word "signified," which was introduced by linguist Ferdinand de Saussure as the exact analogue of *madlul*.

rational elaboration or in new evidence, indicia that help them discover uneven and diversified meanings for a Qur'anic verse or story, with an inexhaustible set of truths to be renewed day after day.

The purpose of this preface is not to list a comprehensive set of examples, and I will mention only two:

In his famous book on jurisprudence, *Kitab al-makasib* (Book of transactions), Sheikh Murtada al-Ansari quotes the following hadith: "For [God] permits speech and prohibits speech."[21] He interprets it in four ways, each different from the other for clarity and for derivation. All four interpretations, however, are based on the core of the words and the hadith. Modern scholars have interpreted the Prophet's saying "Do not cause harm" in many different ways – five, to be precise – all of which are based on exoteric aspects that do not go beyond the meaning of each word.[22]

This principle clarifies the following for the reader:

First, Qur'anic verses have been revealed in a way that can be understood by everyone. They are based on plain and verbal meaning by coinage, rather than on symbolic or obscure rational derivations, a science of numbers, ciphers or alphanumeric codes.

This is the method adopted by the tradition in interpreting divine rules and verses, and the Prophet's successors and the Imams followed in this path.

The Qur'an confirms this method in several verses, for instance verses 15 and 16 of al-Ma'ida: "... There certainly has come to you from God a light and a clear Book through which God guides those who seek His pleasure to the ways of peace, brings them out of darkness ..."; "It is a Book whose verses are perfectly explained – a Qur'an revealed in Arabic

[21] [*Original footnote by Musa Sadr: Kitab al-makasib* (Book of transactions), by Sheikh Murtada al-Ansari.] Murtada al-Ansari (d. 1864) was the most famous Shi'i scholar of the nineteenth century and the author of an elaborate treatise of fiqh about "earning transactions" (*makasib*) focusing on contracts of sale. The treatise consists in its modern edition of five volumes edited by Muhammad Kalantar and first published in Najaf in 1972. An edition in seventeen volumes published by Noor Press in Beirut in 1986 is accessible at https://alfeker.net/.

[22] [*Original footnote by Musa Sadr:* See the letter entitled "No Harm" by Sheikh Ansari and the letter entitled "No Harm" by Grand Ayatollah Mohammad-Hossein Naini Gharavi.] The "no harm" (*la darar*) principle is part of a central hadith in the law of compensation, *la darar wa-la dirar*, which can be translated as "no harm whatsoever will go uncompensated." For a discussion of the legal principle, see Mallat, *Normalization of Saudi Law*, 72–75.

for people who know, delivering good news and warnings. Yet most of them turn away, so they do not hear" (Fussilat, 3–4); and verse 185 of al-Baqara: "Ramadan is the month in which the Qur'an was revealed as a guide for humanity with clear proofs for guidance and for distinguishing right and wrong . . ."

The Sunna also adopts this method. This is evident in several hadiths, as in the famous hadith "If you do not understand the waves of calamities that come onto you like the dark night, seek refuge with the Qur'an" (*al-Kafi: Abwab al-Qur'an*).[23]

These verses and hadiths deny symbolism in the Qur'an and confirm that the Book is a gift to all humans, regardless of their degree of knowledge. It was revealed in plain Arabic with no symbolism or ambiguity.

Second, degrees of understanding the Qur'an are as different as understanding the different aspects and implications of truth. The more sophisticated the study of a verse, the more expressive it becomes, as it explores new meanings, gains new knowledge and probes the verse in deeper ways and new directions. All these meanings are true and accurate, and they are by no means contradictory.

This is very different from the principle of symbolism and allegory, which considers that the key to understanding symbols and allegories is held by their enunciators, as the Author argues. Meditation (*tadabbur*) on the Qur'an is the same as the meditation on laws and conventions, only more profound. God orders us to meditate on the Qur'an: "Do they not then meditate on the Qur'an?" (al-Nisa', 82). The method of the Prophet's companions and the Imams, the logic of discourse and the conventions of human interaction are all based on this approach.

Third, this method is different from superficial understanding.[24] As the Prophet said in the celebrated hadith, the Qur'an "is its own interpreter." We read in the Qur'an: "On that Day some faces will be bright, looking at their Lord" (al-Qiyama, 23). God sees all on Judgment Day: "No vision can encompass Him, but He encompasses all visions" (al-An'am, 103). The verse "the Most Compassionate is the one who is sits on the throne" (Taha, 5) should not be interpreted, as the first

[23] Kulaynī, *al-Kāfī*, 2:598. This work is a major compendium of Shi'i hadith.

[24] The formulation here is awkward. Sadr probably suggests that the clear reading of the Qur'an is not necessarily superficial, and that a mystical reading can be excessive in distorting the otherwise plain meaning of a verse.

Ash'aris believed, as a sign of [human] incarnation. Other verses of the Qur'an reject this interpretation, for "there is nothing like Him" (al-Shura, 11).[25]

Every author has the right to ask their readers to interpret certain terms as concepts specific to him in his own work. The reader of a scholarly book cannot but pay attention to the meaning intended by the author in his choice of terms.

The Qur'an declares this as a principle:

> It is He who has sent down to you the Book in clear (*muhkamat*) verses that form the Book's foundation, and other verses that are unclear (*mutashabihat*). Those with evil in their hearts will follow what is unclear in search of discord and in support of an interpretation suitable to them. No one knows the true interpretation except God. But those with firm knowledge say, "We believe in it. All of it is from our Lord." And no one will be reminded except those with [the right] understanding. (Al 'Imran, 7)

Clear (*muhkamat*) verses are the heart of the Book and guide unclear (*mutashabihat*) verses that cannot be understood on their own. Unclear verses must be read together with the other, clear verses; they are similar to them in some ways and different in others. If we rely on the unclear verses, with their multiple meanings, and try to interpret them according to our personal preferences or some arbitrary evidence, we lose the Qur'anic path. The Qur'an requires us to rely on the clear verses and use them as a reference to understand those which are unclear. This method allows us to avoid a simplistic understanding or a superficial interpretation of the sacred Book.

In short, proper exegesis differs from the Author's view that Qur'anic verses are exoteric symbols with esoteric truths behind them; it also differs from the method that relies on superficial meanings and fails to go beyond the exoteric aspect of some verses, for it does not rely on the meaning of clear verses to reach the understanding of other, unclear ones.

Here, I would like to engage the Author and read again the well-known hadith "The Qur'an possesses an external appearance and a

[25] Against early Ash'aris, who drew parallels to the Christian belief in God's incarnation in His son Jesus, Sadr argues that this interpretation of the Qur'anic verse in Surat Taha cannot stand against the verse in Surat al-Shura, which defends the absolute uniqueness of God since nothing is like God, let alone a divine expression in Christ.

hidden depth, an exoteric as well as an esoteric meaning. This esoteric meaning in turn conceals another esoteric meaning, and this goes on for seven or seventy hidden depths." I understand this hadith differently. In my view, this refers to the multiple meanings of the Qur'an, which are seven or seventy – the numbers are likely a metonymy for "abundance" and "harmony." Another hadith tells us that "the Qur'an was revealed in seven letters (*ahruf*)." This is explained in yet other hadiths as a type of Qur'anic analysis: "It is an order, an injunction, a preaching message, a warning, a book of morals and wisdom."

In the hadith cited by the Author, "every verse of the Qur'an has an outer meaning, an inner meaning, a limited (*hadd*) meaning, and a higher opening (*matla'*)," I believe the "outer and inner meanings" refer to the "clear and unclear" (*al-muhkam wa-l-mutashabih*) verses. The limitation (hadd) is the limiting meaning of the verse itself, while the higher opening (matla') is the interpretation of the unclear verse by reference back to the meaning of the clear (muhkamat) verses.

5.4 Sura Incipits

Overreliance on the abovementioned principle leads some interpreters to deny any symbolism in the Qur'an. They go as far as rejecting even the cryptic letters at the incipit of several chapters, *alif-lam-mim* in al-Baqara, *alif-lam-ra* in Ibrahim and *kaf-ha-ya-'ayn-sad* in Maryam.

The attempts by scholars to explain these incipit letters are evidence of their rejection of all symbolism in the Qur'an, for they consider that all the words in the Book are clear and are available for all to understand.

Some Shi'i scholars fall into this wrong reasoning. They explain these letters by assuming that the Qur'an challenged pagan Arabs to come up with anything similar to the Qur'an, even if it were only ten verses, or even one verse, to prove that it is man-made. The Qur'an went further with the challenge, they argue, of the opening letters in the mysterious chapters. For you find them composed of the letters *a* (*alif*), *l* (*lam*), *m* (*mim*), *r* (*ra'*) and so on . . . To reinforce this interpretation, they say that the incipit *alif-lam-mim* figuring at the beginning of al-Baqara is formed by the letters most used in this sura. The same applies to the letters in *kaf-ha-ya-'ayn-sad* in Maryam, and so on for the rest of the incipits.

Their reasoning is further supported by the argument that these opening letters are often followed by the word "this" (*dhalika* or *tilka* in Arabic), with "this" referring to the Book and the chapters – that is to say, God is telling us that those letters themselves compose the chapters and the Qur'an.

Acknowledging the allegory in these letters does not prove that the [whole of the] Book is allegorical, for such letters are few and far between.

Still, several Shi'i and Sunni scholars acknowledge the symbolism of the opening letters. And many who interpret these incipits use the phrase "These letters are only understood by God and His Prophet . . ."

5.5 The Imam

In Twelver Shi'ism, the Imam does not constitute a reference for the interpretation of Qur'anic symbols, as there is no symbolism or attempt to uncover the esoteric meaning of rules in the Prophet's legacy. As the Qur'an tells us, the Imams do not receive divine revelation; they provide instead a religious role model (*al-mathal al-kamil*) to be followed, and their existence and contributions are clearly specified.

The Imams' opinion must be followed in all affairs. In their words and deeds, in their opinions on all that exists and their outlook on the universe, they are role models (*al-namuzaj al-kamil*) as perfect exemplars; they provide guidance for all intellectual journeys and emotional experiences. Their leadership requires a serious sense of responsibility that is only attained by unique individuals who undergo difficult trials and work to continuously better themselves: "Remember when Abraham was tested by his Lord with certain commandments, which he fulfilled. God said, 'I will certainly make you into a role model for the people.' Abraham asked, 'What about my offspring?' God replied, 'My covenant does not extend to the wrongdoers'" (al-Baqara, 124).

The Imam's interpretation of Qur'anic verses is to be preferred. He is the best reference for the Islamic understanding of God's words, and he carries the religious legacy and knowledge of the Prophet. In Ja'far al-Sadeq's words, "all that which I tell you has been told to me by my father, al-Baqer, who had heard it from his father Ali b. Hussein, who had heard it from his father, Hussein, who had heard it from his father, Ali b. Abi Talib, who had in turn heard it from the Prophet."[26]

The Imam's interpretation of religious rules must be adopted. In the Prophet' words, "truly the people of my house are like Noah's ark:

[26] Kulaynī, *al-Kāfī*, 1:53.

whoever takes refuge therein is saved, and whoever opposes it drowns."[27] In the same vein, the Author mentions a famous hadith: "I leave among you two treasures that, if you cling to them, you shall not be led into error after me: the Book of God and my progeny."[28]

Imam Jaʿfar al-Sadeq discusses the role of the Imam in similar terms, when he asks a scholar from Syria: "Who guides Muslims to the true path if they disagree after the Prophet?" The Syrian scholar answers that the Qur'an shall be the arbiter between Muslims if they disagree and shall guide them if they lose their way. The Imam then asks him how to resolve disagreements among Muslims about the meaning of a Qur'anic verse, to which the scholar reluctantly answers that the logical way would be to return to the Qur'an, as the cause of the disagreement is over the meaning of the verse. When the scholar eventually acknowledges the need for a person to interpret the Qur'an and resolve disagreements among Muslims, the Imam confirms this conclusion and describes how the Qur'an should be understood by him.

Shʿi Imams always trained their students on how to interpret the Qur'an. For example, when Imam al-Sadeq was asked by a companion of his how to wash one's foot during ablution when a healing bandage is placed over a wound and cannot be removed, the Imam answered: "Wipe over the bandage," adding, "That and the like is known from the Book of God," for "He laid upon you no hardship in religion" (al-Hajj, 78).

The Imam also plays a central role in distilling Islamic rules, and here is a primary difference between Jaʿfari thought and other schools in Islam. This, I believe, is why the Author says:

> Alternatively, does not this zahir, exoteric aspect, which, it is claimed, is sufficient for the regulation of one's behavior in everyday life, envelop something which is the batin, the inner, esoteric aspect?

[27] This saying by the Prophet is known as *hadith al-safina*, the hadith of the ark (*safina* literally meaning ship), and is related by Shiʿi tradents in reference to "the people of my house" (*ahl bayti*) as Ali and his successors.

[28] This is a key hadith in the Shiʿi tradition, known as *hadith al-thaqalayn* (also *thiqalayn*), the hadith of the two treasures, to assert the leadership of Ali and his successors (the two treasures being the Qur'an and the progeny of Muhammad, through his daughter Fatima, the wife of Ali and the mother of the Imams Hasan and Hussein). The hadith can be found in both Sunni and Shiʿi collections. See, e.g., for Sunnis, al-Nīsābūrī (d. 1014), *Ṣaḥīḥ Muslim* (Beirut: Dār Iḥyāʾ al-Turāth al-ʿArabī, 1955), 4:1873; for Shiʿis, Kulaynī, *al-Kāfī*, 1:294.

> If the answer is yes, the entire meaning of one's everyday behavior undergoes a modification, because the letter of positive religion, the sharia, will then possess a meaning only within the *haqiqa*, the spiritual truth, which is the esoteric meaning of the divine revelations ... The hidden meaning can be transmitted only by way of a knowledge that is a spiritual heritage; and this spiritual heritage is represented by the vast corpus containing the traditional teachings of the Shiʿi Imams, the "heirs" of the prophets.

The Twelve Imams have greatly contributed to the expansion of jurisprudence (fiqh) and the explanation of religious rules, particularly because they lived during times vastly different from those of the Prophet and his companions and followers. They lived through historical turning points and witnessed innovations resulting from the Arabs' interaction with other peoples, cultures and civilizations such as the Greeks, the Persians, the Indians, the Assyrians ... In the speeches and statements of the Twelve Imams, there is an abundance of rules and guidance on new developments. In fact, Shʿi jurisprudence was named "Jaʿfari" jurisprudence because of Imam Jaʿfar al-Sadeq's invaluable novel contributions.

Such contributions do not consist of revealing the esoteric meaning or the truth behind religious rules. They express the transmission of Islamic views and the Prophet's Sunna, which has been documented and verbally transmitted. Ali b. Abi Talib committed these hadiths to writing or to memory, and he transmitted them to his sons or his companions keen on learning from him, while others refused to transmit these hadiths for political or other reasons. History tells us that at the time of the companions there were wide discussions about the position of Islam toward sundry issues. People often solicited the guidance of Ali, who transmitted to them the sayings of the Prophet to be used as a rule.

The life of Imam Ali and his constant quest for religious teachings from the Prophet are eloquently expressed in his saying "I followed him, wherever he went, like a baby camel which follows its mother." As a result, Imam Ali managed to learn a great deal about the rules and views of Islam and to transmit them. And in one famous hadith, the Prophet said, "I am the city of knowledge, and Ali is its gate." I see no point in explaining the term knowledge as "gnosis" as the Author does; the knowledge of the Prophet is Islam, and Islam in its diverse aspects is greater and broader than any limiting field of knowledge. The Prophet's knowledge – that is, the Islamic sharia – can be accessed through the city's gate, Imam Ali, living up to this expectation: Ali transmitted the texts and taught them to his children, to his companions and to any Muslim who wished to learn.

The Twelve Imams transmitted this wealth of Islamic knowledge from Ali, who in turn transmitted it from the Prophet. The Imams understood the texts of the Qur'an and the Sunna best and diligently applied the general principles they derived from them to new topics and issues. Their words are compelling, and they themselves turned into references. They form one of the Prophet's two treasures. They are Noah's ark.[29]

5.6 The Continuity of the Religious History of Humanity

The Author poses the following question in his book: "How can the religious history of humanity continue after the 'seal of the prophets'? This question, and its answer, form the expression of Shiʿi Islam."

We agree that his question and answer are valid, but the reason he gives is not, for it is based on the same esoteric/exoteric dichotomy that he develops in his book. He argues that the role of the city guardian (*wali*) is to clarify all esoteric meanings after the departure of the Prophet, who provided us with mere exoteric ones. We prefer to this reading what the Prophet himself says: "I leave among you two treasures that, if you hang on to them, shall not lead you into error after me: the Book of God and my progeny. These two shall not be parted until [the Day of Judgment]."[30]

As the Book of God in God's words, the Qur'an is universal truth in its arrested form. This makes it different from words uttered by humans. The universal truth of the Qur'an becomes clearer to humans in every step they take, as they gain more awareness and their degree of knowledge increases.

The universe is the object of the progress of civilization and the evolution of culture, and the carriers of this progress of civilization and culture are humans. Humans and the universe are two fundamental realities that manifest themselves in new ways at each stage of civilization. The Qur'an, a third fundamental reality, also manifests itself in

[29] Sadr fuses the two well-known references (see nn. 26, 27), hadith al-thaqalayn (the hadith of the two treasures) and the salvation story of Noah's ark in hadith al-safina (the hadith of the ark).

[30] Again, hadith al-thaqalayn (see n. 27).

ways similar to the universe and human ways. It guides humans to a better future in the universe.

This genuine harmony between the universe, humans and the Book of God is an a priori. It is revealed in the previously mentioned stages of understanding the Qur'an and its different aspects. It shows us how the universe (or the book of creation, according to kalam theologians) is organized by the legislation of the divine book– the Qur'an – for all times and for all stages of evolution.

The Imam represents the culmination of Islamic understanding for the meaning of the Qur'an, as he is the role model and the perfect example of such understanding. The Imam interprets the words of the Qur'an. This is how he contributes to the development of Islamic thought and renders it suitable for guiding modern human life.

In light of the above, the Imam plays two main roles: he explains religious rules and he interprets Qur'anic verses.

a. The Imam enriches Islamic thought with his profound understanding of the Qur'an, thereby expanding the community's knowledge of the teachings expressed in the Qur'anic verses; and
b. He recounts the Prophet's hadiths and Sunna (practices). By doing do, he transmits the Prophet's Sunna, but he also contributes to its expansion by adding elements from his own life. That is our understanding of the Prophet's hadith in which he confirms that the Qur'an and his progeny shall not part.

The fact that some Qur'anic verses concern specific individuals or events does not do away with their general and comprehensive reach. A particular event provides a tangible example to elucidate the verse. Religion is not a series of instructions; it is a method of upbringing and education, and one of the best pedagogical methods is to have people learn from practical examples.

To conclude this discussion of the Imam's role, I would like to draw the reader's kind attention to the Author's claim that Shiʿism is not a fifth legal school (madhhab) alongside the four legal schools of Sunni Islam. We believe that Shiʿi law (fiqh) is a new form of Islamic jurisprudence (fiqh) based on the Qur'an, the Sunna and the hadiths conveyed by the Imams, which represent a deeper and broader understanding of the Qur'an and the Sunna. Shiʿi law provides a substitute for the Sunni tools of interpretation based on public interest (*masalih mursala*) and analogy (qiyas).

Jurisprudence in other Islamic schools of thought is based on the Qur'an, the meanings inferred by the Prophet's companions and followers from the Qur'an and the Sunna as told and documented during the time of the Prophet and his successors. This covers a small part of the Prophet's teachings and practices, for he prohibited recording and passing on the Sunna [in his lifetime]. [Sunni] jurisprudence relies on the Prophet's companions, whose views are similar because they all lived during the same era generally, who experienced only one way of life and who were not exposed to the developments and events resulting from the encounter with [other] civilizations.

When law was faced with new challenges and events, it could not find an answer to the emerging problems and challenges in its interpretation of the Qur'an in the few documented sections of the Sunna and the opinions of the Prophet's companions. As a result, law had to rely on those unclear (mutashabihat) verses of the Qur'an, and this made them have recourse to analogy. Yet this failed to resolve the problem, and the lack of rules to address new events persisted.

In response, [Sunni] jurisprudence turned to the concept of public interest, which is largely similar to laying down statutes and legislation. This enabled it to evolve and resolve some of problems, but it was soon faced with a new challenge: the lack of consensus, unity or similarity in jurisprudential opinions within an adequate and unified school of thought. In fact, there was a multitude of opinions, which kept drifting apart to the point that they almost caused rifts among Muslims, forcing jurists to put an end to the practice of ijtihad.

As we revisit the Author's statement on Shiʿism, we conclude that similarities among the four Sunni schools of law, in terms of their sources, history and development, do not allow us to consider the Shiʿi school of law as a "fifth" school alongside the other four. By definition, Shiʿi jurisprudence is necessarily opposed to Sunni jurisprudence, which is in turn split into the four schools of law that the Author mentions.[31]

[31] It is not clear in this passage whether Sadr considers the Shiʿi Jaʿfari school of law (madhhab) to be different from the Sunni schools of law. Corbin sees them as different, insofar as the theological message carried by Shiʿism differs fundamentally from its Sunni counterpart. Sadr seems to oppose this distinction yet defends at the beginning of this section the fundamentally different law adopted by Shiʿis. In other writings, however, rapprochement (which was dominant at the time) is preferred. On balance, the rapprochement advocated between Shiʿis and Sunnis prevails over separation in Sadr's humanism.

5.7 Walaya

We find a grave misreading of the term *walaya* in the book. Any student of the various books of Shiʿi scholars on kalam, philosophy, hadith and history would agree that it is immensely difficult to define the concept of walaya in Shiʿism. While we respect the Author's opinions and analyses, they do not reflect the Shiʿi doctrine, despite the genuine belief he and other interpreters have of these doctrinal principles.

The term *walaya* was mentioned in the doctrinal form adopted by Shiʿi scholars in *hadith al-ghadir*, which is a sermon delivered by the Prophet in Ghadir Khumm near al-Juhfa on his journey back to Medina after completing the Farewell Pilgrimage.[32] During this sermon, the Prophet asked his Muslim companions: "Am I not a better guardian to you than you are guardians to yourselves?" To which they answered: "By God, yes!" The Prophet then said: "Whoever has me as his guardian (*mawla*), Ali is his guardian. O God! guard whoever guards him and make an enemy whoever shows enmity to him!"

The term *mawla* appears in the Prophet's talk in reference to the Qur'anic verse "The Prophet is a better guardian to believers than they are guardians to themselves" (al-Ahzab, 6).[33] The verse clarifies the meaning behind the term *mawla* in the hadith.

To further clarify the meaning of walaya, we should examine Islam's views on various powers. When a person reaches adulthood and maturity, she becomes free and independent, with no power set over her own life other than hers. She must obey God's law, conveyed to her by the Prophet, who does not talk here whimsically: "Had he [the Prophet] falsely attributed some statements to Us; We would have seized him by the right arm; Then slashed his lifeline" (al-Haqqa, 44–46).[34]

[32] Hadith al-thaqalayn (see n. 27) was given by the Prophet in a location near Mecca known as Ghadir Khumm. The next section renders a variation on the hadith.

[33] The verse is understandably translated in various forms. We have adapted the translation here to the context. The word *mawla* itself, which, like *wilaya*, derives from the root *waw-lam-ya*ʾ, has a rich polysemic history, including for a long time with reference to slave categories. The text accompanying the previous note combines the Qur'anic verse in al-Ahzab with the hadith al-thaqalayn.

[34] These verses vesting God's message in the Prophet Muhammad in Surat al-Haqqa (The Reality, or Truth) are better understood with the verses preceding them, which the audience would probably recognize as an important Qur'anic topos for both Shiʿis and Sunnis: "40. It is the speech of a noble messenger. 41. And it is not the speech of a poet – little do you believe. 42. Nor is it the speech of a fortune-teller. Little do you reflect. 43. A revelation from the Lord of the Worlds. 44. Had he falsely attributed some statements

The verse "The Prophet is a better guardian to believers than they are guardians to themselves" (al-Ahzab, 6) laid down a new principle, which is the Prophet's authority to educate and guide the believers so that they aim for perfection, for they are God's successors on earth and masters of their own lives. This authority is similar to executive or judicial authority. It is a form of leadership as expressed in the following verse: "In the Messenger of God you have an excellent example" (al-Ahzab, 21), and it is further clarified by the verse "Whatever the Messenger gives you, take it, and whatever he forbids you, leave" (al-Hashr, 7).

The Prophet was given this authority to establish a pious, perfect society, where every individual is provided with livelihood and opportunities for continued development and evolution, and where the proper social environment is the main factor educating and guiding human beings.

The Prophet was given this exclusive authority because of its crucial importance in achieving the aims and objectives of Islam. Only those whom God makes infallible and who are free from reckless emotional behavior deserve to exercise such authority. The wali must possess perfect knowledge of the principles, rules and branches of the law.

The exercise of this authority requires proper enforcement and disciplinary rules in governance and adjudication. This makes the position of wali yet more sensitive and critical.

As described to us in the Islamic chronicles, the Prophet performed these functions after the hijra, and laid down principles and foundations in ways and methods consistent with his divine authority – that is, his authority over believers. It is of benefit for us, in the context of this analysis, to examine how the Prophet did so, for the way he governed sheds light on his teachings and enables us to follow his example.

Accordingly, walaya is a status that complements prophecy, as the Author rightly claims, in the sense that the purpose of divine authority is to enforce the sharia and build a proper Islamic society, an authority only given to the Prophet, the conveyer of God's message, or to the one who follows the Prophet's model scrupulously and becomes the ideal successor.

Conversely, the Author's interpretation that "the walaya is the esoteric aspect of prophecy (*batin al-nubuwwa*)" is unique to him.[35] It is not

to Us. 45. We would have seized him by the right arm. 46. Then slashed his lifeline" (Qur'an 69:40–46). English translation at www.corequran.com/69/#7.

[35] Corbin, *Tārīkh al-falsafa al-islāmiyya*, 89.

recognized by Shiʿism or by Islam generally, notwithstanding that some prominent Sufi scholars or philosophers have adopted this view.

In Shiʿi thought, walaya is a divine authority, and the only reason for its existence is the divine text. It is a status that can be attained only by those who represent the Prophet in their words, their deeds and their thoughts, those whose hearts and intentions have been tested by God, those who abandon their selves and dedicate their lives to God and to Islam, those whose lives reflect every aspect of Islam.

We understand that the special focus on walaya by Imams and scholars in their words and speeches led the Author to explain that walaya is the esoteric aspect of prophecy as well as the truth behind the law, and that the very idea of walaya proves that Shiʿism does not disprove Sufism. The Author also argues that Shiʿism is the only true origin of Sufism and so forth.

In reality, walaya plays a unique role and stands as the highest status in Shiʿism, but it is entirely different from what the Author and the sources he uses claim.

Walaya is the power that allows the divine society ensured by a perfect Muslim education. This education is the primary aim of the Muslim message. Walaya is the sole means to achieve the aim of Islam. That is why the Shiʿi hadith say: "Islam is built upon five [pillars]: prayer, zakat (almsgiving), fasting, hajj (pilgrimage), and walaya; and not one of them was as forcefully proclaimed as walaya."[36]

This hadith supports our reading. It considers walaya a pillar of Islam and a way to ensure the conditions that enable people to practice worship, economics and politics to their fullest extent. Walaya is a duty, and people will be asked about it before all else on Judgment Day. We can even consider walaya to be the primary foundation for all Islamic rules.

The Messenger of God was the incarnation of both prophecy and walaya, but his successors only enjoyed the status of walaya, and they did not have any of the qualities of prophecy (contrary to what the Author claims). The Qur'an emphasizes the unity of God's religion and its gradual revelation through His successive prophets and messengers.

[36] This is a typically Shiʿi hadith, which includes walaya; Sunni hadith mention instead the profession of faith (that there is no god but God, and Muhammad is His slave and messenger) as the first pillar of the faith. Note that the Sunni profession of faith does not mention the Imams.

It considers the Prophet Muhammad to be the final prophet and the culmination of religious revelation. The perfect form of Islam is the set of individual and social laws, which were only practiced after the Prophet's hijra and his assumption of the status of wali [in Medina]. That is why Muslims adopt the hijri calendar to chronicle Islamic history, rather than the day of *mab'ath*, for example.[37] This shows the importance of walaya, which we find expressed in the words and speeches of Shi'i scholars, without exaggeration or interpretation alien to these scholars [such as Corbin's].

The Shi'i scholars' analyses and statements constitute the basis of the Author's conclusions. But the truth is that his conclusions are not found in Twelver Shi'ism in any form. The Twelve Imams are not the recipients of divine revelation, they are not the locus of the angels' visitation, they do not possess the truth behind religious rules and they do not provide the key to the interpretation of symbolic verses or the esoteric aspects of sharia. Their walaya does not constitute the hidden, esoteric aspect and truth of prophecy.

5.8 Sufism and Shi'ism

The Author's views on [the convergence of] Shi'ism and Sufism is odd. Shi'i jurists, scholars and philosophers deny any equivalence between the two worlds.

Sufism is an independent and global school of thought that entered Shi'ism after seeping into the Islamic world as a whole and after pervading Christian doctrines. Sufism nowadays is seen as a way for all religions and sects to be open to one another. It is not specific to Shi'ism, and Sufism finds no foundation or basis in Shi'ism.

Separating sharia and truth is not accepted by any of the major Muslim groups. Sharia in Islam is the absolute and divine truth: "Seeking a way outside Islam will not be accepted" (Al 'Imran, 85). The proposition that prominent Sufi scholars and successive *qutb*s ["poles"] are connected to certain Shi'i Imams, and that others such as Imam Muhammad al-Jawad, known as al-Taqi ["the pious"], are leaders of sharia but not Imams or poles for the truth, only represents the view of their proponents.

[37] *Mab'ath* is the first revelation and commencement of the Prophetic mission.

This duality of sharia and truth is but a reflection of the duality of mind and body, which is a main pillar of Sufism. One consequence of this duality is Sufi disregard of the body and its energy in favor of strengthening the soul and allowing it to strive for perfection. In reality, Islam values the human body and considers it to be a blessing from God; it prohibits monasticism, calls for the unity and interaction between mind and body and makes analogies between the ephemeral world and the afterlife.

God is worshipped in the mihrab of the mosque, in the market, in administrative offices, in agricultural fields and by practicing jihad, maintaining peace, working hard for one's family, being devoted to one's spouse and properly raising one's children. Those who die defending their livelihood are considered martyrs, just as those who die defending their religion.

Bodily needs and natural desires are manifestations of God's blessings and kindness; we must therefore take care of our bodies by avoiding sin and by thanking God for His blessings. Islamic morality wants us to thank God while enjoying our food, drink and other bodily pleasures. The performance of Islamic teachings on marriage, commerce and agriculture is considered a noble form of worship.

These rules and morals cannot be found in Sufism, which opposes mind and body and urges people to suppress their bodily desires and cravings with every fiber of their being.

5.9 Qutb: "The Pole"

The concepts of Imam and wali in Twelver Shiism are completely opposed to the concept of qutb in Sufism. As previously mentioned, the Imam is the perfect role model, and the wali is the ruler; these two concepts carry profound meanings, far-reaching impacts and significant importance.

The term *qutb* in the temporal sense in Sufism refers to the mentor who guides the seeker step by step on an arduous journey filled with perils to eventually reach human perfection. The qutb – who is the perfect human being – undertakes this process through his supporters and assistants, and he walks that path alongside them.

In the cosmic sense, the Sufi qutb refers to the perfect human, the Imam of the age, the reflection of the Prophet and of the Divine. The seeker sees the qutb as a mediator between God and humans as expressed in the verse "You alone we worship and You alone we ask for help" (al-Fatiha, 5). He is a true reflection of the Divine.

These two meanings are very different from the concepts of Imam and wali and their roles (both in terms of their methods and their aims) [in Shiʿism]. There is no truth hidden behind the sharia, nor are there journeys specific to the seeker of truth; there is no direct leadership, nor are there manifestations and reflections of the divine [vesting in leadership].

Shiʿism does not only oppose the methods and behaviors of Sufis; the disagreement runs much deeper, as the two schools have entirely different visions, and the roles of their leaders are very dissimilar.

Some Shiʿi Sufis believe that their qutb is the Imam of their age, and they believe in qualified Mahdism.[38] This is consistent with their general view that the Imams, from Ali b. Abi Talib to Ali b. Musa al-Rida, are Imams of the sharia as well as qutbs of the Sufi way (*tariqa*). This interpretation is deeply rooted in their view of the Imam.

5.10 The Hidden Imam

The role of the Hidden Imam,[39] which, according to the Author, the concept of the Sufi qutb has surpassed, should be more closely considered. This is needed especially since the Author links this role to the esoteric aspects of Shiʿism, and claims that Shiʿis await the revelation of the truth, rather than the advent of a new prophet – that is, they await the advent of a ruler (wali) who reveals the truth behind all religious rules. The Author also claims that the idea of the Hidden Imam refers to the concept of the unseen guide who will lead the nation and reveal the truth.

In order to determine whether the Author's conclusions are valid and to clarify the differences between Twelver Shiʿism and Ismailism, as well as between the Hidden Imam and the Sufi qutb, we must clarify the concept of the Hidden Imam according to Twelver Shiʿism.[40]

[38] The missing Imam is also known as the *mahdi* (literally, "the guided one"). Mahdism is a belief often shared by both Sunnis and Shiʿis, but the Shiʿi Twelvers limit it to the Twelve Imams of their tradition.

[39] *Imam ghaʾib*, variously translated as the occulted or vanished Imam.

[40] Ismailis were originally Shiʿis, but they differ with the Twelvers theologically in their belief in seven Imams, the last being Ismaʿil, the older son of the sixth Imam, Jaʿfar al-Sadeq. Twelver Shiʿis believe that the successor to Jaʿfar al-Sadeq was his second son,

The idea of the Hidden Imam refers to the appearance of the perfect reformer who heralds the ultimate ordering of reality and prepares humans to reach perfection by establishing a perfect society, governed by a perfect system where justice reigns supreme. This would enable people to reach the zenith of knowledge, the utmost quality of life and the most accomplished human interaction. The basis of this idea is the instinctive drive toward improvement in all fields of knowledge and all aspects of life, which propels human beings forward on the journey toward progress and perfection. That is why humans might experience drawbacks, but they inevitably recover and continue their forward motion even after decades or more of deterioration.

Knowledge is constant progress. People accumulate information and experiments and use them to establish new laws that further expand their knowledge. Knowledge grows in all its aspects and enables humans to progress consistently.

Perhaps the heritage left behind for humans by most religions has inspired them to anticipate the coming of the perfect reformer who will restore what is right and fully implement the teachings of the prophets.

Several verses of the Qur'an make reference to the future: "Surely, following the heavenly record, which We decreed in the scriptures: 'My righteous servants shall inherit the land'" (al-Anbiya', 105); "God has promised those of you who believe and do good that He will certainly make them successors on earth, as He did with those before them; and will establish for them the faith which He has chosen for them; and change their fear into security – provided that they worship Me, associating nothing with Me" (al-Nur, 55).

Despite some inconsistencies, the Sunna also refers to the advent of the perfect reformer who will fully apply the teachings of Islam, fill the earth with justice and fairness and rid it from all oppression and tyranny.

Based on such evidence, Muslims believe in the concept of the Hidden Imam, who heralds this new and perfect world. Where humans fail and recognize the fruitlessness of their methods, they expect a world where they can find peace in all aspects of their life. This anticipation facilitates the task of the Imam, whose calling (*da'wa*) will more easily succeed against people's destructive powers and deadly weaponry.

Musa al-Kazem. Ismailis follow the leadership of a descendant of al-Kazem, and their leader is known in modern times as the Aga Khan.

According to Shiʿis, the Hidden Imam is one of the Twelve Imams; he is their final link, and together they constitute one ray of light and bear one message. His role is to implement what his predecessors preached in furtherance of the message of the Prophet. Without prejudice to what we noted regarding the concept of the Imam-ruler, this role consists in giving an opinion on religious matters and clarifying religious teachings, rather than revealing the esoteric aspects of religious rules.

That is the role of the expected Imam in the future. As for his role during his occultation (*ghayba*), it consists of maintaining religious rules and preventing the formation of a consensus at the expense of the truth.[41] By disagreeing with other fatwas, he manages to prevent the emergence of a wrong consensus and a failed jurisprudence. The difficulties that jurisprudence encounters when faced with modern events and developments are evidence of this important role. This disagreement is not contingent on the knowledge of the Hidden Imam or on his reputation. Much has been written about this in books of jurisprudence (*al-kutub al-usuliyya*) and in opinions on the validity of consensus during the age of occultation.

In Shiʿism, the awaited Imam is one person, rather than an all-inclusive concept, and therefore the nomenclature cannot apply to the qutb in every age. The role of the awaited Imam is different from the qutb's. It does not consist of revealing hidden truths or esoteric aspects; rather, his role is to apply Islamic rules through God's successors on earth.[42]

5.11 On the Esoteric Principle

The Author states problematically his view that "Islamic esotericism possibly does not contain a single theme that was not mentioned or initiated by the Shiʿi Imams, in sermons or scholarship."[43]

It is true that some hadith books by Shiʿi and other scholars express belief in esoteric principles. While they overstate a given issue, any fair examiner of such books and statements and their sources would realize

[41] Consensus here is the ijmaʿ attributed to Sunnis.

[42] This is where the thought of Sadr appears as a precursor of *wilayat al-faqih*, established by the Islamic Revolution and at the heart of the Constitution of Iran since 1980. Of note, however, is that he also refers in this section to the role of the scholar in "maintaining religious rules and preventing the formation of a consensus at the expense of the truth."

[43] Corbin, *Tārīkh*, 72.

that they are invalid and poorly referenced. For example, many of the hadiths in *Kitab al-kafi*, which is the most important Shiʿi hadith collection, are criticized and put into question by Muhammad Baqer al-Majlisi in *Mirʾat al-ʿuqul*.[44] Other books of biographies[45] by prominent scholars also criticize these sources and question the chains of transmission in *Kitab al-kafi* and in other important hadith collections. The reader should therefore rest assured that several of the hadiths quoted [by the Author] are fabricated.

Perhaps the most obvious of these fabricated hadiths are those analyzing the number of the Twelve Imams, claiming that the number twelve was selected for being that of the towers of heaven, the number of months or the number of springs that Moses produced with his staff. Those who read the many books that criticized *Kitab al-kafi* and other well-known books will agree that such claims are mere fabrications.[46]

[44] The *Kafi* is by Kulayni (see n. 22). Majlisi (d. 1699) wrote an encyclopedic critical assessment of Kulayni's *Kafi*. It is available in twenty-six volumes in the modern edition, *Mirʾāt al-ʿuqūl fī sharḥ akhbār al-rasūl* (Tehran: Dār al-Kutub al-Islāmiyya, 1989).

[45] The biographical genre of legal scholars is known as *kutub al-rijal*, more generally *tabaqat*.

[46] The text stops here somewhat abruptly. One would have expected Sadr to have given examples of the "fabricated" hadiths and their misuse by Corbin. Missing also is a conclusion to his elaborate review of Corbin's book, where both Sadr's high praise and heady criticism for Corbin's "esoteric" approach to Shiʿi philosophers would have been brought together.

Part II
Social and Economic Values

6

The Social Dimensions of Islam

Before starting the lecture,[1] I wish to thank the Muslim Students' Association in Dakar, which has generously undertaken to arrange this meeting, and to express my gratitude for the generosity of the university in facilitating our gathering. Thanks also to the Senegalese authorities, who provided us with the means to invest energy and bring our efforts to fruition in cultural meetings with our brothers in the local community [Lebanese expatriates in Senegal] along with our Senegalese brothers over this period, for which this evening is for me the grand finale, or the "icing on the cake," in Arabic *misk al-khitam*.[2]

At the beginning of this lecture, we should answer one question: Why is Islam concerned with social issues, and why does it concern itself with society? Is it not possible for Islam to conserve its energies, simply to offer teachings on, and understandings of, faith, morality and the individual? Would it not be better for Islam to content itself with the upbringing and education of the individual, without becoming involved in broader social affairs?

6.1 Individual and Society

The answer to this question is that, if we want the truth, we find that the individual clearly influences and is influenced by society, that the

[1] Lecture delivered in Dakar, Senegal, on May 15, 1967. In this talk, Musa Sadr thanks in the last section (reference here removed) Nimer Sabbah, professor of Arabic language and literature at Dakar University, who helped with arrangements for the visit. Sadr meets during the visit the president of Senegal, poet and statesman Léopold Senghor.

[2] Literally, "an ending in musk." Reflecting the great value placed on musk as a scent in Arabic culture, the expression denotes ending an event with something, or with a person, greatly valued. There is a reference to musk in paradise, in the Qur'an: "They shall be given pure nectar to drink, securely sealed, whose very dregs are musk; for this let all men emulously strive" (83:25–26).

individual is an integral part of his or her society. The human being in her makeup, in her life, in her culture, in her needs, in almost everything, is part of her society, and she is influenced by her society. We cannot care about an individual's reality[3] and ignore the state of society. We cannot devise a comprehensive plan for the individual and her education and then let her live in a society that is not commensurate with our teachings and our planning. If we want the individual to be a decent and upright believer, we cannot ignore society. Islam recognizes this in the words of the Prophet: "I was sent to attain the highest nobility of character."[4] Is it possible to maintain and preserve the highest nobility of an individual's character and let her live in a society that is incompatible with such ethics, faith and noble acts? Definitely not.

We do not need an investigation to establish the impact of society on individual human beings. Islam, which seeks to educate and edify the individual, strives to create for this individual a society that is consonant with the individual's upbringing, faith, ethics and deeds. This is the reason for Islam's concern with the affairs of society.

6.2 What Is Society? How Does Society Take Shape?

There is no doubt that society consists of individuals, but is the existence of individuals sufficient to form societies? Not at all.

If we assume 1,000 people without any kind of interaction, no giving and taking, no selling or buying – no exchange between them – then there is no society. The formation of society is based upon there being individuals who interact and exchange their work, their skills and abilities, one with another. When a person gives and takes, and so does another, and then a third . . . and so on, society takes shape. Short of this, it does not take shape. Therefore, the formation of society depends upon exchange. How does exchange between members of the society come about? It occurs for one of three reasons.

The first reason is disparity in abilities. Just as human beings are physically different from one another, human beings differ in their psychological makeup, in their inclinations, in their aptitudes and talents.

[3] *Wad'*, station, position.

[4] This is a hadith reported by several tradents. See, e.g., https://dorar.net/hadith/sharh/113995. "Highest nobility of character," *makarim al-akhlak*, refers both to ethics and manners. It is also the title of a prayer by Imam Zayn al-'Abidin (d. 713), the fourth Imam for the Shi'i Twelvers.

Disparity among human beings makes for a flow of reciprocity between individuals. As an analogy, if you compare two cups of water, one cold and the other warm,[5] when the two are mixed the colder water immediately takes in heat from the warmer water, and the warm water absorbs coldness from the cold water – so that a reciprocal flow obtains. In contrast, if we suppose the two waters each have the same levels, there would be no exchange and no flow between them. Flow indicates exchange, the give and take that is the basis of the formation of societies, and it arises from differences in individuals' abilities or qualifications. This, then, is the first reason.

The second reason is that humans have goals, interests and aims that are greater than those of the individual. The individual alone cannot reach those goals nor fulfill these interests, and needs to cooperate with others to develop the necessary strength and capacity.

The third reason is that human beings confront dangers, enemies and difficulties that are stronger than their individual energies. Alone and without cooperating with others, individuals cannot overcome these difficulties, fight adversaries and defend themselves.

These three factors – the disparity in abilities; goals and interests beyond the individual's capacity; and some losses and disadvantages being greater than the individual's capacity – require people to form societies and communities. All three factors have been innate to humankind since creation. Therefore, civilization[6] is the outcome of the human desire to form societies, a desire that is natural and inherent in humankind. The widespread view that human beings are by nature *civil* beings derives, as I understand it, from these three reasons, and there may be others.

This brings me to the following point: the desire and feeling to form societies, that is, the desire and feeling of wanting to give and to receive, the desire to fulfill obligations and duties toward others, and the enjoyment of having rights and obligations fulfilled by others, this is what we call "civic feeling." It is innate, inherent and natural in human beings.

[5] The original Arabic says "sweet" instead of "cold," obviously an editorial mistake.

[6] *Madaniyya*, which comes from *madina* (town) and is the style of living of the town. "Civilization" is often translated into Arabic as *hadara*, while the English "civilization" is often equated with the onset of writing. Writing did begin in urban societies; see Stephen Bourke, *The Middle East: The Cradle of Civilization* (London: Thames & Hudson, 2018). But the root of "civilization" in Latin is linked to citizenship and to citizens (*civis*) having rights.

When Islam comes to this feeling it tries to make it more profound by approaching it philosophically.

6.3 The Authenticity of Society

First: these feelings exist in humankind, but Islam philosophizes them to deepen them, to nourish them within the human soul. Secondly: Islam sanctifies these feelings and gives them a sheen of holiness, rendering them even more beautiful. Third: Islam consecrates these feelings by setting guidelines and yardsticks, defining broad and diverse forms of religious societies.

Let us look into the three above points. These feelings exist in humanity. How does Islam deepen them? How does it sanctify them? How does it consecrate them?

As an example of deepening the feelings, when we want to raise our children, we may tell them not to lie, that is, we may address our children with words to forbid them from doing something. This is a superficial kind of education. But if we draw on our wider philosophy, then we are explaining that we should not lie because lying is ugly. This kind of education will go deeper, and we may help create a healthy atmosphere in which our children do not need to lie and feel alienated if they do. This kind of education is deeper and stronger.

We return to our conversation to see how Islam deepens the sense of the human being's role in forming societies. Islam does not just say to people, "Be faithful in your obligations, take and give, just keep the trust!" Rather, Islam tries to give the human being a clear picture of the universe in which humankind lives and says to people: "This universe in which you live, which is your environment and which has the most powerful effect on you, this universe is highly organized, and everything in it, each part of the universe, performs its cosmic role meticulously and masterfully. Therefore, if you want to live in such an atmosphere and in harmony with this universe, you should be organized and precise, you should be meticulously faithful in carrying out your obligations."

We find in the Qur'an this verse: "He raised the heaven on high and set the balance of all things."[7]

[7] "He raised the heaven on high and set the balance of all things, that you might not transgress that balance. Give just weight and full measure" (Qur'an 55:7–9).

What balance is this? True balance means justice in creation, and precision in manufacture.

Then, also from the Book: "who has created all things and gave them due proportion."[8] So, everything is precise, firm and orderly: "He raised the heaven on high and set the balance." Why? "So that you might not transgress that balance."

I say to you that the universe is organized in this fine balance, leading to trust, that is to say: human beings living in this universe weigh finely in the balance, they should not disrupt it; that is, they will not give less than they take, and they will not find themselves unjust in the order of things. The way to deepen this sense in Islam is to understand that the universe is organized, the universe gives, the universe is delicate. You, human beings, if you wish to be in harmony with this universe, you must act delicately. Religion creates depth for humankind, such that humans feel the obligation to fulfill trust and reach to heaven from earth. There is no superficial demand or formality here, but work based on these deep roots. This is how religion brings to humankind a deep sense that it must perform its duties and obligations, and exercise its rights, in the formation of society, as we have explained.

Secondly, Islam tries to sanctify this emotion, this human feeling, for civility and civilized behavior in society, for a sense of rights and obligations, of give and take. How does it sanctify this feeling and make it glow with holiness? In several ways.

The first way is to acknowledge that giving in Islam is part of one's religious duties. At the outset in the Qur'an we read in al-Baqara of what it means to be "pious" as "a guide for the righteous."[9] Who are the pious? The Qur'an describes them as those who meet five criteria:[10] "those who believe in the unseen" is first; "those steadfast in prayer" is the second; "those who give in alms from what We gave them" is the third; "those who believe in what has been revealed to you and what was revealed before you" is the fourth; and "those who have absolute faith in the life to come" is the fifth.

[8] "Praise the Name of your Lord, the Most High, who has created all things and gave them due proportions, who has ordained their destinies and guided them, who brings forth the green pasture, then turns it into withered grass" (Qur'an 87:1–5).

[9] "This Book is not to be doubted. It is a guide for righteous" (Qur'an 2:2).

[10] Musa Sadr cites the five criteria from Qur'an 2:3–4.

The third principle does not mean paying money, but more broadly "spending" what God has provided as sustenance by *giving*. Therefore, the pious believer is one who gives her knowledge, her standing and fame, her expertise, her competence, everything generally.

The person who gives is pious, and so giving – which forms societies – is an element of piety. Social activities, and the performance of social obligations, are inherently religious duties. Let us clarify that *spending* in this sense, as an expression of *giving*, is quite different from an expression of *charity*.[11] Spending in the sense of giving is the term used for what a husband gives his wife, and this is her right; it is in no way a question of generosity: it is a performance of his duty. In this way, giving in Islam takes on the glow of religious duty and the glow of holiness. What the individual gives to society is effectively the rights that society expects of the individual, while the individual at the same time exercises her rights within society; in effect the individual is returning rights to society. We can express and fulfill all these duties in terms of honoring trust, meaning giving all people their undiminished and full rights. The pious Muslim fulfills all duties, and that means fulfilling the trust in what Islam places in her.

We can therefore express the act of giving, the cornerstone of the formation of societies, by fulfilling trust in Islam, and thereby return to the meaning of "trusts" as sanctity and holiness; this is performance of the creed, in all of its beauty and distinctive benefit to humankind. And we then come to understand the meaning of the verse:

> We offered Our trust to the heavens, to the earth, and to the mountains, but they refused the burden and were afraid to receive it. Man undertook to bear it, but he has proved a sinner and a fool.[12]

Man is the only creature who has managed to carry out and perform the trust. And here we come to a second point, namely, to explain the cosmic role played by the sun, the moon and other parts of the universe that are described in the Qur'an as performing prostration, praises and

[11] *Sadaqa* is linked by its Arabic root to *sidq*, "to tell the truth." *Sadāqa* is friendship, but carries an Islamic connotation of giving to the less well-off in order to be close to God (to be a friend of God). The English word "charity" is rooted in *caritas/carus* (Latin, "loved," "dear") but has become almost synonymous with almsgiving. Sadr is talking about giving as something that creates and develops society, not just as an expression of individual goodwill or satisfaction.

[12] Qur'an 33:72.

prayer – while the role of other [nonhuman] creations is not expressed in terms of trust.

Trust is a choice. Humankind performs these duties entirely voluntarily, while the sun, the moon and all other parts of the universe perform duties due to their nature, and not voluntarily, not through exertion of will. They are led to carrying out obligations. Only humankind has free choice, and that is the implementation of the trust given expression by humankind alone.

Human giving, the act of spending, is part of the five characteristics of the pious in proving themselves worthy of the trust. Showing yourself worthy of the trust is a duty, as we find reflected in common expressions and words that shine with the tenderness of holiness. In religious exegesis books[13] we find the saying "All of creation are the children of God, and the most favored of God are those who are most beneficial to His children."[14] Giving to society is beneficial to God's children and brings one closer to God. With these words we underscore what we have already briefly mentioned: Islam sanctifies social ties; it considers them sacred and attending to them a form of worship.

Thirdly, when Islam consecrates these ties and links, it establishes ways of measuring them: this is explicitly stated in the teachings of Islam. We may here mention a few examples; there is no room for detail. Religion has diverse fields such as:

1. The field of culture: the concepts that Islam offers, including explanations given by religion.
2. The field of belief: belief in God, in the Day of Judgment and in prophecy.
3. The field of judgments: this means duties and prohibitions, obligations and prohibitions, what is correct and what is corrupt or decayed, what is permissible and what is not permissible.
4. The field of virtues.[15]

So, we have four major domains, and the consecration of social connections is clear in all four.

[13] Tafsir, "interpretation," the Qur'anic commentary genre.

[14] Hadith related, e.g., at https://bit.ly/46gWB88.

[15] *Akhlaq* – "morals" or "virtues." The third area Musa Sadr cites is what would usually in English be regarded as (religiously based) precepts or rules, and the fourth area personal virtues. "Ethics," as generally understood in the English context, would cover both in the sense that they are prescriptive.

In term of concepts, we look at Islam's interpretation of society and find it saying: "The believers are a band of brothers."[16] Islam considers members of society to be brothers and sisters. It seeks to bestow compassion, and emotional and logical connections, among the members of society. It then expands this interpretation beyond brotherhood and says: "Believers are like one body: if one part is suffering all the other parts become afflicted, feverish and watchful."[17] The parts and members of society are parts of a single body. This meaning appears in many Qur'anic verses that express individuals as "a part" or as "some people." You know that in logical terms there is a difference between "part" and the individual; "part" denotes a piece of a thing, and "individual" is a complete individual. This reflects in teachings on "wealth" or "your wealth": "Do not consume your wealth among yourselves in vanity, but rather trade with it by mutual consent."[18] This means that all wealth, or "your" wealth, is considered part of the wealth of society as a whole. [When we read in the Qur'an,] "Fulfill your contracts," they are considered as a single entity with multiple parts. Islam's interpretation of society, and the understanding it conveys of society – in the cultural field – is that of brethren in a single body.

In faith and belief, Islam commands diligent exercise of reason[19] in the fundamentals of religion. It means that Muslims know the unity of God through proof and logic. Just having faith is not enough. Why insist on the exercise of reason, and expect us to know and understand religious principles as deeply as possible? Islam expects such understanding so that we really live our faith!

[You may ask:] What's the benefit of this?

Believing in one God means that all creation is one, as He has no child, no father, no equal, no cousin, no one who is like Him in His mercy. Consequently, all human beings are as equal as the teeth of a comb.[20] When all human beings are equal, it is easier for them to cooperate

[16] Qur'an 49:10.

[17] This is a well-known hadith in both the Sunni and Shi'i traditions, related by Bukhari (d. 870) and others; see, e.g., https://dorar.net/hadith/sharh/4340.

[18] Qur'an 4:29.

[19] Ijtihad, "effort," literally, "the act of making an effort" or "sustaining an effort," but used to mean the exercise of reason. The word *ijtihad* is often reserved for the reasoning of someone religiously qualified, a mujtahid, but Musa Sadr is here saying it is the duty of every Muslim.

[20] This reference to equality among human beings "like the teeth of a comb" comes from a well-known hadith; see, e.g., https://dorar.net/h/a299eb2d7392665bf974bf861846e797?sims=1.

because there is no one who ranks above the other or who is richer than another, impeding cooperation or making it impossible; instead, each individual is in need of other individuals. Our recognition that all human beings are equal facilitates giving and receiving, and the range of cooperation. There is no one who is simply wealthy, or who is simply poor: everyone is rich in some ways and poor in others, and so must give and take.

On the other hand, if we were to believe, and say to ourselves, that some people are dispensable for others, it becomes difficult to cooperate. Among human beings there is no saint immune from error; every individual is susceptible to making mistakes, and therefore needs counsel. This is something that consecrates intellectual cooperation and exchange among human beings. Human beings need intellectual collaboration and mutual care. This follows from our recognition that all human beings are equal. Then, once we agree that the one God is the source of all our actions and our initiatives, there arises something of a unity in our principles, and our actions come into harmony to facilitate cooperation among human beings.

This concept is enshrined in several texts. God is one and the Creator of all. Human beings and humanity are all from one father and one mother; they are brothers and their destiny is shared: "Say: 'We belong to God and to Him we shall return.'"[21] Roots, destiny and path are all one. This facilitates cooperation, coordination and the formation of human society. There is no disparity in, or advantage to, a person's offspring: there may be a disparity in competence, but this is not a disparity between their *selves*.

On this occasion, I would like to remind my brothers of a well-known saying. One might claim, looking into the Qur'an, that there is superiority for some human beings:

> It is they who apportion your Lord's blessings? It is We who deal out to them their livelihood in this world, exalting some in rank above others, so that the one may take the other into his service. Better is your Lord's mercy than all their hoarded treasures.[22]

Some say that Islam recognizes the superiority of some human beings to others, which contradicts the saying that "people are equal and like the teeth of a comb."

[21] Qur'an 2:156. [22] Qur'an 43:32.

If we consider the meaning of the verse and its interpretations, we find it does not consecrate differences among people or assert the superiority of some people over others, but rather focuses on differences in their talents. Every person in his or her specialization can be superior to others: the doctor in his practice of medicine ranks above the patient; the religious cleric within his area of competence ranks above the supplicant; and the engineer in his specialty ranks above less expert colleagues. The doctor in his or her superiority within his specialty leads others, and others follow his or her lead in this field. However, the same doctor who leads me in his specialty is led by me in mine, and both of us follow the lead of the engineer in his or her specialization. The three of us are guided by the lawyer in his jurisdiction. The four of us follow the lead of the merchant or the farmer in their particular areas of specialization. Therefore, some are raised above others in their specialities "so that the one may take the other into his service." This is the meaning of disparity in expert competence.

Humans are therefore equal like the teeth of a comb, while disparities in competence facilitate and sanctify further cooperation among members of society, as well as faith in God's justice and perfection.

"In the name of God, the Merciful, the Compassionate." God is the summation of the attributes of perfection. God is merciful, benevolent, friendly, just, knowing, beloved. He created us in His image and that is why we have some of His traits reflected in us; this is normal. There is a harmony between cause and effect, and there is a proportionality between them. The effect always takes the shape of the cause. This consecrates a second principle: humankind is in itself good, good by nature. There is no vile or wicked person in humanity who cannot be reformed and cooperated with. If such a person were to be found it would be an aberration in God's creation. This makes it easier for people to cooperate and allows God to extend His hand to every human being in order to cooperate with them: "the upright faith that God created for mankind to embrace."[23]

Belief in the one God and faith in the justice of the Creator facilitates cooperation, while faith in the hereafter and the Day of Judgment brings a person to feel responsibility and to shoulder religious duties toward society, giving freely and unstintingly. Culture provides this beautiful

[23] Qur'an 30:30.

concept of society, and faith consecrates means suitable to the creation of society.

In the field of rules,[24] we find that much research has been undertaken in social affairs. In reviewing their findings on the formation of societies, we can see how much Islam consecrates relationships. In the family, Islam sanctifies the ties between husband and wife, considering them sacred duties par excellence. Islam considers the building of marriage better than the construction of a mosque, and the demolition of marriage, or shortcoming in performing the duties it requires, to be more wayward than any deficiency in building mosques. Ties between husband and wife are strong and sacred links.

Islam also sanctifies relations between children and parents. So consecrated, they are duties associated with obedience to God. There are dozens of Qur'anic verses reminding us of the importance of honoring and respecting parents, [placed only] after obedience to God. Honor and respect are due to husband and wife, children and parents, and to the womb itself. Rupture of the womb and its ties [family relationships] is prohibited, and the prohibition strengthens ties between families.

Then we come to the domain of the neighbor, where Islam commends and affirms the value of neighborliness. As Ali observed, "the Prophet commended our neighbors to us so persistently that we almost thought that neighbors could be our heirs."[25] And Ali's commendation of neighbors is no less than his commendation of blood kinships: "There are forty houses between you and your neighbor,"[26] meaning you are in an entire country composed of neighbors – and so he seeks for us to consolidate and strengthen these links. Then he says in his directives that the responsibility of the people of one country is shared. If someone dies in a town or a country from poverty, hunger or disease, God will not take care of the people of this town or country. Every individual has a binding duty to other individuals from his own country and cannot fail in

[24] Rulings, judgments, *ahkam*. Musa al-Sadr was a jurist, trained both in classical law in the seminaries (hawza) of Qom and Najaf, and in modern law at the School of Law at the University of Tehran. He was attuned to jurisprudence, understood both as classical law (fiqh) principles and modern statutes and court decisions (ahkam).

[25] In the Sunni tradition, this is attributed to the angel Gabriel; see www.dorar.net/hadith/sharh/4089.

[26] The forty houses reference is to a hadith; see, e.g., al-Ḥurr al-ʿĀmilī (d. 1693), *Wasāʾil al-Shīʿa* (Beirut: Muʾassasat Āl al-Bayt li-l-Turāth, 1993), 12:132.

fulfilling it: "No one who believes in God and the Last Day can remain satiated while his neighbor goes hungry."[27] The mutual and reciprocal ties between members of the community and society are strongly consecrated. This is intensified and enhanced by prohibiting seclusion or concealing oneself from others, just as maltreatment, injustice, abandonment and slander are prohibited, along with everything else that weakens social ties and creates a distance between people.

As for acts of worship, you will find that Islam takes absolute care of each act and gives all of them a social aspect. You may be aware that prayer, when first commanded in revelation, was a communal, collective prayer. Only later were Muslims allowed to pray individually. Prayer by its nature is performed in a group and all the Muslims face in one direction, the qibla,[28] synchronizing the prayer and bestowing it, with its single time and single qibla, with a social status – where the time of prayer is one, the qibla is one and the preferred place of prayer is the mosque. And of course, fasting in Ramadan is a social occasion.

The hajj,[29] as you know, involves thousands of people performing a special act of worship and wearing the same kind of garment, moving in one movement, at one time and within a unified pattern and shape. How beautiful and how social this worship is!

Zakat,[30] in all its aspects, is also a social duty. Zakat is different from government taxes imposed by Islamic states in their day. Zakat and charity, as evidenced in the holy verses, are duties that have been specified to solve the problem of economic class differences, not to replenish state coffers or fund state employees and other works, but to bring classes closer materially to each other, in ways appropriate to the age.

The promotion of virtue and the prevention of vice are the two basic foundations for social cooperation, social security and solidarity among

[27] A well-known hadith; see, e.g., https://dorar.net/hadith/sharh/135234.

[28] The qibla is the direction of the ritual prayer (salat) toward the Kaaba in Mecca, and is usually marked in a mosque by the mihrab ("prayer niche").

[29] Hajj is literally "pilgrimage," but is often meant to be the "greater pilgrimage" of Muslims to Mecca, one of the five pillars of Islam. It is a duty that all adults are required to undertake once in their lifetime, and is carried out in the month of Dhu al-Hijja.

[30] Zakat is generally translated into English as "mandatory charitable contribution." Musa Sadr has already made clear in the lecture that such giving should not be seen simply as "charity" but rather as a part of exchange between individuals that both enriches them and creates society. The Arabic noun is derived from the verb *zaka*, which is to thrive, or to be wholesome. For Sadr, the process is simultaneously individual and collective, spiritual and material, religious and social.

society's members. "All of you are shepherds and you are all responsible for your flock."[31] We could look here also more extensively into [social aspects of] acts of worship, [but] we cannot, as time is short.

The fourth domain is ethics. After covering culture, faith and jurisprudence, we come to the field of ethics, or morality. In ethics, there are vast provisions, recurrent teachings that create a broad sensibility in humankind, and a sense that the human being is greater than him or herself. In its moral teachings, Islam seeks to suggest to individuals that they are not alone, that they are part of the group – and this is enshrined in Islam's moral teachings. Ethics makes it easier for individuals to cooperate with each other. We cannot go into all the varieties and aspects of ethics in a single lecture, but we can briefly review some of the main headings.

Sublime virtues fall under headings such as these: love for people; generosity; humility; good faith (trust); flexibility; sincerity and truthfulness; assisting the weak; teaching the mute; deference to elders; mercy toward the lowly; propagating peace; joyfulness in one's face; concealing one's sadness; visiting the ill; politeness and decorum in public; showing appreciation for the righteous; rebuking the corrupt; modesty; forgiveness; acceptance of apology; acceptance of sacrifice; serving the companion; helping the hard of hearing to hear without agitation; gathering large number of people for discussions . . .[32] and there are a thousand more examples like this. Each example strengthens the human feeling of empathy and the sense of the sublime. It facilitates cooperation, love and the strengthening of social ties between people.

If we wanted to go into the details of rules (*akham*) governing social affairs,[33] we would have to reference half of Islamic jurisprudence, which includes sections on commerce and politics that make up at least half of the legal field, if not more, all devoted to organizing and defining different matters: personal status, civil laws and the like. This needs many more lectures, but I must mention here a few points:

31 Hadith reported by several early tradents; see www.dorar.net/hadith/sharh/66037/.

32 The word *majlis*, translated as "council" or "parliament," derives from the Arabic "to sit," as invariably such discussions were conducted while sitting. The English "parliament" has its root in the French word for "talking." Sadr seems to have a preference for the parliamentary system.

33 Musa Sadr here suggests ethics shape jurisprudence, implying the ethics come first, thereby taking a position within Islamic jurisprudence that would align him, in the debate, going back many centuries and well beyond Islam, between "ethicists" and positivists.

Islam deepens, sanctifies and consecrates civic feeling in human beings; Islam tries to convey an idea about society to the individual. It seeks to show people that society is their own creation and not something imposed from the outside, and this point is fundamental. If people feel that they fashion and develop society they will be able to give and take as needed, according to an organized plan. This is seen in several Qur'anic verses:

> God does not change a people's lot unless they change what is in their hearts.[34]

> Corruption has become rife on land and sea in consequence of man's misdeeds.[35]

We find here a consecration of the idea that what you see in society is the result of systems, and these systems are products created by your own hands, by your leave – they are your creation. After God gives them aspects of holiness, profundity and consecration, He bestows the potential to fashion these through education to create the desired society. A person then does not consider that this system is something God wanted and imposed on themself and on others, simply to obey and be submissive. Not at all! There is no trace of this in Islam.

6.4 Islam and Development

The last point is the answer to a question that we often hear about Islam wanting to safeguard the individual while caring for the community, for which it lays out broad guidelines in the organization of society. The question is: How does Islam provide guidelines in caring for development?

Societies, as we know, evolve according to the development of human beings, according to the ascendant level of human culture. How can a religion provide consistent, fixed teachings consistent with the development of societies?

Before answering the question, we must ask, What is development? Does development consist of creating something new in the world, or extinguishing something existing in the universe? No. Nothing is created and nothing is extinguished. Development is the interaction between

[34] Qur'an 13:11. [35] Qur'an 30:41.

human beings and the world. Human beings experiment, read and think, and then go on to discover something new. By building on this discovery, human beings can develop their lives and societies. The discovery and harnessing of electricity helped develop human society.

Development is a new interaction, or continuous interaction, between humankind and the world. Nothing new is brought into the world. There are new interactions, new readings of the universe, a more profound examination of the book of the universe. This is development, and evolution. Islam considers the Qur'an to be the word of God, whose words and culture are unlimited. God's culture is not defined by any one age or era, or by one century rather than another. For God knows everything, the depths of things, their outward and inner aspects, their appearance and their hidden interior, information regarding humanity in the past centuries and in the centuries to come. God most exalted and most sublime knows everything. When we realize that culture, once given due expression, is limitless, we understand in every age something new from the word of God, as we continuously come to understand something new in the same universe. Has the universe changed today from the universe as it was 1,000 or 5,000 years ago? The universe remains the same universe, but you have studied it further and deepened your understanding of it in a new way. It is the same with the Qur'an, the word of God: you are entitled to go into it as much as you can. Yesterday you understood something from the Qur'an and today you will understand something else. You can go deeper into the word of God as you deepen your understanding of the universe. So, we have three factors, the first two being humankind and the universe through whose interaction societies develop.

We have a third element, the word of God. You can interact with the word of God just as you interact with the universe, in harmonious coordination between you, your universe, the development of your communities and God's word. I do not wish to go into specific examples of various new kinds of understanding of the word of God, because it is a vast domain and would take too long. Islam can give broad instructions and guidelines for the formation of societies, and within this framework you develop and understand new things, in light of your culture and the development of your experience, until you discover new branches of knowledge and details of the formation of the society you wish to create. Then you can live in your evolving society just as you wish and whenever you wish.

This was a summary of general ideas on the social aspects of Islam. There are without doubt many more details and issues for research. I hope that we will succeed in our future meetings, in coming years, in these places prepared for intellectual interaction, and be able to listen to discussions undertaken by young people. Thank you again to the members of the Muslim Students' Association in Dakar. And God's mercy and blessings be upon you.

7
Labor in Islam

Having previously discussed the issue of labor and workers,[1] and after a brief introduction on the meaning and types of labor and workers, and on the ways the power of labor can be harnessed, I will present today the Islamic view from two perspectives:[2]

The first perspective concerns the privileges of labor according to Islam, including labor-driven forces and the means of production. The second perspective is that of Islamic rules on the value of labor or, in modern terms, on the "labor theory of value."

Let us begin with the first perspective. We notice that any type of production around the world, be it agricultural, industrial, commercial or other, has three common components, at least in form. These are labor, the means of production and what is referred to as "capital" or, nowadays, the "employer."

I will mention a few examples to clarify this definition, which will make the distinction easier later on. Any given factory produces certain goods in certain quantities; this could be fabric, silk or matchsticks. The purpose of the factory is to produce these goods.

[1] Musa Sadr was early on part of a group of young modernist scholars in Iran and Iraq who sought to bridge the gap between the traditional, quietist tradition of Islamic scholars and the urgent need for a renewed language in Muslim countries to address pressing issues like the economy. In the late 1950s and early 1960s, he published a series of articles on Islamic economics in Persian and in Arabic, on which see Chapter 1 on his editorship in Tehran of the journal *Maktab-e Islami*. This chapter provides a more mature approach to the topic. Sadr's mention of a "previous" talk refers to a previous lecture on "*al-ʿamal wa-l-ʿamil*" (labor and the worker), read at the Shiʿi Council to the "cadres" of the party a week earlier, on December 26, 1970, which can be found in his *Abḥāth fī al-iqtiṣād* [Economic studies] (Beirut: Markaz al-Imām Mūsā al-Ṣadr li-l-Abḥāth wa-l-Dirāsāt, 2007), 193–208.

[2] Lecture delivered at the Supreme Islamic Shiʿi Council on January 2, 1971. On the Council, see the Introduction and Chapter 1.

To enable this production, workers operate machines, transport materials from warehouses to their destination, move goods from one machine to the next, remove end products from machines and so on, depending on the level of automation in each factory. This is an important process no matter how advanced the factory is. We know today that some factories receive raw materials and produce fully manufactured, packaged and ready-to-use products through automated processes, with little direct intervention from workers. Still, the worker is a factor of production, and without the worker the factory would grind to a halt.

There are several categories of workers. Some perform simple tasks, such as moving goods from one machine to the next, transporting materials from warehouses to their destination or from the factory to vehicles. Other workers perform administrative tasks, such as the manager of a company, who operates at a higher level and whose energy, experience and intellect allow them to manage the company effectively. Organizational management has become an important science nowadays, as it helps distribute work and allocate resources to enhance the means of production. Workers are the first factor of production, whether they perform simple tasks or assume management, accounting, inspection, marketing or outreach duties. In this sense, labor, no matter the type, is the first factor of production.

The second factor is a direct contributor to production: it is the machine. We will adopt a broad understanding of the term "machine," not limited to mechanical apparatuses. Our definition encompasses everything that contributes directly or indirectly to production at the factory, such as land, machines, marketing tools such as vehicles, outreach tools and so on. In other words, it includes all the means used by workers, whether they perform simple or "complex" tasks, and whether they are office experts, engineers or otherwise.

Of course, machines play a vital role in the production process. Without factories, our output would be one-thousandth of what it currently is, if not less. Factories amplify production, which is why they are also included in our definition of "machine" – the second factor of production.

As for the third factor, it is "capital," or what is currently referred to as the "employer" – regardless of the nomenclature, this third factor certainly comes into play. What comes to mind when we hear the term "capital" is money invested in production. But what does this money include? It includes the raw materials that are procured and transported;

the salaries paid to workers in advance, which incentivize them to work; and the money spent on marketing, means of production, outreach and the distribution of goods to viable markets around the world for consumers to purchase. Even if we have the most advanced factory, the most experienced engineer and the most dedicated and productive workers in the world, these three factors combined would not produce anything if there were no consumer willing to pay money to buy their goods or if they did not have the funds to transport these goods to markets. Producers either have to give advance payments to farmers in conventional ways, or monopolize the purchase of goods, or buy them legitimately from various regions and transport these goods – wheat, cotton, wool and so on. These purchased raw materials then must be manufactured, in a process involving the factory, the engineer and the worker. This necessitates machines, which consume fuel, and other costs ... Afterwards, when the raw materials are procured and when the factories begin to produce, the goods must be marketed, transported to different regions, advertised or otherwise handled. These are all processes that require more money.

Whether you refer to this money as "capital," which is the traditional name, or "employer," which is the modern term used in Lebanese law, capital remains a necessary component.[3] What matters to us is that there are three factors of production: capital, machinery and labor (the latter term includes simple workers, engineers, accountants, inspectors, all the way up to the head of the company, the chairperson or general manager – that is, those who recruit workers but are also workers themselves).

As mentioned, there are several types of labor: simple, complex, normal, skilled. If we were to view the three factors of production (capital, machine and labor) through the lens of modern sociology, how would we assess the production and contribution of each? How would we set their salaries? How do we distribute goods among them? How would we split the output among these three partners in production? With what percentage, quantity and quality?

[3] In Arabic, *rabb al-ʿamal*, literally, "the work master." Sadr refers to Lebanese labor law, which defines the employer, *rabb al-ʿamal*, as "any person, natural or juridical, in an industrial, trading or agricultural enterprise [who] employs a worker in some capacity in exchange for a salary, even if this salary is paid in kind or as a share in the profit." Art. 1, Lebanese Labor Code of 1946.

Scholars have tried to answer this very common question. I believe that it is at the heart of social justice or what is known as fair distribution. The system of government – or, in more accurate terms, the regime – should protect these three factors. It should not give priority to money or capital over labor, as in capitalist systems, which value profit and accumulation above all else. All means are legitimate in capitalist systems. My intention is not to criticize capitalism or lecture you; I am merely analyzing the facts. As we all know, capitalism is the cornerstone of Western governments; it is part of Western civilization, which, as I have previously mentioned, is not founded on any specific ethical ideology or philosophy.

At the end of the Middle Ages, because of negative reactions to Church practices, the founders of modern civilization abandoned the Church altogether; they took revenge on religion itself, on God and on metaphysics as a school of thought. They dismissed anything beyond nature and built their civilization with no moral foundations. They said: "Let us forsake God and abandon the search for what is beyond nature; let us build a civilization, turn to our civil affairs and produce without restrictions or conditions." And so they did. When you talk to them about commerce, industry or production, they say: "I am not a priest or clergyman; I am a trader. Commerce and principles do not go well together."[4] The reason for this separation can be traced back to the very origins of Western civilization.

So how did "civilization" come to be? It was not built on ethical principles. When Western civilization emerged, it gave no thought to human rights, to famines and other scourges. Western civilization does not distribute production fairly among the three above factors.

It does not ask what the role of each factor is and how much each has produced ... Does this or the other factor account for 10, 20 or 50 percent of production? The question is skirted and turns into conflict. Capital, which is given precedence over all else and is supported by law and the political system, seeks to lower workers' wages as much as possible. If it could make workers toil with no pay, it would. It would not even blink an eye if workers died in the process. Workers are given only the bare minimum to survive. They are exploited like cattle and are offered no sympathy whatsoever; they are only fed to be kept alive and to

[4] Sadr seems to imply that such a separation is inherent to capitalism in Western civilization.

keep serving their owners. That is how capitalist systems treat workers, both in form and in substance. They give workers the bare minimum and resort to a plethora of vicious theories and practices to undermine the rights of workers.

Everything is subject to competition and speculation in such a system. Western civilization impeded agricultural production and subsistence farming, forcing thousands of workers to transition to factory labor. It asked these workers: "How much do you want to be paid per month? 150 liras? It is out of the question because others will accept 120, 100, even 90 . . ." That is the capitalist concept of competition, one which favors employers who are part of the established system of injustice and riba (usury). In this system of injustice, the capitalist imposes on the worker a bare minimal compensation to survive.

This reality persisted for a long time, and several philosophical and other types of ideological justifications were used to convince workers that the position of the capitalist is right. The law, of course, protects the powerful. Long-standing oppression naturally led to the reaction that we refer to as "class struggle." Class struggle emerged not for the sake of social conflict itself, as I will explain later, but because of the exploitation of workers by employers, who own the capital. The worker had no choice but to take action: At the beginning, the worker's reaction was spontaneous and personal, but it gradually became collective, with well-structured movements. Some were successful, others failed.

This is a brief survey of the position of the capitalist system on the distribution of wealth among the three factors of production. Whenever the system was able to give the fruits of production exclusively to employers, it did; and when employers sensed tensions and discontent that could threaten the system, such as when the British factory owner Robert Owen, commonly referred to as "the father of socialism," tried to give workers benefits in the form of reduced working hours, or exempt children, pregnant women or women in general from the obligation to work by amending certain laws. Owen is one of the most celebrated figures in economic history. This is one position.

There was a second response to the oppression practiced by capital or employers, one which, contrary to the first position, sought to deny any role to employers in production, considering instead that only labor – whether simple or complex, direct or indirect – contributes to production. According to this approach, raw materials should be given directly to workers, because they constitute the only factor of production. This opposite theory, which emerged in response to the injustice of capitalists, gave rise to scientific socialism or communism. This is the origin of Marx's philosophy, which is based on the labor theory of value. The theory argues that the value of a good or service is determined by the total amount of labor required to produce it. As a result, even if the employer takes a minimal amount of profit, he is a thief, since the workers are entitled to the entirety of the profit. This theory distributes investment between worker and machine, and any excess value produced determines how the production and distribution process is allotted.

This topic is related to next week's discussion on value and how to determine it.[5] On the one hand, we have oppression, and, on the other, people's reaction to it. We need to analyze this reality calmly, without bias or excess. We need to examine how these three factors – labor, machine and capital – contribute to production. As we have already established, no production can take place without them, but the main question is how we ought to distribute production output among them.

In principle, Islam distributes the output of production among these three factors on the basis of two considerations: the first is related to the strengths and privileges that Islam gives to each factor of production; the second is related to the Islamic theory of value.

With regard to the first dimension, let us consider Islamic law generally. When we talk about an Islamic economy or Islamic views on the economy, we do not mean that the Prophet Muhammad dedicated a special chapter in the Qur'an to economic theory, or that Muslim scholars created a branch in Islamic law dealing solely with economics. Rather, we refer to the opinions and views on economic affairs that any reasonable analyst can deduce when reading the Qur'an and reviewing the different Islamic rules and the jurisprudence bearing on economics.

When reading the Qur'an, you will not find a chapter or verse on economics. This has led poorly informed readers, including a prominent scholar I once heard, to believe that there are no teachings pertaining to economic affairs in Islam. This, of course, is a superficial interpretation. If we were to give a designation to Islamic economics, would they be classified as capitalist? Socialist? On which grounds do we base our analysis? On Islam's positions. In other words, we should explore

[5] See n. 1. The next lecture, in what appears to be a series of three, is entitled "*Nazariyyat al-qima*" (Theory of value), in Sadr's *Abḥāth fī al-iqtiṣād*, 209–22. It was delivered at the Supreme Shi'i Council on January 9, 1971.

Islam's position on wealth distribution, workers' rights and other economic issues and conceive on their basis an overall Islamic opinion. To do so, we must review all jurisprudence on transactions, and possibly even on worship. That is why I present before you today Islamic teachings and law references so that we may explore together what Islam tells us about distribution.[6]

How does Islam view the three factors of production, and which of the three does it value the most? Labor, without a doubt.[7] Why? Because the general principles and conditions that Islam has introduced in the production process bestow on labor privileges that are not available for the other two factors. Before considering these privileges further in detail, we must consider the following points:

First, Islam prohibits riba (usury) and considers it to be a grave sin. A famous hadith by the Prophet is: "One dirham gained by riba is worse than committing adultery seventy times."[8] Some versions of this hadith go even further, but this shall suffice to get my message across. Riba is one of the most serious sins in Islam, and it can never be seen as legitimate, no matter how small the profit is.

But what does riba truly signify?[9] And how does it help us apply Islamic teachings to economics?

Riba is prohibited. As we know, riba is the production of cash (or capital) without any labor involved. The legal interpretation of riba considers it to be every loan that entails interest. That is what scholars tell us. In practical terms, riba is when I borrow money from you, and you rest and do nothing while I struggle and toil. You do not care whether I work or not, whether I eat or starve to death ... All you care about is that you receive your 4 percent interest every month or any

[6] The method and references to Islamic law are common to Musa al-Sadr and a number of contemporary scholars in Iran and in Iraq, in particular Muhammad Baqer al-Sadr (d. 1980) (see n. 7).

[7] One will find close similarities between Musa Sadr's economic views and those of his relative Muhammad Baqer al-Sadr in the latter's *Iqtiṣādunā*. On Muhammad Baqer al-Sadr's methods and their rooting in classical law, see Mallat, *Renewal*, 113–46.

[8] This is a hadith common to Sunnis and Shiʿis; for the Sunnis, see Aḥmad Ibn Ḥanbal, *al-Musnad* (Beirut: Muʾassasat al-Risāla, 1999), 36:288; for Shiʿis, Kulaynī, *al-Kāfī*, 5:144.

[9] On riba definitions and controversies in the twentieth century, see Ibrahim Warde, *Islamic Finance in the Global Economy* (Edinburgh: Edinburgh University Press, 2000); Chibli Mallat, "The Debate on *Riba* and Interest in Twentieth-Century Jurisprudence," in Mallat ed., *Islamic Law and Finance* (London: Graham and Trotman, 1988), 69–88.

agreed amount every year. In this case, your money is increasing without any labor on your part. That is riba. It is the accumulation of capital without labor. It is a loan that entails interest. In economic terms, it is the accumulation of pure capital without the other factors of production. That is prohibited in Islam, which teaches us that it is prohibited (haram) for one to use his/her capital, even if it is valued at billions, to accumulate wealth without effort. Capital must not grow without labor. That is the first principle to consider in Islam's economic teachings. Can we charge 3 percent then? No. One percent? Also no. The entire riba-based system is rejected in Islam.[10]

The second principle is related to machinery – to modern industrial machines in factories, or agricultural machines, previously cattle, used before the invention of tractors: The nature of the machine does not matter, because its purpose is the same. Today, we have tractors and other tools, such as those small shops use for commercial, economic or industrial production, looms and other simple means of production. There is no specific book on agriculture in Islamic jurisprudence, but we do have several different books on the rules of muzaraʿa, musaqat and *mugharasa*,[11] as well as on *ijara* (tenancy or waged labor). These books teach us the following:

We must not allot the machine a share in the fruit of production. Islamic legislators, such as Imam al-Sadeq and others,[12] have been asked: If a person has a piece of land – an orchard, say – worked by farmers and cattle, how are the fruits of production distributed among them? Should a percentage be given to each – that is, to the owner of the orchard, the worker and the cattle, no matter how small, even if it is 5 or 10 percent? The Imam answered in the negative;[13] we cannot give a share to the machine. This also applies to large factories. Islam tells us that we cannot give the machine a percentage of the profit. But how do we benefit from the machine then? Machines are at the service of people. Let us say I am

[10] For a book-length treatment of an alternative banking system, see al-Ṣadr, *al-Bank al-lā ribawī*.

[11] Muzaraʿa, musaqat and *mugharasa* are different contractual forms of share-based farming: crop-sharing, water-sharing and plant-sharing, respectively.

[12] Jaʿfar al-Sadeq (d. 765) is the sixth Imam in the Twelver Shiʿi tradition, and the one considered its paramount legal scholar. Islamic law for Shiʿis is known after him as the Jaʿfari school. Note the use of "legislator" by Sadr.

[13] Sadr relates a hadith of Jaʿfar al-Sadeq; see Kulaynī, *al-Kāfī*, 5:267.

the employer, the owner of a factory, and you are a worker. I built my factory to make profit, and you have a right to a wage – a fixed wage depending on the value generated in the future. This is part of the costs of production, rather than a contribution to production. The machine is rented for 100, 200 or 2,000 pounds, and this capital is simply invested in production. This is the second principle. You may wonder why that is, and we will answer that question later. For now, we simply want to deduce the economic principles in Islam that guide us on how to distribute the output of production.

The third principle is related to workers. How does Islam enable workers to share in production? This is done in two ways:

First, we have rented work (*ijar*). There is a section dedicated to wages (ijara) in law books. The wage is an amount of money paid to someone in return for leasing their services. For example, a person may work for another in one of the three categories in return for a sum of money. She works for a certain number of hours and receives an agreed wage. This is entirely permissible. But at what percentage? This is where state protection comes into play. But, in principle, people are permitted to lease their services in return for a wage.

Second, we have partnership for profit and loss (mudaraba):[14]

In Islamic law, mudaraba is a transaction whereby one party uses the money of another (for example, 1,000 pounds) to work in commerce, industry, agriculture and the like. Say the worker makes 100 pounds of profit, which is split between the two parties – the owner of capital and the worker who puts in her personal effort. The worker's labor and the investor's capital together are able to produce goods or services, and this production is split on the basis of a half, one-third, one-fourth or whatever is agreed between the two. We will discuss this in more detail later, but it is allowed under Islamic law.

Workers can accordingly sell their services either in return for a fixed amount (a wage), or they can partner with someone by receiving a share of the profit. If a worker agrees to receive a fixed wage (say 100 pounds),

[14] *Mudaraba*, the equivalent of the medieval Latin *commenda*, is translated generally as partnership for profit and loss. See for the standard work on mudaraba in classical Islamic law, Abraham Udovitch, *Partnership and Profit in Medieval Islam* (Princeton, NJ: Princeton University Press, 1970). Elsewhere in this chapter, Sadr also uses mudaraba in its modern understanding as commercial competition.

that will not change depending on the production output (which may be valued at 5,000 pounds, for example), regardless of how much the worker contributes to this production. That is the other side of the coin. When the worker makes a profit in a mudaraba, that profit is shared between him and the owner of capital; but if the worker suffers a loss, that loss is only borne by the owner of capital. All scholars agree on this. These principles paint a clear picture when considered together. They reveal to us Islam's position on how to distribute the output of production among the three factors. Workers have an option: they may sell their services for a fixed amount (a wage) or receive a percentage of the profit (under mudaraba), but they are also shielded from loss. That is the first factor (labor). As for capitalists (or employers), they cannot receive a fixed profit, because that would be riba. When there is a fixed return on capital, it is considered riba, because that would be similar to a loan that entails interest, money that increases without labor. Capital does not have benefit. Rather, it has the right to receive a certain percentage of the profit, which is referred to as mudaraba, and it is not shielded from loss. The capitalist in the economic teachings we have inferred has merely one benefit, which is to receive a percentage of profit. He may not receive a fixed amount because that would be considered riba, and he may not be shielded from loss because that is unjust. As for tools, such as cattle, factories and shops, they may be assigned monetary compensation, as we previously mentioned, but they cannot be assigned a percentage of the profit. They also do not bear losses.[15]

When we consider the three factors of production, we notice that the worker benefits from three rights:

1. The right to receive a fixed wage, regardless of the increase or decrease in profit (referred to as risk).[16]
2. The right to receive a percentage of the profit.
3. The right to be shielded from loss.

As for capital and machine, they each have one benefit only. Workers clearly have more. But we are then faced with two main sets of questions:

[15] The passage in Arabic includes some errors probably deriving from the oral nature of the lecture, and Sadr's repetition to clarify some of the more delicate points. We have adjusted the translation accordingly.

[16] "Risk" in inserted in English in the original text.

1. Are there any limits to the share of labor, capital and machine? Our answer is that there should be.
2. What are these limits? Why are they set? Why is the machine not given the right to be assigned a percentage of the profit? Why is capital not given the right to receive a fixed amount? Why do laborers have three benefits? How to analyze these issues? The limits of the distribution process are based on the theory of value. We must first examine the value of things. Why does a box of matchsticks cost ten piasters? How is this box priced? If it costs ten piasters, who is this money for? We should seek answers to these questions in order to arrive at a fair distribution.

That is the general principle for our talk tonight. We must first explore the theory of value to understand the benefits assigned to each factor of production. Then we must determine the contribution of each factor to the process of production.

8

Economic and Social Justice in Islam

The Islamic World Today

The first part of the title has been well covered in this forum, with discussion and analysis involving leading scholars and thinkers, so this lecture takes up the second part,[1] with a focus on some central points that give justice in Islam a distinctive character.

First, justice in Islam, in all fields and in the social and economic fields in particular, rests on Islamic ideology. Justice itself is one of the cornerstones of Islamic ideology and has a great impact on the other pillars. Justice in all domains of human life, at both the level of the individual and of the community, appears in the Qur'an as the outcome of a universal [notion of] justice.

In the Islamic conception, justice and truth are the basic foundations of the universe. As a result, whoever is moved by the mission of Islam and seeks to pursue it successfully must be just in their conduct and in harmony with the universe – or else be consigned, as an alien body in the universe, to rejection and failure, and therefore to be ignored and forgotten. This principle is applicable to both individual and society. Perhaps the most eloquent of the verses of the Qur'an affirming this connection appears in Surat al-Rahman: "He raised the heaven on high and set the balance of all things, that you might not transgress that balance. Give just weight and full measure."[2]

Being just stands among the most prominent of divine attributes, and we find justice reflected in all creation. For as the philosophers say, cause is the perfect realization of effect, and effect is the imperfect realization

[1] Lecture at the Ninth Forum of Islamic Thought, Tlemcen, Algeria, on July 24, 1975.
[2] Qur'an 55:7–9.

of cause. Furthermore, the Qur'anic description of God as the Master of Justice means that universal justice is intrinsic to divine justice, without any need for philosophical consideration or scientific analysis.

This approach is commonly adopted in the Qur'an, which states the educational value of truths and facts, without debating their challenging aspects or considering their consequences, and without going into the history and details of narrated events and realities.

In short, universal justice is an Islamic vision, the outcome of faith in the justice of the Creator. This universal justice has established the foundation for economic, political, social and other types of justice, in the life of both the individual and the collective.

The scholar inquiring into the fundamentals of the Islamic religion and into the foundations of the creed clearly sees that the main entry point for sending the apostles is based on the Day of Judgment and its accounting for lives lived. The original entry points, then, are that of divine justice and the importance of justice for the foundations of the Islamic faith, and the extent of this principle's influence through educational guidance upon the behavior of human beings in general, especially in social and economic justice for the individual and society.

Second, overall Qur'anic justice affirms the equality of human labor in this verse: "that each man shall be judged only by his labors."[3] This equality also exists as justice, in that that justice exists to the extent faith exists, while faith cannot exist without human efforts to realize justice.

> Have you thought of him that denies the Last Judgment? It is he who turns away the orphan and has no urge to feed the destitute.[4]

This principle is reflected, in other words, in a hadith of the Prophet: "No one who believes in God and the Last Day can remain satiated while his neighbor goes hungry."[5]

Hundreds of Islamic rulings place social and economic justice at the heart of worship. Depending on the situation, these principles of justice are neither secondary nor simple, ordinary duties. Rather, they stem directly and indivisibly from the principles of faith and creed. Islam does not recognize faith that does not bring the fruits of justice to the life of the individual and the community. Economic and social justice in Islam runs deep, constantly and comprehensively, as it joins the essence of the

[3] Qur'an 53:39. [4] Qur'an 107:1–3.
[5] Hadith available at https://dorar.net/hadith/sharh/135234.

believer's being, arising from the believer's very self, both as an individual and as a member of a collective.

Third, Islam, in firmly grounding the principle of justice, sets clear limits to prevent instability or laxity, offering guarantees to enable its development and expansion to infinity. This is a very important attribute.

The interdependence between individual responsibility and group responsibility for achieving justice is one of the parameters that Islam sets. The individual is responsible for the safety and welfare of his community according to the principle "You are all shepherds, and every shepherd is responsible for his flock,"[6] and because he is called on to "enjoin justice, and forbid evil."[7] All the individual's wealth, all his energy, talent and experience, even his health and physical strength – all that he possesses – are not simply a fruit of his own effort but are matters which others have contributed to forming, whether they are his contemporaries or have preceded him. He is like a tree, whose branches, leaves and roots all play a part in producing fruit, and which benefits from air, sun, water, earth and other natural factors, as well as sometimes from human efforts.

In short, the individual is responsible for what he owns, responsible toward society, responsible in light of both the past and the future. Such an analysis confirms that the individual has no right to monopolize what he owns, nor to neglect it or let it go to waste. One should not harm or injure oneself, so how could one commit suicide? All these and other similar injurious actions violate the rights of the collective, of the community. This sheds light on the advice on accountability, bequests and the understanding of succession conveyed in the Qur'an, viewing wealth as a trust: "give in alms of that which He has made your inheritance."[8]

In return for the individual's responsibility to ensure the safety of the community, the community has a responsibility toward the individual. Hadiths and fatwas of Islamic jurists[9] all affirm a village's responsibility, shared among all its members, for the death of anyone from starvation. The truth is that this responsibility exists for any person's death, harm, injury or abuse, as we read in the hadith "The people of the village have turned their back on God and His Messenger," when they betray God's

[6] Hadith available at www.dorar.net/hadith/sharh/66037/. [7] Qur'an 3:104.
[8] Qur'an 57:7. [9] *Fuqaha'*, plural of *faqih*.

trust and violate His covenant by shirking their responsibility toward that person.[10]

What applies to the village holds for the city and the homeland, and throughout the territories of the community[11] that together form an integrated unit.

Ali then asked, in anger:

> Do I sleep with my belly full, with growing bellies and burning livers all around me? ... Perhaps even there are in the Hijaz or Yamama people who have given up hoping for a loaf and have never known satiation?[12]

As to how individuals relate to one another, the vision that we discover in Qur'anic verses and narratives is that they together make up one body, so that if one member complains of suffering so do the others. So much so that their wealth, souls, contracts and covenants are all owned by all. This sheds new light on society and its composition, as revealed in the following verses:

> Do not devour one another's property by unjust means.[13]

> Do not spy on one another, nor backbite one another.[14]

> You are the offspring of one another.[15]

... as well as in the passages regarding contracts and covenants in the Qur'an.

Across a range of topics, the Qur'an describes a society where justice prevails and warns of dangers if justice is not prevalent.

Where justice reigns, everyone is encouraged to work toward constructive actions. Giving benefits all, while an absence of justice leads to a large part of society being deprived of some or all their rights, with some or all their abilities stymied; and this spreads to afflict everyone in society, to the community as a collective. The consequences of diseases and other dangers – like malnutrition and inadequate living

[10] We were unable to document the hadith. The general meaning relates to Surat al-'Ankabut (Qur'an 29), where the "people of the village" defied God's injunctions and paid a heavy price for turning their back on His message.

[11] *Umma*, the community of believers: the Arabic root is *amma*, to go, or to go and see, linking the concept to both *imam*, who leads prayer, and *umm*, which is mother or source.

[12] 'Alī b. Abī Ṭālib, *Nahj al-balāgha*, ed. Muḥammad 'Abduh (Beirut: Dār al-Mā'arif, 1990), 3:72, http://shiaonlinelibrary.com.

[13] Qur'an 2:188. [14] Qur'an 49:12. [15] Qur'an 3:195.

conditions – spread from disadvantaged groups to afflict everyone. If left to fester, these and other dangers faced by the disadvantaged lead to revolt.

Let us examine some of these verses:

> You are called upon to give in the cause of God. Some among you are ungenerous; yet whoever is ungenerous to this cause is ungenerous to himself. Indeed, God does not need you, but you need Him. If you pay no need, He will replace you with others who shall bear no resemblance to yourselves.[16]

> All that you give in the cause of God shall be repaid to you. You shall not be wronged.[17]

> Give generously for the cause of God and do not with your own hands cast yourselves into destruction. Be charitable; God loves the charitable.[18]

In these verses, we must understand spending in its Qur'anic meaning as the universal contribution of all God has "spent" on man in terms of wealth, thought, endeavor and struggle. Contemplation on these verses confirms that the return of goodness to the spender along with protection from injustice or ruin is not something confined to divine reward awaiting a man on the Day of Judgment, which the Qur'an calls the fullest reward. Rather, it includes earthly rewards, referred to as short-term, lower-level penalties and lesser torments.

In short, those who seek to offer opportunities in life for others, be it for one person or a group, really contribute to goodness returning to themselves. They protect themselves from the dangers of injustice and destruction, and the social consequences of attitudes that are today all too obvious.

We note that the last verse came in the context of jihad.[19] We find perfect harmony between the expenditure of self that leads to martyrdom and the absence of any self-inflicted destruction at the hands of an enemy's tyranny or a tyrant's injustice. There all doubts about the meaning of the verse evaporate.

[16] Qur'an 47:38. [17] Qur'an 8:60. [18] Qur'an 2:195.

[19] Musa Sadr is referring to Qur'an 2:195, which he cites above. The verse immediately follows a passage on war, beginning at 2:190: "Fight for sake of God those who fight against you, but do not attack them first. God does not love aggressors."

Another dimension of economic and social justice lies in Islamic doctrine.[20] The degree of justice varies, and the stages of its implementation in different societies seems to be endless, much like other endless religious goals.

This is because justice is not an end in itself but rather a means to give human beings opportunities to strive toward perfection. Effort must be exerted from the first stages of realizing justice. Following from this vision, justice begins with a certain degree of individual sensitivity, then grows into an increasing effort on the part of the individual, before becoming a root growing in society, represented by national authorities, and then spreading to prevail and become deep-rooted among all.

Just as exploration may lead to endeavor and turn into action, justice, when realized to the minimal extent of providing life opportunities, may be transformed into the creation of ever more degrees of opportunity, and ever greater equality among an increasing number of members of society. Then, there is greater scope for solidarity, social security, sacrifice and altruism. This sacrifice should in no way result in forgetting the rights of close relatives, something which may take place when individuals are excessive in their generosity, as may be suggested by the verse "Be neither miserly nor prodigal, for then you should either earn reproach or be reduced to penury."[21]

Let us point here, while enumerating the Islamic dimensions of economic and social justice, to the technical detail that rightly captured interest during this conference, in order to complement the picture, namely, the prohibition of interest.[22]

The prohibition of interest reveals dissatisfaction in Islamic law with the multiplication of capital by any means devoid of effort. In addition, Islamic law[23] states, and provides with ample justifications, that it is not correct to allocate a share of profit to the means of production – whether a cow or any primitive tools. Labor is the favored component of production in the view of Islam, and is entitled to a share of profits without the

[20] Madrasa. The translation of madrasa here is "doctrine" because of the context. Madrasa is also translated into English as seminary, college for the training of clerics, but its most common Arabic meaning is simply "school."

[21] Qur'an 17:29.

[22] Riba (from the Arabic root *raba*, "to grow, increase, exceed") is usually translated as "interest" or "usury": the issue has been discussed in recent decades within "Islamic banking"; Mallat, *Introduction to Middle Eastern Law*, 338–45. See also Chapter 7.

[23] Fiqh, the scholarly aspect of sharia.

risk of loss; and it is entitled to take a fixed amount irrespective of risk – which is what we call a wage.

Further reflection on zakat[24] and the narratives of the Imams and of the classical jurists adds a new dimension to justice as social security for people facing poverty – except for poverty caused by laziness – and for the old, for children, for those facing disease and disability, especially in cases of emergency, for travelers, debtors and prisoners, and for all those seeking the help of God for their needs. Islam assigns wider society responsibility for socially difficult situations, persistent ones like old age, disability, or those incapacitated suddenly or merely temporarily.

8.1 The Situation of the Community Today

If we compare this understanding of economics and social justice, and its doctrinal roots and clear parameters, with the reality of the different societies of the community, we find a vast gap.

Over the past quarter-century, the Muslim world has made significant efforts and witnessed gains in the field of justice and in the application of some of its provisions. However, the necessary foundations have not been even minimally available. The result is that the efforts made and gains achieved have been haphazard, sometimes sparse and unbalanced.

The separation between the principles of economic and social justice and those that obtain from Islamic beliefs is part and parcel of the tragedy in dissociating doctrine from the law.[25] This separation, and the passivity of Muslims, has resulted in a loss of depth and strategy in the foundations of justice, so much so that economic, social and other applications of justice have become simply a social and political demand shorn [from the law].

This isolation of teachings from their social effect, and the fact that the doctrine bears little on people's life and their private or public behavior, makes most Muslims profoundly uneasy. For many, the doctrine has become limited to worship and rituals that they find sufficient to regulate their relationship with their Creator or to ease their journey toward

[24] Zakat is the giving up of wealth, to "purify" what remains, to the poor, travelers or the state. As one of the five pillars of Islam, the amount given up varies according to the kind of wealth, considered variously by jurists to generally amount to an annual 2.5 percent of net assets. It is usually rendered as "alms" but can equally be seen as a kind of tithe. See also Chapter 6, n. 30, on zakat.

[25] Sharia.

death. We do not know exactly when or how this conspiracy occurred. Was it at the hands of an ignorant friend? Or through the cunning of an enemy lurking in ambush? It seems clear that this situation came to exist before any intellectual interaction took place between Europe and the Islamic world,[26] and that it emerged prominently once this interaction had begun, exerting an influence to the point that it became the predominant trend in the community.

God is worshipped in the houses of prayer on Fridays and during the month of Ramadan, and faith is reflected in human beings when they are in difficult circumstances, such as illness, failure, defeat, poverty and old age. However, faith is not there during the hours of life, of youth, health, victory and success ... no! The marketplace, the factory, the field, the office and all other venues of life have all erected barriers in the face of faith, and they remain locked on the other side of its dominion.

Those who founded and propagated such a vision sought to work in areas unchallenged by faith and unobserved by God so that they could give free reign to their ambitions and desires, exploit people without mercy and choose to earn profits unconditionally and dishonestly. Those who wanted this were the emissaries of Western materialist civilization, who considered religious feelings and moral obligations to be obstacles in their way, and therefore set about to uproot and extinguish their roots in the world. They put an end to the days of the "scholastics" and similar thinkers,[27] paving the way for capitalism and its "sacred" mission to set about its business absolutely freely, without restraint or obligation – and then go on to manufacture, produce and expand production, search for markets for consumption, colonize, invest, wage war, annihilate entire peoples and civilizations, fabricate new needs, and all the rest.

[26] Musa Sadr suggests that in a defensive response to European colonialism, some Muslims placed a strong emphasis on ritual while neglecting other aspects of the faith, especially the centrality of justice. But he also suggests that it started before.

[27] Musa Sadr is apparently referring to scholastics in medieval Catholic Europe, and their understanding of man as a being who could reach contentment and satisfaction. "From Aristotle until the seventeenth century [in Europe] it was more usual to see the essence of man as activity rather than consumption, as exercise of one's energies in accordance with some rational purpose, than as the consumption of satisfactions. It was only with the emergence of modern market society ... that this concept of man was narrowed ... the essence of rational behaviour was increasingly held to lie in unlimited individual appropriation ... Man became ... an infinite consumer." C. B. Macpherson, *Democratic Theory: Essays in Retrieval* (Oxford: Oxford University Press, 1975), 5. Sadr argues that such a notion of man was spread by European colonialism.

Once all is said and done, these people will eventually come to confront the evidence that they have dug the very graves of their civilization by destroying the rest of humanity and its civilization. They will realize that they have created in their lives a vacuum of faith and poverty that amounts to heresy, and that they have brought overwhelming difficulties and incurable sorrows upon all the peoples of the world.

We return to the status of our Muslim nation, after this summation of the broader situation, and say: humanity has been cut off from justice, and worship has been emptied of its content to become a hollow ritual, although the Qur'an repeats many times over that observance of worship, and prayers in particular, if combined with neglecting or not caring for the needy, or not meeting the needs of one's neighbors, bring disaster to those who pray.[28]

Perhaps some clerics contributed to acts of worship taking primacy over justice, by their declarations or by their silence, despite the teaching of Islam that the best act of worship is "a just and true word in front of an unjust authority."[29]

The result of this conduct and pedagogy has been exceedingly dangerous, because the loss of justice raises dangers beyond society and politics; it causes deviation in ideas and creates disappointment with religion in terms of its institutions and leading figures, who remain silent over widespread grievances and fail to fight for people's rights.

In short, this separation has created chaos amid efforts to achieve justice in our societies, leaving behind severe social, political and ideological challenges. When some societies realize justice partially and in isolation from the doctrinal basis of the religion, this only increases the difficulties, because such justice sets its own cultural models, which impose a certain kind of consumption on society and with it a new way of life that makes society vulnerable to disorientation, alienation and loss.

The responsibility of religious scholars in this field is great, highly delicate and urgent, as they are the trustees serving the community and its people, especially those deprived among them – these scholars alone can give a true picture of the struggle of the disadvantaged and the oppressed within societies and stand in the way of appeals to extremism

[28] Musa Sadr may be referring to Qur'an 107:4–7: "Woe betide those who pray but are heedless in their prayer; who make a show of piety and forbid almsgiving."

[29] A well-known hadith; see, e.g., www.dorar.net/hadith/sharh/132636.

and atheism. Religious scholars are especially capable of preventing the distortion and deflection of efforts to restore rights to people deprived of them. The oppressors and usurpers of justice and rights typically accuse movements that are struggling for justice of atheism or sectarianism. The best remedy in such cases is for religious scholars to stand with the deprived and oppressed and adopt their cause.

The reality of the community today is not just a lack of awareness of Islamic economic and social justice, and the resulting risks of alienation and absence of a comprehensive vision of justice. The reality is that economic and social justice is honored only in rare cases.

The number of people deprived of a decent life and justice is constantly increasing in Muslim societies; and their sense of deprivation is steadily deepening as they find themselves in the midst of extravagance, richness and luxury.

Muslims are living today in diverse countries with extreme disparities in standards of living, despite emerging natural resources and rises in the prices of raw materials. Both the poverty of many people and the wealth of others have increased. All of this is taking place – a bitter reality is clearly apparent to everyone – without any justification for the absence of the application of justice among people, people who belong to one community.

The richer Arab countries have contributed to funding the military budgets of frontline countries, but this contribution did not amount to even a tenth of the profits these countries garnered from war.[30] Participation in the war against Israel does not diminish the need for contributing to Muslim peoples who struggle with poverty, hunger and underdevelopment.

It goes without saying that the need to achieve justice calls not for contributions, donations and grants but for interest-free loans that enable poor people to improve their lives by implementing development projects. Islam has advocated loans without interest and considered that a dirham in loan is equivalent in God's wages to far more than a dirham in charity.[31]

[30] Reference to the financial support of Saudi Arabia and the oil states in the Arab world to Syria and Egypt during the 1973 war.

[31] From a hadith on the superiority of loans in support of enterprise over donations. The hadith is disputed, with a version that establishes the preference for donations as charity over loans. A vindication of the first position can be found in the hadiths collected by Ibn Majah (d. 887), with the Prophet asking the angel Gabriel (Jibril): "What explains that a loan is better than charity? Jibril's answer: the begger asks when he has something. The

If we continue to study the conditions of the community, we will be astonished to discover that Muslim countries treat other Muslim peoples as foreigners, and sometimes treat them more harshly than other countries.

High duties on products, restrictions on workers' movements, the absence of adequate rights for Muslim workers in most Islamic countries, harsh conditions for Muslim experts that push them to emigrate, the humiliation and insults they are subjected to, tense relations between rulers that impair people's lives, especially the poor; these and many other painful observations confirm the lack of justice in the heart of the community nowadays.

We must consider other dimensions that complete the reality of the Islamic nation and the status of justice in it. This concerns the situation of young people, their anxiety about the future, on the one hand, and the deviation or delinquency that arises from an absence of care and mentoring, on the other hand, as well as the status of women, the circumstances of people in remote or isolated areas and farmers, in most if not all Islamic countries.

Now, at the end of this presentation, I present to this gathering the following suggestions:

1. To address a recommendation to all religious scholars in the Islamic world, and to all believers who wish to uphold their duties, to reaffirm Islamic goals and prioritize standing by the disadvantaged and the oppressed, and to alleviate their grievances in light of the circumstances of their country, notwithstanding cost or sacrifice.
2. To call upon governments in the Islamic world, in a detailed and carefully elaborated appeal, to take stock of the present stage of their history and enable their country to complete the necessary phase of internal construction, focusing on efforts to secure the well-being of deprived groups among their peoples by means of specific projects.
3. To appeal to governments attending the Organisation of the Islamic Conference[32] to establish projects for raising opportunities for

borrower asks for a loan because he needs it." ʿAbd al-Muḥsin al-ʿIbād, *Sharḥ Sunan Ibn Mājah*, 175, available at www.alathar.net/home/esound/index.php?op=tadevi&id=10617.

[32] The Organisation of the Islamic Conference was founded in 1969, changing its name in 2011 to the Organisation of Islamic Cooperation. With fifty-seven members in 2020, it was by then the world's second-largest intergovernmental organization, after the United Nations.

disadvantaged areas and people, to pass laws improving the conditions of workers, resident experts and migrant workers; to develop relevant legislation on customs and export–import activities to achieve greater justice among all Muslim peoples.

4. To undertake a comprehensive study of economic and social justice in Islam, its importance and its position in the religion, and to disseminate it in the media and in school textbooks, especially through universities and religious institutes concerned with social issues.

Part III
Liberal Values and the Rejection of Violence

Lebanon in Crisis

9

Freedom Alone Can Preserve Freedom

May God bestow His mercy upon you, Abu Jamil;[1] you were peerless in death, just as in life.[2] You died in the battle arena, falling in the courtyard of the free press, thrown down into its very mihrab, its prayer niche.[3]

For the press, dear brethren, is a mihrab, a sanctuary for the worship of God and for the service of man. If the press does not fulfill its duty, it will reflect the treachery and deceit of evil. The press is one of the most important and delicate battlefields of jihad.

The press forms and shapes public opinion, contributing to public culture. It also prepares nourishment for the soul, developing it and giving it a new stage that better matches the level of culture in society. Even if we say that the soul, dear brethren, is not physical in origin, there can be no doubt that it interacts with public culture and so instills in itself renewed vigor and shape as it takes on a new dimension. The press, then, while contributing to popular culture and guiding the sentiments and emotions of the masses, refashions the human soul.

At the same time, the press plays a huge role in monitoring and guiding society and its pillars, helping direct the state and governmental institutions and contributing to organizing the economy and politics.

1 Literally, "father of Jamil." In time, Jamil Mroueh (as he writes his name in Latin letters) succeeded his father by reviving both *al-Hayat* and the *Daily Star.*

2 The memorial address given for journalist and publisher Kamel Mroueh (Mruwwe) on May 30, 1966, by Musa Sadr, al-Zirariyyah, South Lebanon. Mroueh had been assassinated two weeks earlier, on May 16.

After working for the Lebanese newspapers *al-Nida'* and *al-Nahar*, Mroue founded the pan-Arab daily *al-Hayat* in 1946 and the English-language *Daily Star* in 1952, consistently exposing the activities of military dictatorships. Mroue was killed by a gunman who entered his office as he was preparing the next day's edition of *al-Hayat*.

3 On mihrab, a niche in the wall of a mosque indicating Mecca as the direction of prayer, see Chapter 1, n. 109.

This is how the press plays a major part in shaping human society and the whole environment that serves the physical body. It is how the press both fashions the new stages of the soul's development and serves the needs of the human body. The press is one of the pillars of civil society.

I do not wish to praise the culture of the Lebanese press here among its leaders and representatives, in their own country, and in front of their own readers. I would rather emphasize a point to remind myself and my brethren here of the sensitivity of the role of the press. A journalist can help create a good and righteous society. He knows that by writing a word, publishing a photograph, composing a headline or offering analysis of events, he is equipping and preparing every human being for a new phase of life and of history; a journalist can be a guiding father and a sincere friend – or he can betray the truth and deviate from it.

This role of the press – as one of the most important fields of jihad, and as a principal pillar of civil society – imposes on the journalist a duty toward society, as well as giving him rights and privileges that society should respect. The rights of the journalist are in turn the duties of society toward the journalist; his duties toward society are in turn society's rights. The journalist has a right to freedom, the freedom to exercise the profession and protect society from corruption and deviation.

Freedom, dear brethren, as you know, is the best means of mobilizing the entire energy and potential of human beings. The service that an individual, any individual, may offer in a society that is not free represents only a part, not all, of his capability. Human beings can mobilize all their capacities and develop all their talents only when at liberty to do so. Freedom is the best way to invest in the capabilities of the individual, and to channel these capabilities into serving society. Freedom also recognizes human dignity and good faith, whereas lack of freedom constitutes mistrust in humankind, a diminution of human dignity and a constant doubting of human worth.

Only someone who scorns human instinct[4] – the instinct embedded deep within man's soul – will act to limit individual freedom:

> Stand firm in your devotion to the true Faith, the upright Faith which God created for mankind to embrace. God's Creation cannot be changed. This is surely the right faith, although most men may not know it.[5]

The upright faith acts as an "internal prophet" for humans.

[4] Fitra (see Chapter 3, nn. 26, 28). [5] Qur'an 30:30.

Freedom is therefore a service *to* journalists, while at the same time freedom – which is journalists' right *from* society – is a service to society.

Freedom alone preserves freedom, and freedom, contrary to what may be said, can never be limited, for its boundaries extend to infinity. Freedom is not even limited, as is often said, by the freedom of others.[6] The truth is that complete freedom is a right; it is from God, and it has no limit.

Genuine freedom is freedom from sources of external and internal pressure, or coercion. In the words of the Imam: "Whoever abandons [worldly] desires is free."[7] If we wish to define and clarify the realm of freedom, we must explain that freedom is both being free from others and being free from oneself.

Once we interpret freedom in this way, we cannot believe it has a limit: freedom that collides with or impairs the freedom of others brings a slavish self and its pursuit of lust. For there is freedom derived from jihad – in the words of the Prophet, from the lesser jihad[8] against an exploitative and domineering force, and also from the greater jihad with the self, to gain freedom from appetites and lust. Perhaps the best way to dedicate oneself to self-liberation is through self-criticism, with the participation of reformers.[9]

It is the right of a journalist to have society secure his freedom, and this is in society's best interests. A journalist has also the right to count on society's protection and security against financial constraints, poverty, bribes and psychological pressure. In this way society serves itself, fulfills its role and makes use of all the energies and capacities of the journalist as its servant and warrior. Freedom, then, is the best way to mobilize the

[6] In his *On Liberty*, published in 1859, the English writer John Stuart Mill argued that freedom of the individual should be limited only when it threatens the liberty of others. Musa Sadr's argument is that in a society enthused with the "right faith" such limitations are not needed as individuals respect others and act responsibly.

[7] Cited in Ibn Shu'ba, *Tuḥfat al-'uqūl 'an al-rasūl* (Najaf: al-Ḥaydariyya, 1953; repr., Tehran, 1972), 99.

[8] On the lesser and greater jihad, see Chapter 10, n. 15. The common Prophetic hadith on the lesser and greater jihad is related in the context of the Prophet's return from battle: "'We came back from the lesser jihad to the greater one.' And when [his companions] asked him, 'but is there a greater jihad than the fight against the heathen? he said, 'yes, the jihad of the soul.'" Majlisī, *Biḥār al-anwār*, 67:71.

[9] *Muslihun*, the "reformers," has connotations of "peacemakers," "those who reconcile differences," and occurs often in the Qur'an.

energies and capability of a newspaper and the energies of each servant of the press. It is the best way to uphold these rights.

A journalist should not be insulted, or coerced. He should not be impoverished, and he should not be assassinated. Assassination is one of the worst, most futile and cowardly ways to reach any goal, no matter what the goal may be. It is also a dangerous social phenomenon, since trial, judgment and execution are undertaken by one single person. Once this door is opened, justice cannot prevail in a society. The person is barred from a setting where offenders deserve to be tried and judged, even subjected to capital punishment, and deprived of the full trial needed to achieve the proper outcome. The duty of society, the duty of the protectors of society where it has protectors, is to treat assassination radically, to eliminate it.

May God have mercy on you, Abu Jamil.

You died, but death is in no way your disappearance, nor your condemnation to nonexistence. Death for the believer is a transformation from the earth to the heavens, and from the finite to the infinite and boundless. Death is an extension and expansion, a destruction of constraints and chains. Do we not believe in the Qur'an, which tells us: "He created death and life"?[10]

Death therefore is creation, not annihilation; it is creation before life, for there is no true life until after death.

The phenomenon of death followed by life expresses the truth of transformation, development and perfection. There can be no transformation from the present phase until after death, and no perfection until a human being abandons the phase in which he now lives. The lifeless seed cannot become a plant if it is not transformed, and the plant, if it does not die as a plant, cannot be transformed into an animal or a human being.

So it is with human beings: in the living human being, the cells of the body are constantly dying as the human engages in thinking, and bodily cells are exploding as they become thoughts. The cells of one's body are transformed in human beings into thought, and this cannot take place fully until after the end of the present phase of life. Death is the path to perfection; death is the introduction to transformation. Death is immortality; it is the path where truth is revealed.

[10] Qur'an 67:2.

God have mercy on you, Abu Jamil, and deliver patience in its beauty to your family, your offspring, your colleagues, your compatriots and your homeland. Inspire them to make of your death the most excellent and sublime life.

Peace be upon you.

10

Religion in the Service of Humanity

We praise and thank You, Lord and God of Abraham and Ishmael, God of Moses, Jesus, and Muhammad, Lord of the downtrodden[1] and God of all creation.[2] Praise be to God, who secures and provides support to the downtrodden, frees the just, elevates the humble and humbles the arrogant; who brings down a monarch and delivers his replacement; destroys the tyrant and castigates the oppressor; helps fugitives, and punishes the despot.[3] Praise be to God, who hears the cry of the desperate.

We praise You, our Lord, and stand before You seeking Your care. We congregate under Your guidance, our hearts united in Your love and Your mercy. We meet here in Your midst in one of Your houses of worship, during the period of fasting for Your sake, our hearts yearning for You, our minds deriving light and guidance from You, and, on Your invitation, we walk side by side in the service of Your creation, to meet around a just testament,[4] for the happiness of human beings, who are

[1] *Mustad'afin* means considered or made weak, and is often translated as "downtrodden" or "oppressed." The word was frequently used by Musa Sadr and by Iranian leader Ruhullah Khumaini (Khomeini, d. 1989) in contrast to *mustakbirin*, the "arrogant."

[2] Lent sermon delivered on February 18, 1975, to the Capuchin Franciscan priests at the Saint Louis Latin Cathedral in Beirut, on the invitation of Bishop Paul Basim in the course of the Lent lecture series. With tensions increasing in Lebanon, protests in Sidon over fishing rights, beginning February 26, and a massacre at a church in Ain al-Rummaneh on April 13 triggered Lebanon's fifteen-year civil war; see Hiro, *Lebanon, Fire and Embers*, 18–19. The Saint Louis Cathedral became in December 1975 a battleground between militias.

[3] This passage is from a well-known Shi'i *du'a'*, or prayer, known as *du'a' al-iftitah* (opening prayer).

[4] "Just testament" is a loose translation of *kalima sawa'*, a phrase from Qur'an 3:64 referencing the call of the Prophet Muhammad to the "people of the Book." *Kalima* is literally "word," and *sawa'* "right," or "leveled," even "sane." The phrase is translated simply by N. J. Dawood as "agreement," but it carries strong connotations in Arabic and

Your representatives. Our destination is Your door, and we turn in prayer toward Your mihrab.[5]

We have come together for the sake of humankind, for whose sake religions, one original religion, are revealed, to bring good tidings and bear witness to God delivering human beings from darkness into light, rescuing people from their many weighty, divisive differences and teaching them right conduct for the sake of peace.

Religions were once one, and they served one objective: to call people to God and to serve humankind. For religions are the expression of the one truth. They quarrelled when they came to serve themselves, when their self-interest grew so that they lost sight of their objective. Conflicts intensified and differences multiplied, increasing the plight and suffering of humankind.

Religions, when they were one, worked to fulfill the one objective of battling worldly gods and tyrants while providing help to the vulnerable and the oppressed, two aspects of the one truth. When religions triumphed, and the oppressed triumphed with them, tyrants were quick to don the mantle of religion and use it to reap rewards, for they had learned to rule and to brandish a sword in the name of religion. This exacerbated the ordeal of the oppressed and the predicament of religions, and it gave rise to all manner of differences between them. Wherever a dispute is found, there too are found exploiters. Where differences appeared between religions, it was because of their exploiters' vested interests.

Religions were originally all one, in the beginning, which is God, who is one. The objective, which is the human, is one; and the path, which is this, our universe, is one. When we lost sight of the objective and abandoned our service of the human, God neglected us, and He distanced Himself from us. We found ourselves fragmented into small parts, sects and groups, and as punishment He cast us into the ways of harm and misery, so that we fight among ourselves and throw our universe into disarray, serve narrow interests, worship gods inferior to the one God and tear the human asunder.

And now we return to the path; we return to the human; so that God will return to us; we must turn again to human suffering and save

Islam of a binding path or set of just teachings and beliefs. "People of the Book, let us come to an agreement: that we will worship none but God, that we will associate none with Him, and that none of us shall set up mortals as deities besides God" (Qur'an 3:64).

[5] On the mihrab, see Chapter 1, n. 109.

ourselves from the wrath of God. We must again seek the human – which was destroyed, torn apart – so that we come together and embrace the whole, and thereby meet God, so that all the religions shall again be one.

"We have ordained a law and assigned a path. Had it pleased God, He could have made of you one community; but it is His wish to prove you by that which He bestowed upon you. Vie with each other in good works, for to God shall you all return and He will resolve your differences for you."[6]

Now, in this church, in times of fasting, in a sermon that committed senior figures[7] have invited me to give, I find myself traveling a road alongside you. I find myself preaching, both discoursing and being counseled – speaking with my voice and listening with my heart.[8] History teaches us, and history testifies, that Lebanon is the land of human encounters, homeland of the oppressed, haven for the frightened. In this sublime setting, with its heavenly horizons, we can respond to the original celestial summons, for we are closer to the springs of the divine.

Here is the Lord, loving in anger, His voice high: "No! God's love shall not meet with human hatred."[9] His voice loud in our conscience, in the last Prophet of mercy: "Never will one believe in God and Judgment Day, who is sated while his neighbor goes hungry."[10]

These two voices interact through the ages. They echo the words of the Pope at Lent: "Christ and the poor are one and the same." In his famous encyclical *Populorum Progressio*,[11] the Pope calls for human dignity, just as the Messiah did in the temple. "They are sorely tempted

[6] Qur'an 5:48. Some translations have "test" rather than "prove."

[7] *Mas'ulin multazimin*: the term is used in Arabic to refer to officials committed to a goal. Musa Sadr is speaking of the senior Catholic clergy. He was particularly close to Catholic Bishop Grégoire Haddad (d. 2015), a leading reformist figure in Lebanon.

[8] *Atakallam bi-lisani wa-usghi bi-qalbi – usghi* is "listening carefully."

[9] This probably refers to John 13:34: "I give you a new commandment, that you love one another. Just as I have loved you, you should love one another. By this everyone will know that you are my disciples, if you have love for one another." This establishes love as the mainstay of Christian theology. All quotations from the Bible are from the New Revised Standard Version (Cambridge: Cambridge University Press, 1989).

[10] This hadith, "*ma amana bi-Llah wa-l-yawm al-akhir man bata shibʿanan wa-jaruhu jaʾiʿ*," is related, for example, in Kulaynī, *al-Kāfī*, 2:668. It is common to Sunnis and Shiʿis.

[11] *Populorum Progressio* ("The Development of Peoples") is an encyclical on Christian social teaching issued in 1967 by Pope Paul VI. It stresses that economic development should benefit all humankind rather than a few, and asserts the right to fair wages and working conditions. Becoming pope in June 1963, Paul VI followed the direction set under his predecessor, Pope John XXIII, during the Second Vatican Council (October 1962–December 1965), which stressed *aggiornamento* ("bringing up to date"), social justice

to redress these insults to their human nature by violent means."[12] And he adds that the basest humanity is that of brutal despots who abuse the rights of kings and princes, steal the rights of workers and conclude exploitative deals.[13]

Does this pristine voice not differ little from the objective expressed in the Muslim tradition? When God says, "I, God, am with those whose hearts are broken, I was with the poor struck by illness, with the poor whom I aid and assist, with the needy to whom I provide relief."[14]

How? Every effort to defend a right and to aid the oppressed is considered a struggle on the path of jihad,[15] a prayer at the minbar. It offers victory.

By means of these testimonies we can return to the human to distill the forces that destroy and the forces that divide. The human being is a divine gift, a creature created in the image of his creator and given to share in His qualities, God's deputy on earth.[16] She, the human being, is

and interfaith discussions. The official text of *Populorum Progressio* was in Latin, although it was originally written by Pope Paul and his advisers in French.

[12] *Populorum Progressio*, paragraph 30: "The injustice of certain situations cries out for God's attention. Lacking the bare necessities of life, whole nations are under the thumb of others; they cannot act on their own initiative; they cannot exercise personal responsibility; they cannot work toward a higher degree of cultural refinement or a greater participation in social and public life. They are sorely tempted to redress these insults to their human nature by violent means."

[13] Ibid., paragraph 21: "What are less than human conditions? The material poverty of those who lack the bare necessities of life, and the moral poverty of those who are crushed under the weight of their own self-love; oppressive political structures resulting from the abuse of ownership or the improper exercise of power, from the exploitation of the worker or unjust transactions."

[14] Sadr is citing in the same sentence a hadith, "I, God, am with those whose hearts are broken" and the gospel of Matthew. The hadith is not generally recognized as authentic by Sunnis; see https://dorar.net/fake-hadith/968. The rest of the sentence draws on Matthew 25:34–36: "I was a stranger and you welcomed me, I was naked and you gave me clothing, I was sick and you took care of me, I was in prison and you visited me."

[15] "Jihad" has become a worldwide word, defined in different ways. "A holy war undertaken by Muslims against unbelievers. The name comes from Arabic *jihād*, literally 'effort,' expressing, in Muslim thought, struggle on behalf of God and Islam." *The Oxford Dictionary of Phrase and Fable*, www.oxfordreference.com/view/10.1093/oi/authority.20110803100020733. In Musa Sadr's understanding, the nonviolent effort is emphasized over the warring acceptation. The difference is commonly expressed in the literature as *al-jihad al-akbar* (the larger, more important jihad) for the first meaning, and *al-jihad al-asghar* (the smaller, less significant jihad) for the latter.

[16] The Arabic *khalifa* is variously translated as "vice-regent," "deputy," "caliph" and "successor." The last can imply, in the English, that the human succeeds God, which is not the meaning of the Arabic. "When your Lord said to the angels: 'I am placing on the earth one that shall rule as My deputy,' they replied: 'Will You put there one that will

the foundation of existence, the beginning and the end of the community and of society, the prime mover of history and its engine. She is equivalent to and the equal of the sum of her capacities and energies – not only when, in this century, philosophy and physics confirmed exchange and transformation between material substance and energy, but also as religions and scientific experiments have long shown: "Each man shall be judged only by his labors."[17] Human work is eternal; humans who do not reach for wide horizons through their labor are not worth much. Only to the extent that we safeguard and develop human energy[18] do we honor the human and give her eternal life.

Faith, in its heavenly spiritual form, gives human beings the possibility of infinite sensitivity and aspiration, and keeps hope constantly alive. When faith is secure, it removes anxiety and worries; difficulties are removed. Faith adjusts human relationships, with other humans and with all other creatures. Faith gives human beings glory and beauty; it repairs, protects and sustains them. It requires self-preservation and conservation. It affirms that faith itself cannot exist without a commitment to serve humanity.

The entire energy of humankind, and the energy of each and every human being, must be conserved and nurtured. It is on this basis that human striving for perfection and self-fulfillment has gone hand in hand with the divine and prophetic mission, from the earliest days of the religious call to the recent appeal of the Holy Father: to be authentic, human development must be well-rounded; it must foster the development of every human being, and of the human being as a whole.[19] This is

do evil and shed blood, when we have for so long sung Your praises and sanctified Your name?' He said: 'I know what you know not'" (Qur'an 2:30). The title *khalifat Allah* was apparently first used to describe Abu Bakr, who led Muslims after the death of the Prophet Muhammad, and from there "caliph" became the title of various Muslim rulers. In the Qur'an, the word *khalifa* is general and does not carry a political connotation. On the later political use of the concept, see Chapter 3, n. 4.

17 Qur'an 53:39.

18 *Taqat*, plural of *taqa*, is generally "energy," "power" (even electrical power), but also "capacity" or "potential." All these senses are carried by *taqa*. Sadr uses the word frequently, and we have generally translated it as "energy."

19 Musa Sadr is here citing *Populorum Progressio*, paragraph 14: "The development we speak of here cannot be restricted to economic growth alone. To be authentic, it must be well-rounded; it must foster the development of each man and of the whole man. As an eminent specialist on this question has rightly said: 'We cannot allow economics to be separated from human realities, nor development from the civilization in which it takes

why we find theft prohibited in the commandments. It is a violation, a usurpation of human energy and its fruit – and look today, we see theft in the form of economic exploitation and monopoly, supposedly to lead to prosperity and industrial development, with ways of operating that impose artificial consumer "needs" upon people, giving them a fraudulent desire for ever-greater consumption. Today's "needs" do not flow from the human soul or self; they are fostered through commercialized media subservient to those who control the means of production.[20]

Every day thrusts a new need upon mankind, or develops a new need from an existing one, taking control of all human energy and transforming so much of it that one ceases to choose how to expend it, or becomes unable to expend it as one wishes. We are witnessing a profound change that obstructs and repels the energy of humankind, destroys and shatters it. These forces remain essentially the same, despite the disparity of their shape or form, and despite the great extent of their "development."

Religion has fought, also, against lies and hypocrisy, and against vanity and pride; when we observe the roots of these traits, we understand better their impact on the energy and potential of individuals and groups. Lying falsifies facts and dissipates the energy marshaled to enable healthy exchange between human beings, and the energy that

place. What counts for us is man – each individual man, each human group, and humanity as a whole.'"

The eminent specialist referred to by Pope Paul VI is Louis-Joseph Lebret (1897–1966), a priest, social scientist and author who pioneered the concept of the "human economy," was called to the Second Vatican Council as an expert by Pope John XXIII and played a part in drafting *Populorum Progressio*. Before becoming a priest Lebret fought as a French marine with the Lebanese squadron in the First World War.

20 Musa Sadr and other Muslim thinkers in the 1960s and 1970s, including the Iraqi Muhammad Baqer al-Sadr and the Iranian Ali Shariati, were in their emphasis on social ills reacting to the growth of communist and leftist ideas in the Middle East (the challenge of the left was recognized in Najaf as early as 1953 by Muhammad Husayn Kashif al-Ghita; see Mallat, *Renewal*, 9). However, Christian and Muslim thinkers alike were reacting – like Marxists, and with partly similar and partly different answers and approaches – to real or perceived growing inequality within and between nations: Christian and Muslim thinkers reached back to the egalitarianism of Jesus or Muhammad that long predated Marx. Musa Sadr's sermon at the Saint Louis Cathedral well illustrates an emphasis on ethics, an area that "deterministic" Marxism struggled with. Eugene Kamenka was among those who rescued a "humanistic" Marx, especially from the early writings; see his *Ethical Foundations of Marxism* (London: Routledge & Kegan Paul, 1972 [1962]).

In addition to Mallat, *Renewal*, on Muhammad Baqer al-Sadr, who developed the most sophisticated "Islamic" economics, see Ali Rahnema, *An Islamic Utopian: A Political Biography of Ali Shari'ati* (London: I.B. Tauris, 1998), on Ali Shariati.

gives the opportunity to grow. Lying stymies energy, distorts human exchange and wastes potential. Vanity and pride freeze and paralyze human relations. When people come to feel self-important and vain, they think that they are self-sufficient, so they cease to receive and they then fail to be complete or fulfilled. Others, in turn, will stop receiving from them. Without giving and taking there is only death, the demise of energy and capacity, the death of human abilities and capacity. It is the same with traits similar to deceit and pride.

Freedom, in contrast, offers an environment enabling the growth of human potential and the blossoming of a person's talents and gifts. Freedom has long been subject to assault, often violated on diverse pretexts. Insofar as it enables the growth of human faculties, energy and aptitude, freedom is the source[21] of all human powers. There have been bitter battles for freedom. When freedom is stolen from a person, that person's potential, and the whole community's, are subject to the whim of the usurper. People are diminished, shrunk to the level forced on them by the usurper. With the intensity and scope of freedom offered to human beings so diminished, and their creative lifeblood drained, both the individual and the community – society at large – become stunted. When a person rejects reduction and bloodletting, and, as we strive with her, in accordance with our faith, to limit or put an end to the tyranny of this divisive and destructive oppression, we are defending together long-term human potential and dignity, whatever historical form is taken by the attempt to undermine freedom.

From despotism to colonialism, from feudalism to the repression of freedom of thought,[22] history is full of those claiming custody over people they say are ignorant and lack understanding. From neocolonialism to the imposition of ideological beliefs on individuals and peoples through economic, cultural or intellectual force – even policies of deliberate negligence[23] and marginalization, depriving people, some people,

[21] *Umm*, literally, "mother." [22] *Al-irhab al-fikri* – literally, "intellectual terrorism."

[23] *Siyasat al-ihmal*. The notion of "deliberate negligence" or "deliberate policy of negligence" is almost self-contradictory, and yet it is encapsulated here in the neglect by the Lebanese state of "peripheral" areas, including those inhabited mainly by Shi'i Muslims. The context would not have been lost on Musa Sadr's Catholic audience, and yet his argument rests on asserting universal rights and not sectarianism, situating the specific situation of the Lebanese Shi'is within a consistent, overall framework. Sadr also believed the worst result of neglect was not material, even with the absence of adequate medical facilities. Ajami quotes a US diplomatic cable of 1966 in which the reporting officer wrote after a meeting with Sadr: "He said that after so many years of neglect by the

of opportunity, and withdrawing opportunity from whole regions, some regions – there have been many measures restricting freedom, destroying human potential and depriving people of health, mobility and development.

And then there is wealth, this greatest of idols and which the Lord Jesus considered more prohibitive of entry to the kingdom of heaven than the size of a camel in trying to pass through the eye of needle.[24] Wealth is temptation and affliction, even though it can be used wisely in its appropriate place to partake of grace and mercy. When, instead of God, wealth becomes the holy of holies pursued by the worshipper, who becomes trapped in its orbit, it grows at the expense of other needs of individuals and the community. And it takes on a destructive, fracturing power that has a profound impact upon people's lives. The large consumes the small.

It is much the same way with any human need, when it grows in a way detrimental to other human needs. Let us consider the category of "desire" or "lust": all such desire is a human drive, an engine that propels humans through life. But when it grows at the expense of other human needs, it turns catastrophic and brings disaster. This is why an enormous responsibility is attached to enjoying property, wealth, prestige, influence and all other areas of human activity and capabilities.

Faith keeps a link between God and humans; it is continuously present and needs persistent attention. Exclusion and rejection of faith as a basis for modern culture and civilization renders culture vulnerable to this imbalance. When we review the history of our modern civilization, we see human beings becoming more inclined to pursue wealth at the expense of other objectives. Because politics, governance, commerce

government, the South had become a depressed area not only materially but psychologically. As a religious leader of his community, Sadr said he felt obligated to restore the spiritual values of his people and to give them a sense of self-respect. Sadr said that this psychological element was probably the most depressing result of the poor economic and social conditions which prevail in the South." Ajami, *The Vanished Imam*, 111–12.

[24] This refers to words of Jesus in the gospels of Matthew (19:23), Mark (10:24) and Luke (18:24). "Then Jesus said to his disciples, 'Truly, I tell you, it will be hard for a rich person to enter the kingdom of heaven. Again I tell you, it is easier for a camel to go through the eye of a needle than for someone who is rich to enter the kingdom of God.' When the disciples heard this, they were greatly astounded and said, 'Then who can be saved?' But Jesus looked at them and said, 'For mortals it is impossible, but for God all things are possible.'" In Matthew, Jesus was approached by a rich young man, in Mark by a rich man and in Luke by a ruler.

and urbanization have not been grounded firmly in faith that adjusts and tempers them to serve everyone and to avoid destroying and fragmenting people's lives, they have expanded over time into colonialism, wars, unfair markets and militarized peace – a peace that rests on armed deterrence.[25] This has cast humanity in its entirety fluctuating between hot and cold wars, between periods of dressing wounds and peace, loaded and primed.

Further, the love of self, the fuel of perfection that humans can draw upon to achieve their aspirations, this fine thing that serves human needs, can also be problematic, as when it grows unchecked inside an individual and morphs into self-worship. Here is the source of conflict, racial discrimination, contempt of others, bitter struggles – from the smallest units within society to international relations. This conflict entails multiple episodes. Although the arena for these circles of conflict is one and the same, the size and scope of the circles vary.

People have wrongly considered such conflict or struggle to be an integral part of creation – an error that is a consequence of self-love growing to the extent it transforms into self-worship. Individual selfishness can become collective selfishness. A group or a collective takes shape in the service of humankind, for a person in her very nature is a collective being who seeks to belong to society. Man has both dimensions – the personal or individual, and the collective. When selfishness takes on a collective meaning, the collective itself, the community, becomes selfish. Here the problem builds into wider frameworks: the selfish self becomes a familial selfishness, which inflicts much evil upon humankind, expands into despotic tribalism and undermines the whole system with myriad consequences. We then see confessionalism[26]

[25] Musa Sadr is referring here mainly to the Cold War, the rivalry short of armed conflict between the United States and the Soviet Union; but he is also alluding to the era being far from peaceful in much of the developing world, where great power rivalries cut across struggles against colonialism and for social justice. See Fred Halliday, *The Making of the Second Cold War* (London: Verso, 1983).

[26] Musa Sadr here refers to the Lebanese system of "confessionalism" (*ta'ifiyya*, from *ta'ifa*, religious group or sect). *Confessionalisme* is the French word used in Lebanon to describe the system during the Mandate (1920–43) and corresponds to "communalism" during the British domination of India. While confessionalism has roots in Middle Eastern antiquity, it was institutionalized in Lebanon as early as 1834 in the "Beirut Council" formed during the Egyptian occupation (1832–40), and then during the Mutasarrifiyya (1865–1914), where a council composed of a specific number of representatives of the main religious communities ruled the country under a non-Lebanese governor of Christian confession appointed by the Ottoman Porte.

or sectarianism, by way of selfishness, upending heaven and earth and emptying religion of sublimity, compassion, coherence and tolerance.[27] This expression of sectarianism buys and sells values at all sorts of prices and forges them into a patriotic nationalism of selfishness. Patriotism may well be one of the most noble sentiments and motivations, yet it can become a racist patriotism when human beings are led to worship homeland and nation before God almighty. This is when human beings build the glory of "nation" on the ruins of the homeland of others,[28] and found their civilization on the destruction and devastation of the civilizations of others, raising up their own people at the expense of others, and, as in the case of Nazi nationalism, burning the world over and over again.

We end up worshipping such expanded egoisms, and turn them into affliction and devastation, whereas original self-love, duty toward parents and love of family and patriotic love of community and nation are all among the finest callings of human life, as long as they are practiced within appropriate limits. This explains the [other] title chosen for this talk: "For human beings, in their needs and potential."

Society that nurtures the human being must be coordinated and harmonious. The individual must be fully integrated and in tune with it. Whenever any particular human need exceeds or prevails over other needs in society, whenever it is fulfilled at their expense, the situation turns unhealthy and noxious. It is no less harmful and unhealthy whenever an individual or an individual's needs grow to the detriment of other individuals. Disaster strikes whenever one group or one group's needs grow at the expense of another group or another group's needs. Moderation is achieved by probing, exploring connections with others, to the point that one comes to feel the pain felt by others as one's own pain. This is exactly the aim – and requirement – of fasting. Such moderation and balance guarantee the individual's healthy and sound growth, together with the safe and sustainable growth of the collective.

[27] The context to this sermon – rising tensions in Lebanon weeks, days even, before the incidents that sparked the fifteen-year civil war – must have been keenly felt by those attending. "The audience that left the Catholic church and those who read about the episode the next day knew the phobias and divisions of the country in which they lived." Ajami, *The Vanished Imam*, 135.

[28] This refers to Israel in particular. Despite Sadr's criticism of the activities of the Palestine Liberation Organization, which was then dominant in Lebanon, his criticism of Israel (which he called *sharr mutlaq*, "absolute evil") as a source of oppression in the Middle East never wavered. See also n. 34 and accompanying text.

Lebanon is our country, and Lebanon's primary and ultimate wealth and capital is its human being. It is the human being who has written the glory of Lebanon through her effort, migration, thought and initiative. It is this human being that must be preserved in this country. If other countries have wealth beyond human wealth, our wealth "beyond" human wealth is also human.[29] Our work in Lebanon looks for this direction; it seeks opportunities, through temples of worship, universities and institutions, to maintain human wealth through humanist administration and management, so that every human being, whichever part of the country they live in, enjoys their many talents, becomes fully human.[30]

If we wish to preserve Lebanon and protect it, if we wish to put our patriotic fervor into practice, if we wish to practice our religious sensitivity through the principles just presented, we must then preserve the human beings of Lebanon, all of them, every one of them, in all of his and her capacities.

In the Lebanon we live in, where every day witnesses deprivation, this deprivation is caused by malpractice. Responsibility falls upon everyone. Forceful verbal expression in the service of human beings, as we heard in the blessed sermon,[31] is allowed to the extent it does not adversely impact the human being or subvert him.

The regions in which our fellow humans live,[32] like all humans in Lebanon, are a trust[33] hanging around our neck, and hanging around the

[29] Musa Sadr is here making a general point, although his 1970s audience might think of Lebanon lacking the mineral wealth of some regional countries, notably oil (Lebanon has more recently found offshore oil deposits). While blessed with precipitation, verdant valleys and some areas of rich agriculture, the Lebanese have always taken pride in their "human capital" and creativity as seen in multilingualism, the arts and commerce. This too would be very clear to Sadr's listeners.

[30] This is both a specific reference to relatively deprived parts of Lebanon, including those inhabited mainly by Shiʿi Muslims, and an illustration of the general principle cited earlier: "The entire energy of humankind, and the energy of each and every human being, must be conserved and nurtured."

[31] This is probably a reference to Jesus, as described in all four gospels, entering the temple and upsetting the tables of moneylenders and merchants. "He said to them, 'It is written: "My house shall be called a house of prayer"; but you are making it a den or robbers'" (Matthew 21:12–13).

[32] Sadr probably refers to the south of Lebanon and to the suburbs of Beirut, where poorer sections of the Lebanese population lived, mostly Shiʿi.

[33] Musa Sadr often mentions trust, amana, both a moral and legal concept. This is in reference to Qur'an 33:72, where God says He vested trust (amana) in human beings after offering it to "the heavens, to the earth, and to the mountains," who "refused the burden and were afraid to receive it." The roots of the word are Semitic and continue in

neck of the authorities in charge. South Lebanon, and all the regions of the country, are trusts to be preserved, by the will of God and the will of the nation. It is essential that we pay heed, in our thought, to practice and implementation. Wrong-headed thinking and misplaced investment are each a double-betrayal of this trust – as they are both a form of corruption and involve missing genuine opportunities by wasting funds and undermining public rights. Privileges and perks, whatever form they may take, serve to differentiate and divide, no matter how they are packaged or labeled.

Our Lebanon, the country of human beings and of humanism, highlights the humane reality through the contrast today of living with the enemy, an enemy through which we can see the formation of a racist society that destroys and discriminates, financially, culturally, politically and militarily. We even see the enemy distorting history, proceeding with the Judaization of the holy city of Jerusalem and disfiguring its historic monuments.[34]

Our nation is not only to preserve for God and for His human beings. It must be preserved for all of humankind, for humankind in its entirety, so that its true expression is promoted worldwide in defiance of many false images. And we find ourselves facing the opportunity of a lifetime in the new episode that Lebanon has begun.[35]

So let us meet, faithful men and women, let us meet for humankind, at the level of humankind, and at the level of every single human

Western liturgy in "Amen." *Amin* (trustworthy, fiduciary) and *amana* appear often in the Qur'an. It is also found in common usage in law, where agencies and partnerships are based on trust. The English "trust" as legal institution or foundation is known under the name of waqf, a transplant in English law from Islamic law for the establishment of the Oxbridge colleges. See also on amana Chapter 12, n. 10.

[34] Sadr is referring to the continuous "Judaization" of Jerusalem, which Israel occupied in the 1967 war. Meron Benvenisti, deputy mayor of Jerusalem from 1971 to 1978, wrote in 1995: "Although Jerusalem's physical space was unified after the Six-Day War in 1967, the city's psychological space did not merge with it. Indeed the absence of physical barriers reinforced the need for emotional ones. Segregation and alienation cut across all levels of communal interaction, from nursery to graveyard ... So basic is the cleavage that a decisive component of the self-identity of Jews and Arabs alike is not who they are, but who they are not." Meron Benvenisti, *Intimate Enemies: Jews and Arabs in a Shared Land* (Berkeley: University of California Press, 1995). Benvenisti was one of the first to argue that Jewish settlements in the West Bank were not benign, and that they undermined the "two-state" proposal for Israel/Palestine.

[35] Again, this is a reference to the impending civil war that would engulf Lebanon in violence. The passage is a particularly premonitory stance by Sadr, warning against the misuse of violence in pursuit of political gain.

being – every human, our humanity in Beirut, in the south, in the Hermel, in Akkar, in the Beirut suburbs from Karantina to Hayy al-Sulum.[36] The human being, every single human being, must never be excluded from opportunity by being isolated, categorized or classified. Let us preserve humankind in Lebanon and Lebanon's humanity, and preserve this country, the country of humankind. It is a trust of history and a trust of God.

[36] Karantina is in northern Beirut, part of the Christian-dominated region that came to be known during the Lebanese wars as "east Beirut," whereas Hayy al-Sulum (literally, "the Staircase Neighborhood") is in south Beirut. Karantina had once been a quarantine area near the Port of Beirut, but at the time of Musa Sadr's sermon was mainly a Palestinian camp, where poor Kurds, Syrians and Armenians also lived, as well as Lebanese Shiʿis from South Lebanon (who had been displaced by Israeli operations) and from the Bekaa (which they left in search of better economic opportunities). In January 1976, Christian militias massacred 1,000 people, leading to a reprisal attack by Palestinians on the mainly Christian town of Damour, south of Beirut, in which at least 500 were massacred. Hayy al-Sulum is part of Beirut's "southern suburbs," a once prosperous and semirural fringe of the city that became home to Lebanese Shiʿis displaced from the south by Israeli invasions in 1978 and 1982 or just seeking work in the capital.

11

Lebanon

A Wake-Up Call

To that brilliant mind and that tender heart;[1] to those whose every thought is guided by their conscience; to Lebanon's conscientious stewards; to the creativity that God has ingrained in humans in Lebanon; to the ember set alight by the All-Knowing, All-Aware, in the hearts of the cultivated, the experts and the intellectuals and kindled by the mercy of God; to university professors; to experiments and experimenters; to every soul that is pained to see the deep darkness of the night engulfing us; to every heart that beats for Lebanon and its people; to you all.

What actions have you taken, O ambassadors of God on this earth, in response to the horrific events in Lebanon, to the raging fire laying to waste crops and human life (al-Baqara, 205) and nearly setting the entire region ablaze?

Where are you? Have you abandoned your duties? Have you reneged on the true nature on which basis God has created human beings? Is anyone holding you back, preventing you from thinking of solutions or making your positions clear? Have you proposed remedies that the ailing nation has refused? Have you been disregarded by officials and citizens and taken this as a pretext to abdicate your responsibilities?

This country is all we have; why leave it to the wolves? Our country is like no other. Its land is a reflection of the sky; its geography, a journey

[1] This chapter appeared as an article in the daily *al-Nahar* on January 6, 1976, and was addressed "to the Lebanese mind (or reason)," *ila al-'aql al-Lubnani*, as renewed battles were raging across the country. It is included in the selection as a sample of Sadr's concern with Lebanon as the country to which he became particularly attached. It also expresses his humanist horror for war, especially civil wars. The Qur'anic references appear within the original Arabic text.

through history. Our soil is pure, creative and alive, a living soul in itself. Our small stretch of land encompasses the world, and the world's fate lies within its borders. God has destined our people for greatness, but they [the warring groups] want us to remain small; God has created us brave and compassionate, but they want us to be reluctant and shy away from our brethren's pain and hardship; and lastly, God has made us pioneering and dedicated leaders, but they want us to be fearful, uncaring and self-absorbed.

At whose mercy have you placed this country and its citizens, O responsible minds, leaving people to fight one another and forcing them to forsake their land, their message, their livelihood and their dignity along the way?

Have you acknowledged your futility – God forbid – and ceded the throne to those who have left our country of great initiatives fruitless for thirty years, if not more? Have you fled the bullets and snipers and left your country to face its adversities alone, melting away like a candle in its long and treacherous night? Have you decided to retire into your measly towers or Europe's ivory towers, watching from afar and only acting when a relative of yours suffers hardship or when your houses are at risk of ruin? Do you wait until then to contact the warlords or their cronies or those to whom you have given no thought so far, those whose very existence has meant nothing to you? Do you gloat over the misfortune of others? Do you lie in wait for their demise? I dare not believe you would!

Have you heard what your friends say about you, let alone your enemies? Has our model country not had its fair share of torment and disgrace? Is it not enough that the death of five members of the Basque separatist group brought Franco's palace and regime to the ground, while no one bats an eye at the unimaginable suffering of our people?[2] Hardly anyone gives a thought to our suffering, to us or to our cities and universities, aside from arms traffickers and our predatory enemy, ever gleeful at our demise.

Where are you, O conscientious and bright-minded stewards of Lebanon, our brothers in fate and our wise friends?

I implore you to think, to study, to delve deep, to propose, to ask, to insist, to plead, to solicit help, to criticize, to stand your ground and to

[2] Sadr makes reference to the last use of capital punishment with the execution of five Basque militants in Spain on September 27, 1975, and the strong reaction it elicited in Europe.

make your demands heard, time and again. I implore you to make your proposals known to the people, who have also forsaken the struggle, to stand witness and make it clear to the world and to history that you stand by your country in times of adversity. With all due respect to their exponents, the proposals at hand today, with the exception of very few, are either sectarian (and sectarianism would wreak havoc in our country), factional (and the victory of one faction over the other is unacceptable), inflammatory and contentious (and these are both unacceptable, for fair and just solutions require proper elaboration and consensus) or inconducive to fruitful discussion (as they involve much talk but no specific demands or well-designed proposals). There is an abundance of attempts, committees, meetings and private and side discussions filled with positive traits, but they all stagnate, and our plight persists.

They condemn mutual fear, but all they do is instill more fear in people, as if their true intention is to kill the patient rather than find the cure. Our country is facing the most severe crisis of its entire history, whose victims outnumber those of war, but its causes, consequences and contributing factors, both within and without, remain obscure – even the physician's every move seems to aggravate the illness.

O conscientious stewards of Lebanon! I implore you – nay, your country implores you – to act before it is too late, to develop a plan that could save us from ruin.

What we need is a future that breaks with the past; a future where competing factions become equal citizens, where citizens have equal rights and responsibilities; a future where our country can rise to meet global challenges and stand up to Israeli military, cultural, economic, civilizational aggression on our military, culture, economy and civilization; a future that nurtures and preserves out nation's global message and where our many sects become civilizational windows to the world, rather than petty, conflicting statelets; a future where every sect contributes to its country's growth and feels proud to do so, rather than grow at its expense and feel oppressed and despised by others; a future where every citizen treasures their country and refuses to trade it even for the entire world; and lastly, a future where our country becomes the focal point of Islamic–Christian dialogue and European–Arab rapprochement,[3] the

[3] This refers to the attempts to institutionalize a European–Arab dialogue; see Chapter 12, n. 9, and corresponding text.

hub of interaction between civilizations and an oasis for successful experiences to be replicated around the world.

What we need is to build a future where our country carries the torch of the Palestinian cause high and spreads the noble message of Jerusalem for all to see and hear, to touch people's conscience the world over and to build the civilization of tomorrow on fairer grounds.

What we need, O brilliant minds, is to build a new country where no deprived person is left behind, where lost talent and untapped genius are invested to raise our country to new heights, to the rank of giants; we need a country that utilizes its squandered water resources and the natural wealth in its land, sea and sky as industriously as our expatriates' toil around the world.

What we need is to develop an action plan to implement solutions so that all of Lebanon may triumph, not Muslims, Christians, individuals or parties, whether right- or left-wing – only the people of Lebanon as a whole.

What we need is to think and exchange views on how to convince people and build consensus among conflicting parties around this vision. How can we win over extremists, zealots and those who have suffered damages or lost loved ones? How do we reward martyrs and redress people's immense pain and suffering? What do we say to those whose trust we have lost, to those we have let down, to those whose well-intentioned gestures we have dismissed, whose interests we have undermined and whose loved ones we have hurt?

The answer to all of these questions lies in developing a comprehensive plan – one that combines sound thinking, effective means for its implementation and a convincing way forward.

Let, then, O brilliant minds, enlightened people harness the power of the human mind, human conscience and our human values to this end. "And those who strive in Our cause, We will certainly guide them to Our ways: For God is truly with those who do right" (al-ʿAnkabut, 69).

12

Lebanon and Human Civilization

Lebanon is a civilizational must for the world.[1] Living together is a planetary trust vested in the Lebanese. If the Lebanese trial fails, humanity as a whole will grow dark.

In this encounter with representatives of the media, we recall from our bitter experience that the media has played an influential role in the Lebanese civil war, to the extent we can say that it was one of the most effective weapons used. One theory suggests that the conflict itself was a media war, impacting political figures by calling on people's emotions and playing up mass sentiment. Naturally, those who fought were convinced their combat was for the sake of a superior patriotic goal.

But the Middle East in this period, and in Lebanon over these years in particular, was an international arena of conflict between the great powers, focused upon a small expanse of real estate. Israel – endowed with historic powers, and by initiating conspiracies,[2] in politics, through

[1] A group from the Lebanese newspaper publishers' trade union visited Musa Sadr at the Supreme Islamic Shi'i Council, February 18, 1977. Following his talk, Sadr took questions, some of which are reproduced here in italics. While specifics of the discussion are now mainly of almost historical interest, several underlying issues remain unresolved. The conversation highlights Sadr as a leader shaping, reacting to and analyzing fast-moving political events from a bedrock of principles.

[2] Various observers have highlighted "conspiracy theories" in the Middle East; for example, Daniel Pipes, *The Hidden Hand: Middle East Fears of Conspiracy* (New York: St. Martin's Press, 1998). Many miss that those most attracted to such theories are often the victims of conspiracies. In *Periphery: Israel's Search for Middle East Allies* (Lanham, MD: Rowman & Littlefield, 2015), Yossi Alpher traces Israel's contacts with the Lebanese Maronites to "schemes launched by David Ben Gurion in 1948 and 1956, but not implemented at the time, to extend Israeli rule to the Litani River in south Lebanon ... [and] Israeli arms deliveries ... during the civil war of 1958" (45). Israeli armed forces reached the Litani River in their 1978 invasion, and Beirut in the 1982 invasion. Israel's links with the Abu Nidal group, responsible for a series of murders, were examined in

the media – defended its "interests" by taking revenge upon all Arabs through Lebanon. It is clear that the October 1973 war was a military victory for the Arabs, and it suffices to compare the wars of 1967 and 1973 to realize that the military equation and balance of power had changed dramatically.[3]

Along with the military confrontation, there was also a political "war" taking place, beginning with the African boycott of Israel, the European boycott[4] and the wars waged with oil and currencies. Finally, there was an ideological war underway, in which a concerted effort was taking place at the United Nations to find ways to expel and silence Israel; this led Israel to seek revenge against the Arab world through Lebanon, given that Lebanon posed an existential challenge to Israel simply through its example of coexistence.

This region was increasingly manipulated by foreign powers, backed by people in the national media,[5] then by the region's own political leaders. In this context, a large number of voices, columnists and others,

Patrick Seale, *Abu Nidal: The World's Most Notorious Terrorist* (London: Arrow Books, 1992), 42–53.

Tensions with Lebanon built up with clashes with Palestinians, originally just with refugees returning to harvest (see Benny Morris, *Israel's Border Wars, 1949–1956* [Oxford: Oxford University Press, 1993], 35–36, 38–39) and more particularly after the Palestine Liberation Organization (PLO) leadership moved from Jordan to Lebanon in 1970.

3 While Arab armies were more successful in the 1973 war than in 1967, the greater impact of 1973 was strengthening conservative Arab forces and encouraging Egypt's 1979 agreement with Israel; see Fouad Ajami, *The Arab Predicament: Arab Political Thought and Practice since 1967* (Cambridge: Cambridge University Press, 1992), 113–14, 179–80. Lebanon did not take part in the 1973 war.

4 Most Arab countries had established an economic boycott of Israel since its inception in 1948, but the boycott intensified and widened in the wake of the 1973 war, especially with the embargo on oil against Western countries, above all the USA, for supplying heavy weaponry to Israel during the war. Several African countries cut their diplomatic ties with the Jewish state, and some European countries distanced themselves somewhat from Israel because of its breach of international law in the Occupied Territories. Yet there was no formal boycott, so Musa Sadr might have mentioned it as a promising feature of the Euro–Arab institutional dialogue (see n. 9). The boycott in place elsewhere started collapsing when Egypt's ruler, Anwar Sadat, decided to go it alone with a separate peace with Israel after his visit to Jerusalem in late 1978. The boycott has since been dropped by Egypt, the Palestinian Authority, Jordan and the Gulf Cooperation Council, while informal boycott campaigns, supported by Palestinian civil-society movements and modeled on boycotts of apartheid South Africa, have focused on settlements in Israeli-occupied territory and Israeli breaches of international law.

5 "National" (*wataniyya*) refers probably to the wider Arab world.

came to prominence, and one can say they participated in the war – if they did not actually cause it.

In this meeting, which I hope might contribute to rebuilding the country, I wish to start from this point. It has become evident that the media has a huge role. Perhaps in Lebanon, its role is especially great; from what we can see in the present atmosphere, we might say that its role is prevalent, because of anxiety in the soul and the absence of any conviction among many Lebanese that they can ever again want to live together. Some feel that no power on earth can impose upon them the undertaking of rebuilding the homeland. Similarly, however, if the Lebanese, with a unified will, resolve among themselves to rebuild a united country, then no one can hope to prevent them. The real reconstruction of Lebanon does not depend on military might, up-to-date laws, constitutional government or economic regulations: it depends upon the will of the Lebanese, and upon the impact of the leaders of the media.

I would like to imagine that the ideas reflected by the media in newspapers and journals might lay foundations for constructing a new and united Lebanon. Lebanon has suffered from the uprooting, scattering and forced separation of so many living souls, and from the fracturing of the people's will. The information and media atmosphere dominated and controlled people's innermost emotions, further dividing and dispersing their souls and ripping their will into shreds. Yet if we could revive the conviction in people's spirits that we can rebuild an enduring, immortal future for our country, Lebanon, then the country would face no real threat. Because Lebanon is a necessity for global civilization – as so many have said.

Lebanon, at this particular stage in history, represents an essential model for the world. Firstly, because of the expansion of transport and communication, we feel that the entire world in the late twentieth century and at the beginning of the twenty-first century lives effectively like a single country. The distance between one country and another, in terms of physical travel time, seems no more than the distance between Beirut and Tripoli. In such an interconnected world as ours, which includes different religions and coexistence among the peoples of the world, any efforts to create a universal state should link closely with and be greatly affected by the success of Lebanon's example.

Further, and equally central to Lebanon's importance, the hopes of migrant and immigrant communities the world over depend upon

Euro–Arab dialogue, itself dependent on Muslim–Christian dialogue – all the more so in the wake of the failure of the experiment in Asian–African unity and the outcomes of this failure.[6] The world found itself tested, prior to the rise of the two superpowers, in convening successfully efforts to establish Afro–Asian encounters, African unity and a European market.[7] Today the World Federation of Parliamentarians[8] calls yet again upon humanity to find a guarantee for the security of human beings confronted with the rivalry between the two superpowers. As things are today, which country, human being or institution can guarantee its safety and security if America and the Soviet Union agree with each other against it? Consequently, the world looks for another force that can remove this duopoly.

People have dreamt of China emerging to take a prominent role, but this hope has not come to fruition. The Arab–European dialogue[9] – given Europe's expertise, long experience and position, and the Arab world's cultural heritage, wealth and geographical location – gave rise to great hopes and to attention and energy being invested in new political forces expected to emerge from Christian–Muslim dialogue. If the experience of Lebanon should falter or fail, this would harm and undermine the whole of human civilization for the next fifty years, at the very least. Therefore, we say that Lebanon is a civilizational necessity, now more than ever.

We ask the Lebanese to allow us to express our view that coexistence and tolerance of diversity is not the property of the Lebanese, not something they can dispose of or dispense with. Rather, it is a trust[10]

[6] Musa Sadr is probably referring here to hopes that had been raised in the early postcolonial period by the 1955 Asian–African Conference held in Bandung, Indonesia.

[7] The Organisation of African Unity (OAU) was established on May 25, 1963, in Addis Ababa, originally with thirty-two states. The European Economic Community was formed in 1957, having evolved from the 1951 European Coal and Steel Community: it became the European Union in 1993, with a single market and a population of around 450 million people before the withdrawal of the United Kingdom in 2020.

[8] This probably refers to the Inter-Parliamentary Union, formed in 1989, which worked both to promote international law and protect parliamentarians. As of 2020, it had 178 member parliaments from around the world.

[9] The Euro–Arab dialogue, which started in the wake of the 1973 war, is probably what Sadr refers to in this passage, as several meetings took place in 1975. See, generally, Alan R. Taylor, "The Euro–Arab Dialogue: Quest for an Interregional Partnership," *Middle East Journal* 32, no. 4 (1978): 429–43.

[10] Amana. Sadr often uses the concept of amana, the trust of people in each other and in institutions. It is also a legal concept. See also Chapter 10, n. 33.

the Lebanese must hold in their hands; it is their responsibility and their duty, not just their right.

Here lies the importance of a persuasive, convincing media and the significance of their role. Where can the Lebanese find satisfaction and in what can they take pride, faced with all the martyrs that have been sacrificed, on both sides of the front lines? All those killed were children of Lebanon; every one of them died believing that the combat was being waged for the sake of Lebanon. What would console the [bereaved] Lebanese mothers? How can we explain to the next generation such a large number of victims, tens of thousands of our finest young people?

This is why we have said we cherish Lebanon's unity and uphold it along with the country's independence, as well as harmony between Lebanon and the region. The maintenance of this entity called Lebanon is a sacred trust of world civilization.

I feel supreme happiness as I meet my siblings in humanity, the men and women of the media. The great importance of your jobs derives from working in what your syndicate chairman has described as a "niche of worship," this office where you use your pens as a prayer tool and your ink to light a torch of unity over this country's future.

The future is not for editors to base their writings just on feelings or interests, God forbid. The future requires editors to be accurate in every word they write, in every title and headline, and with every analysis or image they publish. If editors feel they are in a "niche of worship," then they will feel the holiness of their responsibility in the times ahead. I imagine that the tensions in the minds and souls [of the Lebanese] are in urgent need of being soothed. Newscasting should be reevaluated; unqualified people in position as war-media puppets should have their roles reassessed. You are well informed of your duties and in your areas of expertise; all I have to do is to pray to God for your success, and open myself, my knowledge, my experiences to any questions you may want to ask.

Do you think that the 1943 accord has collapsed, and do you have in mind a new vision for a strong and sustainable future for Lebanon?[11]

[11] The National Pact of 1943 followed independence. "This unwritten agreement enshrined a historic compromise: the Maronites, recognizing Lebanon's Arab character and membership of the Arab family, agreed to renounce any protective links to European powers and the Muslims ... shed their pan-Arab nationalist dream ... The Pact also presumed to regulate the share and status of every religious community ... There were a full

In fact, the vulnerability of the Lebanese political system to what has taken place does not invalidate the sectarian formula for representative government, because the factors involved lay beyond the scope of the Lebanese will. After all, we know this country does not manufacture a single bullet. Yet we can witness the flood of weapons moving toward and into Lebanon. Where do these weapons come from, and why? We know that weapons in today's world today are political commodities, not purely commercial ones; this was clear in the continuation of the civil war's battle for two years.

We say that the pressures that brought the storm to Lebanon and shook the 1943 formula are more powerful than any country could withstand. Yet I think Lebanon did not quite collapse as some of the state's institutions remain standing although they require bolstering. I do not defend the existing system, but I would defend the framework for coexistence it espoused, and the democratic context that exists within society. I was one of the critics of the previous situation.[12] As for the future, there are priorities that are sacrosanct. Through dialogue, the Lebanese should choose the formula that is best to uphold and realize these priorities. Lebanon's leaders, with their knowledge of what is in the hearts of the Lebanese people, should choose a formula that reflects these priorities.

Today, if Lebanon should be seen as a facsimile of any other country, we should see it as a microcosm of far larger countries given its size. For Lebanon not to remain just a microcosm, it must have a special, comparative advantage. Our comparative advantage here is none other than our history of and skill in coexistence. Coexistence is a living feature – leaving aside the especially rich features of Lebanon in its history and the strength of its people and climate; these advantages are already here, and not gifts we need to look for in the future.

seventeen of these ... The Maronites, taking the presidency, command of the army and other key posts, came out firmly at the apex of the hierarchy." Hirst, *Beware of Small States*, 11–12. The outbreak of war in 1975 was in part a challenge to the 1943 pact, and the postwar settlement of the 1989 Taef agreement, 120,000 deaths later, would shift the pact's ratio of parliamentary seats, ending the previous, slight Christian predominance over Muslims and Druze (ibid., 112).

[12] While not endorsing the specific – and by 1975 contentious – arrangements of the 1943 pact, Sadr is expressing support for the principles of coexistence and consensus on which it was based. He frames this in terms of general principles rather than political representation based on religious sect, while acknowledging that his thought has moved away from its total rejection.

Lebanese's primary message lies in coexistence. In order to integrate, the Lebanese religious affiliations should maintain a minimal cultural role, which can be achieved only by keeping personal status law as it is rather than through secularization. The personal status laws that manage marriage and inheritance both complement national culture. These laws must continue, for other than these laws Lebanon is a secular state. It does not emanate from God's rules, from the rules of heaven. Lebanon's presidents are not the shadow of God on earth.[13] Lebanese law is also secular for it does not stem from the Qur'an or from the Bible.

The second point concerns freedom in Lebanon, on which Lebanon's mission of coexistence depends. On a foundation of freedom, civilized groups can coexist within one nation. An individual can sometimes impose himself on his homeland,[14] but one group, contending and coexisting with other groups, cannot impose itself on the homeland.

The third point is respect for the rights of citizens, that is, full and complete justice: upholding political, social and economic rights, and fairness in development.[15]

Do you favor the reunification of the education curriculum? Are you in favor of making Lebanon one single electoral district? And would that, in your opinion, contribute to restoring cohesion among the Lebanese?

[13] Musa Sadr here refers to the notion of the ruler as deriving authority from God, taken by Islamic rulers from the Qur'anic depiction of man as vice-regent or deputy adopted later by the Islamic Republic of Iran. Similar notions were found earlier in Sasanian Iran (Said Amir Arjomand, *The Shadow of God and the Hidden Imam: Religion, Political Order, and Societal Change in Shi'ite Iran from the Beginning to 1890* [Chicago, IL: University of Chicago Press 1984], 95–96). Sadr's point is that Lebanon's rulers root their legitimacy in the country's constitution rather than God's will, and that Lebanese law in general is "secular" in the sense it is not based on holy texts. Family law, referred to by Sadr as "personal status law," is an exception. "Both the family law systems of Israel and Lebanon have run to date with separate jurisdictions for Christians, Muslims, and Jews, and within each large denominational community, between sects and sub-sects. Each community has its own separate laws, and its own separate judge." Mallat, *Introduction to Middle Eastern Law*, 364–65.

[14] Musa Sadr's point is that a system based on coexistence works against the emergence of dictatorship.

[15] Economic and social inequalities were part of the mix that led to the outbreak of war in Lebanon in 1975, two years before this talk. "Between 1970 and 1973 the so-called boom in fact imprisoned the majority of Lebanese, especially Muslim, in a trap of high inflation, falling real incomes ... Industry and agriculture continued to stagnate while fortunes were made in services and property." William Harris, *Faces of Lebanon: Sects, Wars, and Global Extensions* (Princeton, NJ: Markus Wiener, 1997), 156. Development across Lebanon was uneven, while the wealth of some was very evident.

I am 100 percent in favor of unified educational and cultural curriculums, and a unified single countrywide electoral district in Lebanon.

Will the [proposed] religious leaders' summit be held? What do you think about the efforts under way for this summit?

I am among those who are fully convinced by this. I am working hard on the issue, and I believe this summit is at our doorstep. We just need a brief period of time to exchange views on the working paper and then we can have the summit.

Do you consider the constitutional document a valid formula for resolving the crisis?[16]

The constitutional document is an agenda for political dialogue; it did not put forward specific options. Unfortunately, when the Syrian delegation began to talk to the Lebanese parties following the misguided attempts at isolation that occurred at the very beginning of the Lebanese crisis,[17] the Lebanese were not meeting and political dialogue was impossible, even to a minimal extent. "Dialogue" at this time was top to bottom, that is, President Franjiyye would speak to the Lebanese Front,[18] and then proceed to present recommendations to the [Syrian] arbitrating delegation. Prime Minister Rashid Karami[19] would consult in

[16] The Constitutional Reform Document, backed by Syria, was put forward in February 1976 by Suleiman Franjiyye, president of Lebanon from 1970 to 1976. The document proposed changing the sectarian balance within the political system by giving greater powers to the prime minister, a post held by a Sunni under the terms of the 1943 National Pact, and establishing parity between Muslims and Christians in Parliament, so ending the Christian majority of deputies in Parliament. The document failed to satisfy the Lebanese National Movement (LNM), made up of mainly Muslim parties, or end tensions between Christian militias and the PLO. The war continued.

[17] In 1975, the LNM, a coalition of mainly Muslims and leftist parties generally of secular persuasion (including the Communist Party and the Syrian Nationalist Party with a large Christian composition), called for isolating the Kataeb, or Phalangist, Party, led by Pierre Gemayel and his sons, and the National Liberal Party led by Camille Chamoun, which were allied in the mainly Christian Lebanese Front. While Musa Sadr had himself in 1975 established the Amal militia and supported some of the reforms demanded by the LNM, and progressed under the general umbrella that the LNM assembled, he opposed the LNM's call for isolating the Christian parties and advocated dialogue involving all Lebanese parties to stop violence and reach agreement on political representation. This is discussed in Section I.4 of the Introduction on violence.

[18] The Lebanese Front was a coalition of mainly Christian parties (see n. 17).

[19] From Tripoli in North Lebanon, Rashid Karami was prime minister ten times between 1955 and 1987, including between July 1975 and December 1976. A Sunni Muslim, Karami was not part of the LNM. He was assassinated in 1987.

turn with his front and then contact the negotiating delegation. Through the two leaders, President Suleiman Franjiyye and Prime Minister Rashid Karami, and others, the arbitrating delegation would reach a solution commensurate with the feelings of and interests of the parties. In this way, the constitutional document was drawn up after contact with the Palestinian side. On the day the document was promulgated it was decided that its recommendations should be the basis for a meeting of the Lebanese parties, who would then be able to decide on further measures. Of course, if the Lebanese [parties of varying views] meet they may go far beyond what is stated in the constitutional document in order to build the future. The constitutional document remains valid as a working paper or agenda for future political dialogue, and I would say – I hope that it will not be seen as courtesy or my being excessively polite – I believe that the Christmas message of Patriarch Khoreish,[20] on its own, can serve as a discussion paper and basis for dialogue and even the examination of future political options. Let us have a homeland, a motherland, such as the one Patriarch Khoreish sets forth in the latest Christmas message.

How do you view the situation in the south, and will it affect the general situation in Lebanon?

The problem of the south today is a microcosm of the Lebanese problem, and the Lebanese crisis has moved into to the territory of the south ... The solution is for the Arab Deterrent Forces to go to the south.[21] There are some political difficulties over this since Israel has made threats after opposing the dispatch of these forces to the south and there have been some regional negotiations. Until this is resolved, there

[20] From the village of Ain Ebel, South Lebanon, Anthony III Peter Khoreish was the Maronite Patriarch of Antioch and the Levant from 1975 until his retirement in 1986. He was known for his moderate positions, and died in 1994.

[21] The Arab Deterrent Force (Quwwat al-Radʿ al-ʿArabiyya) was endorsed by the Arab Summit in Cairo, October 25–26, 1976, to be stationed in Lebanon, and mandated to disarm militias. It deployed across Lebanon by mid-November 1976, ending a nineteen-month phase of the civil war that had taken 10,000 lives. The situation was more complex in the south, due to the presence of armed Palestinians and Lebanese Christian militias allied to Israel, which under its "Good Fence" policy was offering work to Lebanese Christians in Israel. As other member states comprising the force (mostly from South Yemen) withdrew, Syria became increasingly dominant in Lebanon, but was prevented by Israel from moving to the south. In March 1978, Israel would invade South Lebanon. See Hiro, *Lebanon, Fire and Embers*, 43–51.

should be realistic attempts to create a political reconciliation in the south. Perhaps these could help alleviate the pain.

Do you think Lebanon is paving a way to recovery?

Lebanon is paving its way to recovery and healing; it is rising and moving on. As for the setbacks, they will remain limited and narrow: the al-Akkawi explosion is an example,[22] along with other deep and provocative tragedies. The reaction lacked any reasonable measure, and as a result people were pent up [in their frustration]. Dozens were then killed in response.

Lebanon is on its way to recovery, rehabilitation, restoration and liberation, although I feel not all our leaders agree to live together.

The Lebanese crisis was closely related to the Palestinian presence in Lebanon. What is your perception of the current reality?

The Palestinian presence in Lebanon certainly played a major part in the Lebanese crisis.[23] The solution to the crisis must include clarifying and defining Lebanese–Palestinian relations in detail. I want to stress that given the strong relations I have kept with Palestinian leaders during the ordeal, I believed, and I still believe, that if the Lebanese wanted to organize relations with Palestinian leaders, this could be straightforward and easily conceived.

[22] This is a reference to a car bomb that exploded on January 3, 1977, next to the Phalangist headquarters on Akkawi Street, east Beirut. United Press International (an American press agency), cited in the *New York Times*, reported that twenty-five people were killed and seventy injured, and quoted Phalangist official Karim Pakradouni as saying that "contacts have been initiated through the Arab peacekeeping force to try to contain the incident and prevent renewal of the fighting that ravaged Lebanon for 19 months before the peacekeeping force arrived in November." "Blast Said to Kill 25 at Office in Beirut of Rightists' Party," *New York Times*, January 4, 1977. Car bombs, the terror of Beirutis throughout the civil war, were often "unclaimed" and invariably led to bloody reprisals against other civilians. Ronen Bergman (*Rise and Kill First: The Secret History of Israel's Targeted Assassinations* [London: John Murray, 2019], 242) makes the point that Israel planted car bombs in Lebanon, including the use of drones to detonate them, with Defense Minister Ariel Sharon hoping to draw the PLO into attacks on Israel that would "justify" an Israeli invasion. Car bombs were used by all parties, domestic and international, through the Lebanese wars, as a tool for intimidation and revenge.

[23] The PLO was loosely aligned with the LNM after it was formed in 1969 and broadly supported its aim of reforming the Lebanese political system. Musa Sadr's answer to this question shows his principled support for the Palestinian cause but his unwillingness to see Palestinians in Lebanon dragged into potentially divisive alliances.

This is not a predetermined matter; we must cooperate to help Palestinian leaders implement or develop agreements with Lebanon. They must also help themselves and Lebanon by not interfering in internal affairs and not making alliances with Lebanese parties here and there – with any party. They ought to help clarify, and to apply, these clear principles in Lebanon. So, if the Lebanese and the Palestinians agree, and this is what I hope and believe in, then there need be no difficulties for Lebanon in dealing with the Palestinian cause.

We feel that the leaders do not disagree about the need for coexistence, but what do you think could be a broad outline for coexistence among the Lebanese?

As I said, the Lebanese may differ. My own view, which I offer to the Lebanese and to our friends in the media, is that a formula of coexistence that continues to create more meetings and contacts is the best formula. Today's trend toward political or administrative decentralization is wrong in my view because any shift to postwar decentralization is considered an outcome of the war and will therefore go deeper than the Lebanese would want. In my view, after this war, the Lebanese should return, even if for a period of six years, for example, to a more intensive centralization than in the past. They could turn Lebanon into one single [electoral] district,[24] for example, or, as a result of better transportation systems, succeed in creating more interactions among various regions, to bring about greater coexistence, tolerance and intermixing.

This would be better, I think, because the whole of Lebanon is, as I see it, like a single governorate of bigger countries. This is what I hope for, and what I would propose to the Lebanese. Lebanon enjoys the respect and care of the world, and a high degree of global prominence, solely as a result of its intercommunal tolerance and coexistence.

What about the National Pact, which some believe was built on conditions that no longer exist?

[24] The *qada'* (*kaza* in Turkish) was the smallest administrative unit of the Ottoman Empire, with several making up a *sanjak* or, still larger, a *vilayet*. After independence in 1946, a system developed with eight provinces (*muhafazas*), above districts (qada's) and, below them, municipalities. This increased the fissiparous nature of Lebanese politics, and several reformists supported the transformation of the country's election into a unified national district.

One should not exaggerate the influence of the [1943] National Pact, because it reflected political trends intersecting at one point in time. Lebanese coexistence is far older than the National Charter, indeed older than the authors of the National Pact, or their fathers and grandparents! A thousand years ago the Lebanese [resident] opened his door to discover a neighbor with a religion that was different to his; he ate with him, invited him to be his guest, sought solace and refuge with him. They lived as neighbors sharing hopes and sorrows, forging strong links and ties. These bonds have been more numerous and stronger than those among people in other countries. Coexistence is at the core of Lebanese life, and the situation we see around us today is the result of exceptional circumstances brought about in part by what remains of the wartime [divisive] media. We will overcome this through dedication and strength.

Bibliography

On Musa al-Sadr, no fewer than three book-length biographies are available in English: Fouad Ajami, *The Vanished Imam: Musa al Sadr and the Shia of Lebanon* (Ithaca, NY: Cornell University Press, 1986); Peter Theroux, *The Strange Disappearance of Imam Moussa Sadr* (London: Weidenfeld and Nicholson, 1987); Majed Halawi, *A Lebanon Defied: Musa al-Sadr and the Shiʿa Community* (Boulder, CO: Westview, 1992). A review of various aspects of Sadr's background and life can be found in H. E. Chehabi, ed., *Distant Relations: Iran and Lebanon in the Last 500 Years* (Oxford: Centre for Lebanese Studies, 2006).

Several books on Sadr are available in Persian, including ʿAbd al-Raḥīm Abadhār, *Imām Mūsā al-Ṣadr: Omīd-e maḥrumān* [Imam Musa al-Sadr: The hope of the deprived] (Tehran: Sāzimān-i Tablīghāt-i Islāmī, 1995); and, in Arabic, Ṣādeq al-Nabulsī, *Mūsā al-Ṣadr: Masār al-taḥaddiyyāt wa-l-taḥawwulāt* [Musa al-Sadr: The path of challenges and transitions] (Beirut: Markaz al-Ḥadāra li-Tanmiyat al-Fikr al-Islāmī wa-Ittijāhātih, 2013); Rabāb al-Ṣadr, *al-Falsafa al-iṣlāḥiyya fī ruʾyat al-Imām Mūsā al-Ṣadr wa-aʿmālihi* [Reformist philosophy in the vision of Imam Musa al-Sadr and in his writings] (Beirut: Markaz al-Imām Mūsā al-Ṣadr li-l-Abḥāth wa-l-Dirāsāt, 2022).

An extensive record of Sadr's life and works in twelve volumes can be found in Yaʿqūb Dāher, *Masīrat al-Imām Sayyed Mūsā al-Ṣadr: Yawmiyyāt wa-wathāʾiq* [Journey of Imam Sayyed Musa al-Sadr: Daily chronology and documents] (Beirut: Dār Bilāl, 2000). Dāher's comprehensive compendium lists all the activities, statements and works of Sadr almost on a daily basis. Except for Chapter 1 ("By Way of an Autobiography"), the original Arabic text of the chapters in the present work can be found in Dāher's collection, arranged chronologically. Another set of extensive documents on Sadr's social and intellectual activities has been compiled in four volumes by ʿAlī Jāber, *al-Islām al-Qurʾānī* [Qur'anic Islam] (Beirut: Dār al-Maʿārif al-Ḥukmiyya, 2019).

A more accessible reference to the Arabic texts (and their translation in various languages) can be found on https://imamsadr.net, a dedicated site that keeps all information and texts up to date. The texts in the present book are translated from the latest available copies on the site. Several books that compile Sadr's contributions thematically were also published by the research centers on Sadr in Tehran (www.imamsadr.ir) and Beirut. A selection is listed under Sadr's bibliographic entry below, by date of publication. Another site on Sadr's social activities is https://imamsadrfoundation.org.

Main websites used in the book comprise, on the Qur'an, in Arabic with several English translations, https://corpus.quran.com; on Sunni hadith, https://dorar.net; on Shiʿi hadith and the classical law corpus, https://shiaonlinelibrary.com.

This bibliography only mentions the books, chapters and articles cited in the present study (short articles in newspapers and on websites are not included).

Abrahamian, Ervand. *Iran between Two Revolutions*. Princeton, NJ: Princeton University Press, 1983.

The Coup: 1953, the CIA, and the Roots of Modern US–Iran Relations. New York: New Press, 2013.

Ajami, Fouad. *The Vanished Imam: Musa al Sadr and the Shia of Lebanon*. Ithaca, NY: Cornell University Press, 1986.

The Arab Predicament: Arab Political Thought and Practice since 1967. Cambridge: Cambridge University Press, 1992.

Algar, Hamid. "ʿAllāma Sayyid Muḥammad Ḥusayn Ṭabāṭabāʾī: Philosopher, Exegete, and Gnostic." *Journal of Islamic Studies* 17, no. 3 (2006): 326–51.

ʿAlī b. Abī Ṭālib. *Nahj al-balāgha*. Edited by Muḥammad ʿAbduh. Beirut: Dār al-Maʿārif, 1990. http://shiaonlinelibrary.com.

Dīwān [Collection of poetry]. www.aldiwan.net/.

Alpher, Yossi. *Periphery: Israel's Search for Middle East Allies*. Lanham, MD: Rowman & Littlefield, 2015.

al-Anṣārī, Murtaḍā. *Kitāb al-makāsib* [Book of transactions]. Edited by Muḥammad Kalantar. Najaf: Maṭbaʿat al-Ādāb, 1972.

Arjomand, Said Amir. *The Shadow of God and the Hidden Imam: Religion, Political Order, and Societal Change in Shiʿite Iran from the Beginning to 1890*. Chicago, IL: University of Chicago Press, 1984.

Arminjon Hachem, Constance. *Chiisme et État: Les clercs à l'épreuve de la modernité*. Paris: CNRS, 2013.

Ayer, A. J. *Language, Truth and Logic*. London: Gollancz, 1936.

Batatu, Hanna. *Syria's Peasantry, the Descendants of Its Lesser Rural Notables, and Their Politics*. Princeton, NJ: Princeton University Press, 1999.

Bayandor, Darioush. *Iran and the CIA: The Fall of Mosaddeq Revisited*. London: Palgrave Macmillan, 2010.

Benvenisti, Meron. *Intimate Enemies: Jews and Arabs in a Shared Land*. Berkeley: University of California Press, 1995.

Bergman, Ronen. *Rise and Kill First: The Secret History of Israel's Targeted Assassinations*. London: John Murray, 2019.

Berkey, Jonathan. *The Formation of Islam: Religion and Society in the Near East 600–1800*. Cambridge: Cambridge University Press, 2003.

Blair, Sheila, and Jonathan Bloom. "Art and Architecture: Themes and Variations." In Esposito, *The Oxford History of Islam*, 215–67.

Bourke, Stephen. *The Middle East: The Cradle of Civilization*. London: Thames & Hudson, 2018.
Boyce, Mary. *Zoroastrians: Their Religious Beliefs and Practices*. London: Routledge & Kegan Paul, 1979.
al-Bukhārī. *al-Ṣaḥīḥ*. Beirut: Dār Ṭawq al-Najāt, 2001.
Bulliet, Richard. *Islam: The View from the Edge*. New York: Columbia University Press, 1994.
Chalabi, Tamara. *The Shi'is of Jabal 'Amil and the New Lebanon: Community and Nation-State, 1918–1942*. New York: Palgrave Macmillan, 2006.
Chamussy, René. *Chronique d'une guerre: Liban 1975–1977*. Paris: Desclée, 1978.
Chehabi, H. E., ed. *Distant Relations: Iran and Lebanon in the Last 500 Years*. Oxford: Centre for Lebanese Studies, 2006.
Chehabi, H. E., and Tafreshi Maji. "Musa al-Sadr and Iran." In Chehabi, *Distant Relations*, 137–61.
Corbin, Henry. *L'Imagination créatrice dans le soufisme d'Ibn 'Arabi*. Paris: Flammarion, 1958.
"Eschatologie et réincarnation chez les Ishrâqîyûn (Sohrawardî et Mollâ Ṣadrâ)." *Annuaire de l'École pratique des hautes études, Section des sciences religieuses* (1961–62): 73–79.
"La place de Mollâ Sadrâ (m. 1050/1640) dans la philosophie iranienne." *Studia Islamica* 18 (1963): 81–113.
"Maqâm-e Mollâ Sadrâ Shîrâzî dar falsafa-ye Iran" [The place of Mulla Sadra Shirazi in Iranian philosophy]. Translated by S. H. Nasr. *Revue de la Faculté des Lettres de l'Université de Téhéran* 12 (1963): 1–34.
Histoire de la philosophie islamique, des origines jusqu'à la mort d'Averroës. Paris: Gallimard, 1964.
Tārīkh al-falsafa al-islāmiyya [History of Islamic philosophy]. Beirut: 'Uwaydāt Press, 1966.
En Islam iranien, aspects spirituels et philosophiques. 4 vols. Paris: Gallimard, 1971–73.
"Le Kitâb al-Hikmat al-'Arshîya de Mollâ Ṣadrâ Shîrâzî." *Annuaire de l'École pratique des hautes études, Section des sciences religieuses* 85 (1976–77): 269–74.
Cronin, Stephanie. *Armies and State-Building in the Middle East*. London: I.B. Tauris, 2014.
al-Dabbāgh, 'Abd al-Karīm. *al-Sayyed Muḥammad Mahdī al-Ṣadr*. Qom: Rāfed, 2017.
Dermenghem, Emile. *La vie de Mahomet*. Paris: Plon, 1920 [new ed. Alger: Charlot, 1950].
Mahomet et la tradition islamique. Paris: Le Seuil, 1955.
Donner, Fred. "Muhammad and the Caliphate." In Esposito, *The Oxford History of Islam*, 1–61.
Esposito, John, ed. *The Oxford History of Islam*. Oxford: Oxford University Press, 1999.
Faḍlallāh, Muḥammad Ḥusayn. *Bayyināt* [Proofs]. www.bayynat.org.lb/.
Farrokhiān, Mahdī, ed. *Andīshe-ye rabudeh shodeh* [The thought that was stolen (with the disappearance of the Imam)]. Tehran: Imam Moussa Sadr Cultural Research Institute, 2006.

Flaubert, Gustave. *Salammbô*. Translated by J. S. Chartres. Paris: Michel Lévy Frères, 1862; Project Gutenberg, 2006. www.gutenberg.org/ebooks/1290.

Habachi, René. "Teilhard de Chardin et le drame du XXe siècle. Le génie de l'évolution." Les Conférences du Cénacle 1, Beirut, 1956.

"Teilhard de Chardin. Science, philosophie et foi." Les Conférences du Cénacle 6, Beirut, 1956.

Halliday, Fred. *The Making of the Second Cold War*. London: Verso, 1983.

Harris, William. *Faces of Lebanon: Sects, Wars, and Global Extensions*. Princeton, NJ: Markus Wiener, 1997.

Hillion-Launey, Tristan. "The Islamic Economy according to Musa al-Ṣadr: The Avant-gardist Thoughts of an Original Shiʿi Reformist Cleric." In *Proceedings of the Sixth Annual Conference on Shiʿi Studies*, 33–74. London: Islamic College, 2021.

Hiro, Dilip. *Lebanon, Fire and Embers: A History of the Lebanese Civil War*. London: Weidenfeld and Nicolson, 1993.

Hirst, David. *Beware of Small States: Lebanon, Battleground of the Middle East*. London: Faber and Faber, 2010.

Hourani, Albert. *A History of the Arab Peoples*. Cambridge, MA: Harvard University Press, 1991.

al-Ḥurr al-ʿĀmilī. *Wasāʾil al-Shīʿa*. Beirut: Muʾassasat Āl al-Bayt li-l-Turāth, 1993.

al-ʿIbād, ʿAbd al-Muḥsin. *Sharḥ Sunan Ibn Mājah*. www.alathar.net/home/esound/index.php?op=tadevi&id=10617.

Ibn Abī al-Ḥadīd. *Sharh Nahj al-balāgha*. Cairo: Ḥalabī, 1960.

Ibn Ḥanbal, Aḥmad. *al-Musnad*. Beirut: Muʾassasat al-Risāla, 1999.

Ibn Mājah. *Sunan*. Edited by Muḥammad Fuʾād ʿAbd al-Bāqī. Beirut: Dār Iḥyāʾ al-Kutub al-ʿArabiyya, 1952.

Ibn Shayba. *al-Kitāb al-muṣannaf fī al-aḥādīth wa-l-āthār*. Riyadh: al-Rushd, 1988.

Ibn Shuʿba. *Tuḥfat al-ʿuqūl ʿan al-rasūl*. Najaf: al-Ḥaydariyya, 1953. Reprint, Tehran, 1972.

Jafariān, Ḥabībe. *Sayyed Mūsā Ṣadr: Haft revāyat khuṣūṣī* [Sayyed Musa Sadr: Seven personal narratives]. Mashhad: Sepīdeh Bavārān; Tehran: Markaz-e Imām Mūsā Ṣadr, 2015.

Jurdi Abisaab, Rula. "Sayyid Musa al-Sadr, the Lebanese State, and the Left." *Journal of Shiʿa Islamic Studies* 8, no. 2 (2015): 131–57.

Kamenka, Eugene. *The Ethical Foundations of Marxism*. London: Routledge & Kegan Paul, 1972 [1962].

Kassir, Samir. *La Guerre du Liban: De la dissension nationale au conflit regional*. Paris: Karthala, 1994 [new ed. L'Orient des Livres/Sindbad/Actes-Sud, 2018].

Katouzian, Homa. *Musaddiq and the Struggle for Power in Iran*. Revised ed. London: I.B. Tauris, 1999.

Kelly, Henry Ansgar. *Satan: A Biography*. Cambridge: Cambridge University Press, 2006.

Kerr, Michael, and Craig Larkin, eds. *The Alawis of Syria: War, Faith and Politics in the Levant*. London: Hurst & Company, 2015.

Khātamī, Muḥammad. *Az Doniā-ye Shahr tā Shahr-e Doniā* [From the world of the city-state to the city of the world]. Tehran: Nashr-e Nāy, 1994.

Bīm-e Mawj [In the middle of the waves]. Tehran: Sīmā-ye Javān, 1994.

Khosraw, Nasir. *Le Livre Réunissant les Deux Sagesses (Kitâb-e jâmiʿ al-hikmatain) ou Harmonie de la Philosophie Grecque et de la Théosophie Ismaélienne*. Tehran/Paris: Adrien-Maisonneuve, 1953.

Kulaynī. *al-Kāfī*. Tehran: Dār al-Kutub al-Islāmiyya, 2000.

Lammens, Henri. *La Syrie, précis historique*. 2 vols. Beirut: Imprimerie Catholique, 1921.

Les années "Cénacle." Beirut: Dār al-Nahār, 1997.

Lings, Martin. *Muhammad: His Life Based on the Earliest Sources*. Rochester, VT: Inner Traditions, 1983.

Macpherson, C. B. *Democratic Theory: Essays in Retrieval*. Oxford: Oxford University Press, 1975.

Majlisī. *Biḥār al-anwār*. 2nd ed. Beirut: al-Wafāʾ, 1983.

Mirʾāt al-ʿuqūl fī sharḥ akhbār al-rasūl. Tehran: Dār al-Kutub al-Islāmiyya, 1989.

Makdisi, George. *The Rise of Colleges: Institutions of Learning in Islam and the West*. Edinburgh: Edinburgh University Press, 1981.

Mallat, Chibli. *Aspects of Shiʿi Thought from the South of Lebanon*. Oxford: Oxford Centre for Lebanese Studies, 1988.

"The Debate on *Riba* and Interest in Twentieth-Century Jurisprudence." in Mallat, *Islamic Law and Finance*, 69–88.

The Renewal of Islamic Law: Muhammad Baqer as-Sadr, Najaf and the Shiʿi International. Cambridge: Cambridge University Press, 1993.

"Khatami: A Man amidst the Waves." Daily Star, June 23–28, 1997.

Introduction to Middle Eastern Law. Oxford: Oxford University Press, 2007.

Philosophy of Nonviolence. New York: Oxford University Press, 2015.

ʿAn Kamāl Junblāṭ wa-min waḥyihi [On Kamal Jumblat and his inspiration]. Beirut: Badāʾiʿ, 2018.

The Normalization of Saudi Law. New York: Oxford University Press, 2022.

Democracy Redefined: Michel Chiha and the Lebanese Constitution. Edinburgh: Edinburgh University Press, 2025.

Mallat, Chibli, ed. *Islamic Law and Finance*. London: Graham and Trotman, 1988.

Massé, Henri. *L'Islam*. 5th ed. Paris: Armand Colin, 1948.

Massignon, Louis. *La passion de Hallâj*. 4 vols. Paris: Gallimard, 1975.

Mervin, Sabrina. *Un réformisme Chiite: Ulémas et Lettrés du Jabal ʿÂmil (actuel Liban-Sud) de la fin de l'Empire Ottoman à l'indépendance du Liban*. Paris: Karthala, 2000.

Mill, John Stuart. *On Liberty*. London, 1859.

Mizutani, Makoto. *Liberalism in 20th Century Egyptian Thought: The Ideologies of Ahmad Amin and Husayn Amin*. London: I.B. Tauris, 2014.

Morris, Benny. *Israel's Border Wars, 1949–1956*. Oxford: Oxford University Press, 1993.

Mubarak, Yuwakim. *Pentalogie Islamo–Chrétienne*. Beirut: Cénacle Publications, 1972–73.

al-Muttaqī al-Hindī. *Kanz al-ʿummāl fī sunan al-aqwāl wa-l-afʿāl*. Edited by Bakrī Hayyānī and Ṣafwat al-Saqwa. Beirut: Muʾassasat al-Risāla, 1989.

Nasr, Hossein. *Islamic Philosophy from Its Origin to the Present*. Albany, NY: SUNY Press, 2006.

Nassif, Nicolas. *Raymond Eddé: Jumhūriyyat al-ḍamīr* [Raymond Edde: The moral republic]. Beirut: Dār al-Nahār li-l-Nashr, 2002.

al-Nīsābūrī. *Ṣaḥīḥ Muslim*. Beirut: Dar Iḥyāʾ al-Turāth al-ʿArabī, 1955.

al-Jāmiʿ al-ṣaḥīḥ. Beirut: Dār al-Fikr, 2009.

Pipes, Daniel. *The Hidden Hand: Middle East Fears of Conspiracy*. New York: St. Martin's Press, 1998.

Polybius. *The Histories of Polybius*. Translated by Evelyn Shirley. London: Macmillan, 1889. Project Gutenberg. www.gutenberg.org/files/44125/44125-h/44125-h.htm.

Rahnema, Ali. *An Islamic Utopian: A Political Biography of Ali Shariʿati*. London: I.B. Tauris, 1998.

Randall, Jonathan. *The Tragedy of Lebanon: Christian Warlords, Israeli Adventurers and American Bunglers*. London: Hogarth, 1990 [1983].

Russell, Bertrand. *The Practice and Theory of Bolshevism*. London: George Allen and Unwin, 1920.

History of Western Philosophy. New York: Simon & Schuster, 1945.

Russell, Gerard. *Heirs to Forgotten Kingdoms: Journeys into the Disappearing Religions of the Middle East*. New York: Simon & Schuster, 2014.

al-Ṣadr, Muḥammad Bāqer. *al-Bank al-lā ribawī fī al-Islām* [The interest-free bank in Islam]. Beirut: Dār al-Taʿāruf, 1983 [Kuwait, 1969].

Iqtiṣādunā [Our economic system]. Beirut: Dār al-Taʿāruf, 1984 [Najaf, 1959, 1961].

Ṣadr, Mūsā. "Taṣdīr" [Preface]. In Corbin, *Tārīkh al-falsafa al-islāmiyya*, 7–28.

Iqtiṣād dar maktab-e Islām [Economics in the Islamic school]. Tehran: Mashʿal Dāneshjū, 1989.

"al-Islām wa-thaqāfat al-qarn al-ʿishrīn" [Islam and twentieth-century culture]. In *Les années "Cénacle,"* 463–72.

al-Madhhab al-iqtiṣādī fī al-Islām [The economic school in Islam]. Beirut: Markaz al-Imām Mūsā al-Ṣadr li-l-Abḥāth wa-l-Dirāsāt, 1998.

Risāla ilā al-maḥrūmīn [Message to the deprived]. Beirut: Markaz al-Imām Mūsā al-Ṣadr li-l-Abḥāth wa-l-Dirāsāt, 2000.

Abḥāth fī al-iqtiṣād [Economic studies]. Beirut: Markaz al-Imām Mūsā al-Ṣadr li-l-Abḥāth wa-l-Dirāsāt, 2007.

Rūḥ al-sharīʿa al-islāmiyya [The spirit of Islamic law]. Beirut: Markaz al-Imām Mūsā al-Ṣadr li-l-Abḥāth wa-l-Dirāsāt, 2009.

Kalima huwa qāʾiluhā [Words he spoke]. Beirut: Markaz al-Imām Mūsā al-Ṣadr li-l-Abḥāth wa-l-Dirāsāt, 2022.

al-Ṣadr, Rabāb. *al-Falsafa al-iṣlāḥiyya fī ruʾyat al-Imām Mūsā al-Ṣadr wa-aʿmālihi* [The reformist philosophy in the vision of Imam Musa al-Sadr and in his writings]. Beirut: Markaz al-Imām Mūsā al-Ṣadr li-l-Abḥāth wa-l-Dirāsāt, 2022.

Ṣadrā, Mullā. *al-Ḥikma al-muta'āliya fī al-asfār al-'aqliyya al-arba'a* [Transcendent wisdom in the four journeys of the intellect]. Edited by Muḥammad Kāẓem Muṣṭafawī. 2nd ed. Qom: Maktab al-I'lām al-Islāmī, 1999.

Sartre, Jean-Paul. *L'être et le néant*. Paris: Gallimard, 1943.

Being and Nothingness. New York: Citadel, 1956.

Seale, Patrick. *Asad of Syria: The Struggle for the Middle East*. London: I.B. Tauris, 1988.

Abu Nidal: The World's Most Notorious Terrorist. London: Arrow Books, 1992.

Asad: The Struggle for the Middle East. Revised ed. Berkeley: University of California Press, 1995.

Sejestani, Abu Ya'qub. *Le Dévoilement des Choses Cachées (Kashf al-Mahjûb)*. [Persian text with an introduction by Henry Corbin, 1–25.] Tehran/Paris: Adrien-Maisonneuve, 1949.

Sharafeddin, 'Abd al-Hussein. *al-Murāja'āt*. Sour: al-'Irfān, 1936.

Bughyat al-rāghibīn fī silsilat Āl Sharaf al-Dīn [The object of desire in the lineage of the Sharafeddin family]. Edited by 'Abdallah Sharafeddin. Tyre: Markaz al-Imām Sharaf al-Dīn, 1991.

Sharafeddin, Hussein. *al-Imām al-Sayyed, Maḥaṭṭāt tārīkhiyya, Īrān – al-Najaf – Lubnān* [Imam Sayyed, historical moments, Iran – Najaf – Lebanon]. Beirut: Dār al-Arqam, 1996.

Shehadi, Nadim. *The Idea of Lebanon: Economy and State in the Cénacle Libanais 1946–54*. Oxford: Oxford Centre for Lebanese Studies, 1987.

al-Ṣuyūṭī, Jamāl al-Dīn. *al-Durr al-manthūr fī al-tafsīr bi-l-ma'thūr*. wikisource.com.

al-Ṭabāṭabā'ī, Muḥammad Ḥusayn. *al-Mīzān fī tafsīr al-Qur'ān*. Beirut: Mu'assasat al-A'lamī, 1954–72.

Shi'ite Islam. Translated by Seyyed Hossein Nasr. Albany, NY: SUNY Press, 1975.

A Shi'ite Anthology. Translated by William Chittick. Albany, NY: SUNY Press, 1978.

The Qur'an in Islam. Translated by Assadullah Yate. Tehran: Haeri Trust, 1987.

al-Ṭabāṭabā'ī, Muḥammad Ḥusayn, and Henry Corbin. *Shī'a: Majmū'ah-i muzākarat ba Profesur Hanri Kurbin* [Shi'ism: An assemblage of recollections with Professor Henry Corbin]. Edited by Hādī Khusrawshāhī. Qom: Mu'assasat-i Bustān-i Kitāb, 1960.

Taylor, Alan R. "The Euro–Arab Dialogue: Quest for an Interregional Partnership." *Middle East Journal* 32, no. 4 (1978): 429–43.

Tehrānī, Muḥammad Muḥsin Āghābozorg. *Ṭabaqāt a'lām al-Shī'a* [Biographies of famous Shi'is]. Beirut: Dār Iḥyā' al-Turāth al-'Arabī, 1982 [1962].

Timoviev, Igor. *Kamāl Junblāṭ: al-Rajul wa-l-usṭūra* [Kamal Jumblat: The man and the legend]. Beirut: Dār al-Nahār li-l-Nashr, 2000.

Turner, Colin. *Islam without Allah? The Rise of Religious Externalism in Safavid Iran*. London: Curzon, 2000.

Ṭūsī. *Amālī*. Qom: Mu'assasat al-Baṭḥā', 1993.

Udovitch, Abraham. *Partnership and Profit in Medieval Islam*. Princeton, NJ: Princeton University Press, 1970.

Warde, Ibrahim. *Islamic Finance in the Global Economy*. Edinburgh: Edinburgh University Press, 2000.

Wiesehöfer, Josef. *Ancient Persia*. London: I.B. Tauris, 1996.

Wittgenstein, Ludwig. *Philosophical Investigations*. Translated by G. E. M. Anscombe, P. M. S. Hacker and Joachim Schulte. Oxford: Wiley-Blackwell, 2009.

Index

Page numbers in **bold** refer to content in footnotes.

Index

CAMBRIDGE TEXTS IN THE HISTORY OF POLITICAL THOUGHT

Titles published in the series thus far

Aquinas *Political Writings* (edited and translated by R. W. Dyson)
Aristotle *The Politics and The Constitution of Athens* (edited and translated by Stephen Everson)
Arnold *Culture and Anarchy and Other Writings* (edited by Stefan Collini)
Astell *Political Writings* (edited by Patricia Springborg)
Augustine *The City of God against the Pagans* (edited and translated by R. W. Dyson)
Augustine *Political Writings* (edited by E. M. Atkins and R. J. Dodaro)
Austin *The Province of Jurisprudence Determined* (edited by Wilfrid E. Rumble)
Bacon *The History of the Reign of King Henry VII* (edited by Brian Vickers)
Bagehot *The English Constitution* (edited by Paul Smith)
Bakunin *Statism and Anarchy* (edited and translated by Marshall Shatz)
Bartolus of Sassoferrato *Political Writings* (edited and translated by George Garnett and Magnus Ryan)
Baxter *Holy Commonwealth* (edited by William Lamont)
Bayle *Political Writings* (edited by Sally L. Jenkinson)
Beccaria *On Crimes and Punishments and Other Writings* (edited by Richard Bellamy; translated by Richard Davies)
Bentham *A Fragment on Government* (edited by Ross Harrison)
Bernstein *The Preconditions of Socialism* (edited and translated by Henry Tudor)
Bodin *On Sovereignty* (edited and translated by Julian H. Franklin)
Bolingbroke *Political Writings* (edited by David Armitage)
Bossuet *Politics Drawn from the Very Words of Holy Scripture* (edited and translated by Patrick Riley)
Botero *The Reason of State* (edited and translated by Robert Bireley)
The British Idealists (edited by David Boucher)
Burke *Pre-Revolutionary Writings* (edited by Ian Harris)
Burke *Revolutionary Writings* (edited by Iain Hampsher-Monk)
Caliphate and Imamate: An Anthology of Medieval Muslim Texts on Political Theology (edited and translated by Hassan Ansari and Nebil Husayn)
Cavendish *Political Writings* (edited by Susan James)
Christine de Pizan *The Book of the Body Politic* (edited by Kate Langdon Forhan)
Cicero *On Duties* (edited by E. M. Atkins; edited and translated by M. T. Griffin)
Cicero *On the Commonwealth and On the Laws* (edited and translated by James E. G. Zetzel)
Comte *Conciliarism and Papalism* (edited by J. H. Burns and Thomas M. Izbicki)
Comte *Early Political Writings* (edited and translated by H. S. Jones)
Condorcet *Political Writings* (edited by Steven Lukes and Nadia Urbinati)
Constant *Political Writings* (edited and translated by Biancamaria Fontana)
Dante *Monarchy* (edited and translated by Prue Shaw)

Albert Venn Dicey *Writings on Democracy and the Referendum* (edited by Gregory Conti)
Diderot *Political Writings* (edited and translated by John Hope Mason and Robert Wokler)
The Dutch Revolt (edited and translated by Martin van Gelderen)
Early Greek Political Thought from Homer to the Sophists (edited and translated by Michael Gagarin and Paul Woodruff)
The Early Political Writings of the German Romantics (edited and translated by Frederick C. Beiser)
Emerson *Political Writings* (edited by Kenneth S. Sacks)
The English Levellers (edited by Andrew Sharp)
Erasmus *The Education of a Christian Prince with the Panegyric for Archduke Philip of Austria* (edited and translated by Lisa Jardine; translated by Neil M. Cheshire and Michael J. Heath)
Fénelon *Telemachus* (edited and translated by Patrick Riley)
Ferguson *An Essay on the History of Civil Society* (edited by Fania Oz-Salzberger)
Fichte *Addresses to the German Nation* (edited by Gregory Moore)
Filmer *Patriarcha and Other Writings* (edited by Johann P. Sommerville)
Fletcher *Political Works* (edited by John Robertson)
Sir John Fortescue *On the Laws and Governance of England* (edited by Shelley Lockwood)
Fourier *The Theory of the Four Movements* (edited by Gareth Stedman Jones; edited and translated by Ian Patterson)
Franklin *The Autobiography and Other Writings on Politics, Economics, and Virtue* (edited by Alan Houston)
Gramsci *Pre-Prison Writings* (edited by Richard Bellamy; translated by Virginia Cox)
Guicciardini *Dialogue on the Government of Florence* (edited and translated by Alison Brown)
Hamilton, Madison, and Jay (writing as 'Publius') *The Federalist with Letters of 'Brutus'* (edited by Terence Ball)
Harrington *The Commonwealth of Oceana and A System of Politics* (edited by J. G. A. Pocock)
Hegel *Elements of the Philosophy of Right* (edited by Allen W. Wood; translated by H. B. Nisbet)
Hegel *Political Writings* (edited by Laurence Dickey and H. B. Nisbet)
Hess *The Holy History of Mankind and Other Writings* (edited and translated by Shlomo Avineri)
Hobbes *On the Citizen* (edited and translated by Michael Silverthorne and Richard Tuck)
Hobbes *Leviathan* (edited by Richard Tuck)
Hobhouse *Liberalism and Other Writings* (edited by James Meadowcroft)
Hooker *Of the Laws of Ecclesiastical Polity* (edited by A. S. McGrade)
Hume *Political Essays* (edited by Knud Haakonssen)

Ibn Khaldūn *Political Thought* (edited by Gabriel Martinez-Gros; translated by Anna Bailey Galietti)
Jefferson *Political Writings* (edited by Joyce Appleby and Terence Ball)
John of Salisbury *Policraticus* (edited by Cary J. Nederman)
Kant *Political Writings* (edited by H. S. Reiss; translated by H. B. Nisbet)
King James VI and I *Political Writings* (edited by Johann P. Sommerville)
Knox *On Rebellion* (edited by Roger A. Mason)
Kropotkin *The Conquest of Bread and Other Writings* (edited by Marshall Shatz)
Kumazawa Banzan *Governing the Realm and Bringing Peace to All below Heaven* (edited and translated by John A. Tucker)
Lawson *Politica Sacra et Civilis* (edited by Conal Condren)
Leibniz *Political Writings* (edited and translated by Patrick Riley)
Lincoln *Political Writings and Speeches* (edited by Terence Ball)
Locke *Political Essays* (edited by Mark Goldie)
Locke *Two Treatises of Government* (edited by Peter Laslett)
Loyseau *A Treatise of Orders and Plain Dignities* (edited and translated by Howell A. Lloyd)
Luther and Calvin on Secular Authority (edited and translated by Harro Höpfl)
Catharine Macaulay *Political Writings* (edited by Max Skjönsberg)
Machiavelli *The Prince, Second Edition* (edited by Quentin Skinner and Russell Price)
Joseph de Maistre *Considerations on France* (edited and translated by Richard A. Lebrun)
Maitland *State, Trust and Corporation* (edited by David Runciman and Magnus Ryan)
Malthus *An Essay on the Principle of Population* (edited by Donald Winch)
Marsiglio of Padua *Defensor minor and De translatione Imperii* (edited by Cary J. Nederman)
Marsilius of Padua *The Defender of the Peace* (edited and translated by Annabel Brett)
Marx *Early Political Writings* (edited and translated by Joseph O'Malley)
Abul A'la Maududi *Al Jihad fil Islam and Other Writings* (edited and translated by Humeira Iqtidar)
Medieval Muslim Mirrors for Princes: An Anthology of Arabic, Persian and Turkish Political Advice (edited and translated by Louise Marlow)
James Mill *Political Writings* (edited by Terence Ball)
J. S. Mill *On Liberty and Other Writings* (edited by Stefan Collini)
Milton *Political Writings* (edited by Martin Dzelzainis; translated by Claire Gruzelier)
Montesquieu *The Spirit of the Laws* (edited and translated by Anne M. Cohler, Basia Carolyn Miller and Harold Samuel Stone)
More *Utopia* (edited by George M. Logan and Robert M. Adams)
Morris *News from Nowhere* (edited by Krishan Kumar)
Nicholas of Cusa *The Catholic Concordance* (edited and translated by Paul E. Sigmund)

Nietzsche *On the Genealogy of Morality* (edited by Keith Ansell-Pearson; translated by Carol Diethe)
Paine *Political Writings* (edited by Bruce Kuklick)
William Penn *Political Writings* (edited by Andrew R. Murphy)
Plato *Gorgias, Menexenus, Protagoras* (edited by Malcolm Schofield; translated by Tom Griffith)
Plato *Laws* (edited by Malcolm Schofield; translated by Tom Griffith)
Plato *The Republic* (edited by G. R. F. Ferrari; translated by Tom Griffith)
Plato *Statesman* (edited by Julia Annas; edited and translated by Robin Waterfield)
Political Thought in Portugal and Its Empire, c.1500–1800 (edited by Pedro Cardim and Nuno Gonçalo Monteiro)
The Political Thought of the Irish Revolution (edited by Richard Bourke and Niamh Gallagher)
The Political Thought of Nineteenth-Century Spanish America (edited by Iván Jakšić and Eduardo Posada-Carbó)
Price *Political Writings* (edited by D. O. Thomas)
Priestley *Political Writings* (edited by Peter Miller)
Proudhon *What Is Property?* (edited and translated by Donald R. Kelley and Bonnie G. Smith)
Pufendorf *On the Duty of Man and Citizen according to Natural Law* (edited by James Tully; translated by Michael Silverthorne)
The Radical Reformation (edited and translated by Michael G. Baylor)
Rousseau *The Discourses and Other Early Political Writings* (edited and translated by Victor Gourevitch)
Rousseau *The Social Contract and Other Later Political Writings* (edited and translated by Victor Gourevitch)
Seneca *Moral and Political Essays* (edited and translated by John M. Cooper; edited by J. F. Procopé)
Shundai *Writings on Political Economy* (edited and translated by Peter Flueckiger)
Sidney *Court Maxims* (edited by Hans W. Blom, Eco Haitsma Mulier and Ronald Janse)
Sorel *Reflections on Violence* (edited by Jeremy Jennings)
Spencer *Political Writings* (edited by John Offer)
Stirner *The Ego and Its Own* (edited by David Leopold)
Emperor Taizong and ministers *The Essentials of Governance* (compiled by Wu Jing; edited and translated by Hilde De Weerdt, Glen Dudbridge and Gabe van Beijeren)
Thoreau *Political Writings* (edited by Nancy L. Rosenblum)
Tönnies *Community and Civil Society* (edited and translated by Jose Harris; translated by Margaret Hollis)
Utopias of the British Enlightenment (edited by Gregory Claeys)
Vico *The First New Science* (edited and translated by Leon Pompa)
Vitoria *Political Writings* (edited by Anthony Pagden and Jeremy Lawrance)

Volney *The Ruins and Catechism of Natural Law* (edited and translated by Colin Kidd; translated by Lucy Kidd)
Voltaire *Political Writings* (edited and translated by David Williams)
Weber *Political Writings* (edited by Peter Lassman; edited and translated by Ronald Speirs)
William of Ockham *A Letter to the Friars Minor and Other Writings* (edited by Arthur Stephen McGrade; edited and translated by John Kilcullen)
William of Ockham *A Short Discourse on Tyrannical Government* (edited by Arthur Stephen McGrade; translated by John Kilcullen)
Wollstonecraft *A Vindication of the Rights of Men and A Vindication of the Rights of Woman* (edited by Sylvana Tomaselli)

Printed in the United Kingdom by TJ Clays Ltd.